D1571333

GREAT PREACHING ON

THE NEW YEAR

GREAT PREACHING ON

THE NEW YEAR

COMPILED BY
CURTIS HUTSON

SWORD of the LORD
PUBLISHERS
P. O. BOX 1099, MURFREESBORO, TN 37133

Copyright, 1987, by

SWORD OF THE LORD PUBLISHERS

ISBN 0-87398-326-2

Printed and Bound in the United States of America

Preface

Back at the old home there's a certain door frame marked with smudged penciled lines, each carefully dated. There each child on his birthday was measured carefully to see how much he had grown during the year.

Though the children are grown now, the faint smudges remind us of the days of youthful, joyful growth.

Suppose we stand against an imaginary door frame and measure our spiritual growth of the past year. Have we conquered some of the sins we vowed we would conquer? Is the Word of God sweet and precious, partaken of daily? Is there really victory over a particular sin? Have some of our friends trusted Christ because of our testimony? Is the home life honoring to Christ? Are the children obedient and thoughtful? Could you say you are satisfied with your spiritual growth?

Most of us must honestly confess there are many ways we failed God in that year's time.

Let us resolve, with God's help, that there will be spiritual growth in the days ahead.

In *Great Preaching on the New Year*, the cream of the writings of many authors is included. If you are afraid to be changed and challenged, you will not want to read these piercing sermons. If you don't want some of your illusions shattered and your self-complacency interrupted, don't read them! But if you are a Christian seeking to serve your Lord in a constantly more effective way, then you will want to join the thousands who will find great help in these Spirit-filled messages as they were delivered to crowded audiences. Here they are, practically as they were spoken, for God to bless to thousands.

Curtis Hutson
Editor, SWORD OF THE LORD

Table of Contents

I.

Measuring Life's Success

T. DeWITT TALMAGE

"How old art thou?" —Gen. 48:8.

The Egyptian capital was the focus of the world's wealth. In ships and barges there had been brought to it from India frankincense, cinnamon, ivory and diamonds; from the North, marble and iron; from Syria, purple and silk; from Arabia, some of the finest horses of the world, and from Greece some of the most brilliant chariots; and from all the earth, that which could best please the eye and charm the ear and gratify the taste.

There were temples aflame with red sandstone entered by gateways guarded by pillars bewildering with hieroglyphics, garlanded with brazen serpents and adorned with winged creatures—their eyes and beaks and pinions glittering with precious stones. There were marble columns blooming into white flower beds; there were stone pillars at the top bursting into the shape of the lotus when in full bloom. Along the avenues lined with sphinx and fans and obelisk, there were princes who came in gorgeously upholstered palanquins, carried by servants in scarlet, or elsewhere drawn by vehicles, the snow-white horses, golden-bitted and six abreast, dashing at full run.

On floors of mosaic the glories of Pharaoh were spelled out in letters of porphyry and beryl and flame. There were ornaments twisted from the wood of tamarisk, embossed with silver breaking into foam. There were footstools made out of a single precious stone. There were beds fashioned out of crouched lion in bronze. There were chairs spotted with the sleek hides of leopards. There were sofas footed with the claws of wild beasts and armed with the beaks of birds.

As you stand on the level beach of the sea on a summer day and look either way, there are miles of breakers, white with the ocean foam, dashing shoreward, so it seemed as if the sea of the world's pomp and wealth in the Egyptian capital for miles and miles flung itself up into white breakers of marble temple, mausoleum and obelisk.

It was to this capital and the palace of Pharaoh that Jacob, the plain shepherd, came to the royal apartment to meet his son Joseph, who had become Prime Minister. Pharaoh and Jacob met, dignity and rusticity, the gracefulness of the court and the plain manners of the field. The king, wanting to make the old countryman at ease and seeing how white his beard is and how feeble his step, looks familiarly into his face and says to the aged man: "How old art thou?"

On this first day of the new year I feel that it is not an inappropriate question that I ask you, as Pharaoh did Jacob, the patriarch: "How old art thou?" People who are truthful on every other subject lie about their ages, so that I do not solicit from you any literal response to the question I have asked. I would put no one under temptation; but I simply want to see by what rod it is we are measuring our earthly existence.

There is a right way and a wrong way of measuring a door, or a wall, or an arch, or a tower; and so there is a right way and a wrong way of measuring our earthly existence. It is with reference to this higher meaning that I confront you this morning with the stupendous question of the text and ask: "How old art thou?"

Do You Measure Life by Worldly Gratification?

There are many who estimate their life by mere worldly gratification. When Lord Dundas was wished a happy New Year, he said: *"It will have to be a happier year than the past, for I hadn't one happy moment in all the twelve months that have gone."*

But that has not been the experience of most of us. We have found that, though the world is blasted with sin, it is a very bright and beautiful place to reside in. We have had joys innumerable. There is no hostility between the Gospel and the merriments and festivities of life. I do not think that we sufficiently appreciate the worldly pleasures God gives us.

When you recount your enjoyments, you do not go far enough back. Why do you not go back to the time when you were an infant in your mother's arms, looking up into the heaven of her smile; to those days when you filled the house with the uproar of boisterous merriment; when you shouted as you pitched the ball on the playground; when on the cold, sharp winter night, muffled up, on skates you shot out over the resounding ice of the pond? Have you forgotten all those good days that the Lord gave you?

Were you never a boy? Were you never a girl? Between those times and this, how many mercies the Lord has bestowed upon you! How many joys have breathed up to you from the flowers and shone down to you from the stars and chanted to you with the voice of soaring bird and tumbling cascade and booming sea and thunders that, with bayonets of fire, charged down the mountain side!

Joy! Joy! If there is anyone who has a right to the enjoyments of the world, it is the Christian, for God has given him a lease of everything in the promise: "All are yours."

But I have to tell you that a man who estimates his life on earth by mere worldly gratification is a most unwise man. Our life is not to be a game of chess. It is not a dance in the lighted hall to quick music. It is not the froth of an ale pitcher. It is not the settlings of a wine cup. It is not a banquet with intoxication and roistering. It is the first step on a ladder that mounts into the skies, or the first step on a road that plunges into a horrible abyss.

"How old art thou?" Toward what destiny are you tending, and how fast are you getting on toward it?

Life Should Not Be Measured by Sorrows and Misfortune

Again, I remark that there are many who estimate their life on earth by their sorrows and misfortunes. Through a great many of your lives the ploughshare hath gone very deep, turning up a terrible furrow. You have been betrayed, misrepresented, set upon, slapped of impertinence and pounded of misfortune. The brightest life must have its shadows and the smoothest path its thorns. On the happiest brood the hawk pounces. No escape from trouble of some kind.

While glorious John Milton was losing his eyesight, he heard that Salmasius was glad of it. While Sheridan's comedy was being enacted in Drury Lane Theatre, London, his enemy sat growling at it in the stage box. While Bishop Cooper was surrounded by the favor of learned men, his wife took the manuscript of his lexicon, the product of a long life of anxiety and toil, and threw it into the fire.

Misfortune, trial, vexation for almost everyone. One pope, applauded of all the world, had a stoop in the shoulder that annoyed him so much that he had a tunnel dug so that he could go unobserved from garden to grotto and from grotto to garden. Cano, the famous Spanish artist, was disgusted with the crucifix that one priest held before him because it was such a poor specimen of sculpture.

And so, sometimes through taste, sometimes through learned menace and sometimes through physical distresses—aye, in ten thousand ways—troubles come to harass and annoy.

Yet it is unfair to measure a man's life by his misfortunes because, where there is one stalk of nightshade, there are fifty marigolds and harebells; where there is one cloud, thunder-charged, there are hundreds that stray across the heavens, the glory of land and sky asleep in their bosom.

Because death came and took your child away, did you immediately forget all the five years or the ten years or the fifteen years in which she came every night for a kiss, all the tones or the soft touch of her hand?

Because in some financial Euroclydon your fortune went into the breakers, did you forget all those years in which the luxuries and extravagances of life showered on your pathway?

Alas, that is an unwise man, an ungrateful man, an unfair man, an unphilosophic man, and, most of all, an unchristian man, who measures his life on earth by groans, tears, dyspeptic fit, abuse, scorn, terror and neuralgic thrust.

Do Not Evaluate Life by Amount of Money Made

Again, I remark that there are many people who estimate their life on earth by the amount of money they have accumulated. They say, "The year 1866 or 1870 or 1898 was wasted." Why? "Made no money."

Now, it is all cant and insincerity to talk against money, as though it had no value. It may represent refinement, education and many blessed surroundings.

It is the spreading of the table that feeds the children's hunger. It is the lighting of the furnace that keeps you warm. It is the making of the bed on which you rest from care and anxiety. It is the carrying of you at last to decent sepulchre and the putting up of the slab on which is chiseled the story of your Christian hope. It is simply hypocrisy, this tirade in pulpit and lecture-hall against money.

But while all this is so, he who uses money or thinks of money as anything but a means to an end will find out his mistake when the glittering treasures slip out of his nerveless grasp and he goes out of this world without a shilling of money or a certificate of stock. He might better have been the Christian porter that opened his gate or the Christian workman who last night heaved the coal into his cellar. Bonds, mortgages and leases have their use, but they make a poor yardstick with which to measure life.

"They that trust in their wealth, and boast themselves in the multitude of their riches; None of them can by any means redeem his brother, nor give to God a ransom for him: (For the redemption of their soul is precious, and it ceaseth for ever:) That he should still live for ever, and not see corruption." —Ps. 49:6-9.

Measure Life Partly by Spiritual Development

But I remark, there are many—I wish there were more—who estimate their life by their moral and spiritual development. It is not sinful egotism for a Christian man to say, "I am purer than I used to be. I am more consecrated to Christ than I used to be. I have gotten over a great many of the bad habits in which I used to indulge. I am a great deal better man than I used to be." There is no sinful egotism in that.

It is not base egotism for a soldier to say, "I know more about military tactics than I used to, before I took a musket in my hand and learned to 'present arms,' and when I was a pest to the drill-officer."

It is not base egotism for a sailor to say, "I know better how to clew down the mizzen topsail than I used to, before I had ever seen a ship."

And there is no sinful egotism when a Christian man, fighting the battles of the Lord, or, if you will have it, voyaging toward a haven of eternal rest, says, "I know more about spiritual tactics and about voyaging toward Heaven than I used to."

Why, there are those among us who have measured lances with many a foe and unhorsed it. We know Christian men who have become swarthy by hammering at the forge of calamity. They stand on an entirely different plane of character from that which they once occupied. They are measuring their life on earth by golden-gated Sabbaths, by pentecostal prayer meetings, by communion tables, by baptismal fonts, by hallelujahs in the Temple. They have stood on Sinai and heard it thunder. They have stood on Pisgah and looked over into the Promised Land. They have stood on Calvary and seen the cross bleed. They can, like Paul the apostle, write on their heaviest troubles "light" and "but for a moment." Even on the darkest night their soul is irradiated, as was the night over Bethlehem, by the faces of those who have come to proclaim glory and good cheer. They are only waiting for the gate to open, the chains to fall off and the glory to begin.

Life Best Measured by Good Done

I remark again: There are many—and I wish there were more—who are estimating life by the good they can do.

John Bradford said he counted that day nothing at all in which he had not, by pen or tongue, done some good.

If a man begin right, I cannot tell how many tears he may wipe away, how many burdens he may lift, how many orphans he may comfort, how many outcasts he may reclaim.

There have been men who have given their whole life in the right direction, concentrating all their wit, ingenuity, mental acumen, physical force and enthusiasm for Christ. They climbed the mountain, delved into the mine, crossed the sea, trudged the desert and dropped, at last, into martyrs' graves, waiting for the resurrection of the just.

They measured their lives by the chains they broke off, by the garments they put upon nakedness, by the miles they traveled to alleviate every kind of suffering. They felt in the thrill of every nerve, in the motion of every muscle, in every throb of their heart, in every respiration of their lungs, the magnificent truth: "No man liveth unto himself." They went through cold and through heat, foot-blistered, cheek-smitten, back-scourged, tempest-lashed, to do their whole duty. That is the way they measured life—by the amount of good they could do.

Do you want to know how old Luther was; how old Richard Baxter was; how old Philip Doddridge was? Why, you cannot calculate the length of their lives by any human arithmetic. Add to their lives ten thousand times ten thousand years, and you have not expressed it—what they have lived or will live. Oh, what a standard that is to measure a man's life by!

There are those among us who think they have only lived thirty years. They will have lived a thousand—they have lived a thousand. There are those who think they are eighty years of age. They have not even entered upon their infancy, for one must become a babe in Christ to begin at all.

Now, I do not know what your advantages or disadvantages are; I do not know what your tact or talent is; I do not know what may be the fascination of your manners or the repulsiveness of them; but I know this: there is for you, my hearer, a field to cultivate, a harvest to reap, a tear to wipe away, a soul to save.

If you have worldly means, consecrate them to Christ. If you have eloquence, use it on the side that Paul and Wilberforce used theirs. If you have learning, put it all into the poor-box of the world's suffering.

But if you have none of these—neither wealth nor eloquence nor learning—you, at any rate, have a smile with which you can encourage the disheartened; a frown with which you may blast injustice; a voice with which you call the wanderer back to God.

"Oh," you say, "that is a very sanctimonious view of life!" It is not. It is the only bright view of life, and it is the only bright view of death.

Contrast the death-scene of a man who has measured life by the worldly standard with the death-scene of a man who has measured life by the Christian standard.

Quinn, the actor, in his last moments, said, "I hope this tragic scene will soon be over, and I hope to keep my dignity to the last."

Malherbe said in his last moments to the confessor, "Hold your tongue! your miserable style puts me out of conceit with Heaven."

Lord Chesterfield in his last moments, when he ought to have been praying for his soul, bothered himself about the proprieties of the sick room and said, "Give Dayboles a chair."

Godfrey Kneller spent his last hours on earth in drawing a diagram of his own monument.

Compare the silly and horrible accompaniments of the departure of such men with the seraphic glow on the face of Edward Payson, as he said in his last moment: "The breezes of Heaven fan me. I float in a sea of glory." Or with Paul the apostle, who said in his last hour, "I am now ready to be offered up, and the time of my departure is at hand. I have fought the good fight, I have kept the faith. Henceforth there is laid up for me a crown of righteousness which the Lord, the righteous Judge, will give me." Or compare it with the Christian deathbed that you witnessed in your own household.

Ah, this world is a false god! It will consume you with the blaze in which it accepts your sacrifice, while the righteous shall be held in everlasting remembrance; and when the thrones have fallen and the monuments have crumbled and the world has perished, they shall banquet with the conquerors of earth and the hierarchs of Heaven.

The New Year—a Good Time to Start Measuring Life Aright

This is a good day in which to begin a new style of measurement. "How old art thou?" You see the Christian way of measuring life and the worldly way of measuring it. I leave it to you to say which is the wiser and better way. The wheel of time has turned very swiftly, and it has hurled us on. The old year has gone. The new year has come. For what you and I have been launched upon it, God only knows.

Now let me ask you all: Have you made any preparation for the future? You have made preparation for time, my dear brother, but have you made any preparation for eternity? Do you wonder that, when that man on the Hudson River, in indignation, tore up the tract which was handed to him and just one word landed on his coat sleeve—the rest of the tract being pitched into the river—that one word aroused his soul? It was that one word, so long, so broad, so high, so deep—*eternity*!

Some of you, during the past year, made preparation for eternity, and it makes no difference to you really as to the matter of safety, whether you go now or go some other year—whether this year or the next year. Both your feet on the rock, the waves may dash around you. You can say, "God is our refuge and strength—a very present help." You are on the Rock, and you may defy all earth and Hell to overthrow you. I congratulate you, I give you great joy. It is a happy New Year to you.

I can see no sorrow at all in the fact that our years are going. You hear some people say, "I wish I could go back again to boyhood." I would not want to go back again to boyhood. I am afraid I might make a worse life out of it than I have made. You could not afford to go back to boyhood if it were possible. You might do a great deal worse than you have done. The past is gone! Look out for the future! To all Christians it is a time of gladness. I am glad the years are going. You are coming on nearer Home. Let your countenance light up with the thought—nearer Home!

In 1835 the French resolved that at Ghent they would have a kind of musical demonstration that had never been heard of. It would be made up of the chimes of bells and the discharge of cannon.

The experiment was a perfect success. What with the ringing of the bells and the report of the ordinance, the city trembled and the hills shook with the triumphal march that was as strange as it was overwhelming.

With a most glorious accompaniment will God's dear children go into their high residence, when the trumpets shall sound and the Last Day has come. At the signal given, the bells of the towers and of the lighthouses and of the cities will strike their sweetness into a last chime that shall ring into the heavens and float off upon the sea, joined by the boom of bursting mine and magazine, augmented by all the cathedral towers of Heaven—the harmonies of earth and the symphonies of the celestial realm making up one great triumphal march, fit to celebrate the ascent of the redeemed to where they shall shine as the stars forever and ever.

II.

A New Year's Wish

CHARLES SPURGEON

"But my God shall supply all your need, according to his riches in glory by Christ Jesus."—Phil. 4:19.

Several times the Philippians had sent presents to Paul, to supply his necessities. Though they were not themselves rich, yet they made a contribution and sent Epaphroditus with "an odour of a sweet smell, a sacrifice acceptable, well pleasing to God."

Paul felt very grateful; he thanked God, but he did not forget also to thank the donors. He wished them every blessing, and he did as good as say, "You have supplied my need, and my God shall supply yours. You have supplied my need of temporal food and raiment out of your poverty; my God shall supply all your need out of His riches in glory."

"As," he says in verse 18, "I have all and abound: I am full; so my God shall supply all your need. You have sent what you gave me by the hand of a beloved brother, but God will send a better messenger to you, for He will supply all your need by Christ Jesus."

Every single word sounds as if he had thought it over and the Spirit of God had guided him in his meditation, so that he should to the fullest extent wish them back a blessing similar to that which they had sent to him, only of a richer and more enduring kind.

This verse is particularly sweet to me; for, when we were building the orphanage, I foresaw that, if we had no voting and no collecting of annual subscriptions but depended upon the goodness of God and the voluntary offerings of His people, we should have times of trial. Therefore, I ordered the masons to place upon the first columns of the orphanage entrance these words:

My God shall supply all your need, according to his riches in glory by Christ Jesus.

The text is cut in stone upon the right hand and upon the left of the great archway. There stands this declaration of our confidence in God. And as long as God lives, we shall never need to remove it, for He will certainly supply the needs of His own work. While we serve Him, He will furnish our tables for us.

The text might suggest to us a field of gloomy thought if we wished to indulge the melancholy vein, for it speaks of "all your need." So, first behold

A Great Necessity

". . . all your need."

What a gulf! What an abyss! *"All your need."*

I do not know how many believers made up the church at Philippi, but the need of one saint is great enough; what must many need? It would not be possible to tell the number of God's children on earth, but the text comprehends the need of the whole chosen family, *"all your need."* We will not ask you to reckon up the wonderful draft upon the divine exchequer which must be made by all the needs of all the saints who are yet on earth, but please think of your own need; that will be more within the compass of your experience and the range of your meditation. May the Lord supply your need and *all* your need!

There is *our temporal need*, and that is no little matter. If we have food and raiment, we should be therewith content; but there are many of God's people to whom the mere getting of food and raiment is a wearisome toil; and what with household cares, family trials, sickness of body, losses in business and sometimes the impossibility of obtaining suitable labor, many of God's saints are as hard put to it as Elijah was when he sat by the brook Cherith. If God did not send them their bread and meat in a remarkable manner, they would surely starve. But their bread shall be given them, and their water shall be sure. "My God shall supply all your need." You have, perhaps, a large family; and your needs are therefore greatly increased; but the declaration of the text includes the whole of your needs, personal and relative.

After all, our temporal needs are very small compared with *our spiritual needs*. A man may, with the blessing of God, pretty readily provide for the wants of the body; but who shall provide for the requirements of the soul? There is need of perpetual pardon, for we are always sinning, and Jesus Christ's blood is always pleading for us and cleansing us from sin. Every day there is need of fresh strength to battle against inward sin; and, blessed be God, it is daily supplied, so that our youth is renewed like the eagle's. As good soldiers of Jesus Christ, we need armor from head to foot. Even then we do not know how to wear the armor or how to wield the sword unless He who gave us these sacred implements shall be always with us.

Warring saint, God will supply all your need by His presence and Spirit.

But we are not merely warriors; we are also workers. We are called, many of us, to important spheres of labor (indeed, let no man think his sphere unimportant), but here also our hands shall be sufficient for us, and we shall accomplish our life's work.

You have need to be helped to do the right thing, at the right time, in the right spirit and manner. Your need, as a Sunday school teacher, as an open-air preacher, and especially as a minister of the Gospel, will be very great; but the text meets all your requirements: "My God shall supply all your need."

Then comes our need in suffering, for many of us are called to take our turn in the Lord's prison house. Here we need patience under pain, hope under depression of spirit. Who is sufficient for furnace work? Our God will supply us with those choice graces and consolations which shall strengthen us to glorify His name even in the fires. He will either make the burden lighter or the back stronger; He will diminish the need or increase the supply.

Beloved, it is impossible for me to mention all the forms of our spiritual need. We need to be daily converted from some sin or other which, perhaps, we have scarcely known to be sin. We need to be instructed in the things of God. We need to be illuminated as to the mind of Christ. We need to be comforted by the promises. We need to be quickened by the precepts. We need to be strengthened by the doctrines.

Oh, what do we *not* need! We are just a bag of wants, a heap of infirmities. If any one of us were to keep a *want book*, as I have seen tradesmen do, what a huge folio it would need to be; and it might be written within and without, crossed and recrossed, for we are full of wants—from the first of January to the end of December; but here is the mercy: "My God shall supply all your need."

Are you put in high places? Have you many comforts? Do you

enjoy wealth? What need you have to be kept from loving the world, to be preserved from wantonness and pride and the follies and fashions of this present evil world. My God will supply your need in that respect.

Are you very poor? Then the temptation is to envy, to bitterness of spirit, to rebellion against God. "My God shall supply all your need."

Are you alone in the world? Then you need the Lord Jesus to be your Companion, and your Companion He will be.

Have you many around you? Then you have need of grace to set them a good example, to bring up your children and manage your household in the fear of God. "My God shall supply all your need."

You have need, in times of joy, to be kept sober and steady. You have need, in times of sorrow, to be strong and quit yourselves like men. You have needs in living, and you will have needs in dying, but your last need shall be supplied as surely as your first. "My God shall supply *all* your need."

That first thought, which I said might be a gloomy one, has all the dreariness taken out of it by four others equally true, but each of them full of good cheer.

So, second, for our enormous wants here is

A Great Helper

"*My God* shall supply all your need."

Whose God is that? Why, Paul's God. That is one of the matters in which the greatest saints are no better off than the very least, for though Paul called the Lord, "My God," He is my God, too. My dear old friend who sits yonder and has nothing but a few pence in all the world can also say, "And He is my God, too. He is my God; and He is as much my God if I am the meanest, most obscure and weakest of His people, as He would be my God if I were able, like Paul, to evangelize the nations."

It is, to me, delightful to think that *my God is Paul's God*, because, you see, Paul intended this; he meant to say, "You see, dear brethren, my God has supplied all my wants; and as He is your God, He will supply yours."

I have been in the Roman dungeon in which Paul is said to have been confined, and a comfortless prison indeed it is. First of all, you descend into a vaulted chamber into which no light ever comes except through a little round hole in the roof; and then, in the middle of the floor of that den, there is another opening through which the prisoner was let down into a second and lower dungeon in which no fresh air or light could possibly come to him. Paul was probably confined there. The dungeon of the Praetorium in which he was certainly immured is not much better.

Paul would have been left well nigh to starve there, but for those good people at Philippi. I should not wonder but what Lydia was at the bottom of this kind movement, or else the jailor. They said, "We must not let the good apostle starve"; so they made up a contribution and sent him what he wanted. When Paul received it he said, "My God has taken care of me. I cannot make tents here in this dark place so as to earn my own living, but my Master still supplies my need; and even so, when you are in straits, will He supply you."

"*My* God." It has often been sweet to me, when I have thought of my orphan children and money has not come in, to remember Mr. Mueller's God and how He always supplies the children at Bristol. His God is my God, and I rest upon Him.

When you turn over the pages of Scripture and read of men who were in sore trouble and were helped, you may say, "Here is Abraham, blessed in all things, and Abraham's God will supply all my need, for He is *my* God.

"I read of Elijah, that the ravens fed him; I have Elijah's God, and He can command the ravens to feed me if He pleases."

The God of the prophets, the God of the apostles, the God of all the saints that have gone before us, "this God is our God for ever and ever."

It seems to be thought by some that God will not work now as He used to do. "Oh, if we had lived in miraculous times," they say, "then we could have trusted Him! Then there was manifest evidence of God's existence, for He pushed aside the laws of nature and wrought for the fulfillment of His promises to His people." Yet that was a rather coarser mode of working than the present one, for now the Lord produces the same results without the violation of the laws of nature.

It is a great fact that, without the disturbance of a single law of nature, prayer becomes effectual with God; and God, being inquired of by His people to do it for them, does fulfill His promise and supply their needs. Using means of various kinds, He still gives His people all things necessary for this life and godliness. Without a miracle, He works great wonders of loving care; and He will continue so to do.

Beloved, *is the God of Paul your God?* Do you regard Him as such? It is not every man who worships Paul's God. It is not every professing Christian who really knows the Lord at all, for some invent a deity such as they fancy God ought to be. The God of Paul is the God of the Old and New Testament—such a God as we find there. Do you trust such a God? Can you rest upon Him?

"There are such severe judgments mentioned in Scripture." Yes, do you quarrel with them? Then you cast Him off; but if, instead thereof, you feel, "I cannot understand Thee, O my God, nor do I think I ever shall; but it is not for me, a child, to measure the infinite God or to arraign Thee at my bar and say to Thee, 'Thus shouldst Thou have done, and thus oughtest Thou not to have done.' Thou sayest, 'Such am I,' and I answer, 'Such as Thou art, I love Thee; and I cast myself upon Thee, the God of Abraham, of Isaac, and of Jacob, the God of Thy servant Paul. Thou art my God, and I will rest upon Thee.' " Very well, then, He will "supply all your need, according to his riches in glory by Christ Jesus." Just think of that for a minute.

If *He* will supply you, you will be supplied indeed; for God is infinite in capacity. He is infinitely wise as to the manner of His actions and infinitely powerful as to the acts themselves. He never sleeps nor tires; He is never absent from any place but is always ready to help.

Your needs come, perhaps, at very unexpected times. They may occur in the midnight of despondency or in the noonday of delight, but God is ever near to supply the surprising need. He is everywhere present and everywhere omnipotent; and He can supply all your need, in every place, at every time, to the fullest degree. "Remember that Omnipotence has servants everywhere"; and that, whenever God wishes to send you aid, He can do it without pausing to ask, "How shall it be done?" He has but to will it, and all the powers of Heaven and earth are subservient to your necessity. With such a Helper, what cause have you to doubt?

A Great Supply

"My God shall *supply* all your need."

Sometimes we lose a good deal of the meaning of Scripture through the translation; in fact, nothing ever does gain by translation except a Bishop! The present passage might be rendered thus, "My God will fill to the full all you need."

The illustration which will best explain the meaning is that of the woman whose children were to be sold by her creditor to pay the debts of her late husband. She had nothing to call her own except some empty oil jars, and the prophet bade her set these in order and bring the little oil which still remained in the cruse. She did so; then he said to her, "Go among your neighbors, and borrow empty vessels, not a few." She went from one to another till she had filled her room full of these empty vessels, and then the prophet said, "Pour out." She began to pour out from her almost empty cruse; and to her surprise, it filled her largest oil jar. She went to another and filled that, and then another and another. She kept on filling all the oil jars, till at last she said to the prophet, "There is not a vessel more." Then the oil stayed, but not till then.

So will it be with your needs. You were frightened at having so many needs just now, were you not? But now be pleased to think you have them, for they are just so many empty vessels to be filled. If the woman had borrowed only a few jars, she could not have received much oil; but the more empty vessels she had, the more oil she obtained.

So the more wants and the more needs you have, if you bring them to God, so much the better, for He will fill them all to the brim; and you may be thankful that there are so many to be filled. When you have no more wants (but, oh, when will that be?), then the supply will be stayed, but not till then.

How gloriously God gives to His people! We wanted pardon once; He washed us and made us whiter than snow.

We wanted clothing, for we were naked. What did He do? Give us some rough dress or other? Oh, no! He said, "Bring forth the best robe, and put it on him." It was a fortunate thing for the prodigal that his clothes were all in rags, for then he needed raiment, and the best robe was brought forth.

It is a grand thing to be sensible of spiritual needs, for they will all be supplied. A conscious want in the sight of God—what is it but a prevalent request for a new mercy?

We have sometimes asked Him to comfort us, for we were very low; but when the Lord has comforted us, He has so filled us with delight that we have been inclined to cry with the old Scotch divine, "Hold, Lord, hold! It is enough. I cannot bear more joy. Remember I am only an earthen vessel."

We, in relieving the poor, generally give no more than we can help, but our God does not stop to count His favors; He gives like a king. He pours water upon him that is thirsty and floods upon the dry ground.

We must pass on to the next thought and consider for a minute or two

The Great Resources Out of Which This Supply Is to Come

"My God shall supply all your need, *according to his riches in glory.*"

The preacher may sit down now, for he cannot compass this part of the text. God's riches in glory are beyond all thought.

Consider *the riches of God in Nature;* who shall count His treasures? Get away into the forests; travel on league after league among the trees which cast their ample shade for no man's pleasure, but only for the Lord. Mark on lone mountain side and far-reaching plain the myriads of flowers whose perfume is for God alone.

What wealth each spring and summer is created in the boundless estates of the great King! Observe the vast amount of animal and insect life which crowds the land with the riches of divine wisdom, for "the earth is the Lord's, and the fulness thereof."

Look towards the sea; think of those shoals of fish, so countless that, when only the fringe of them is touched by our fishermen, they find enough food to supply a nation. Mark, too, the sunken treasures of the ocean, which no hand gathereth but that of the Eternal.

If you would see the wealth of the Creator, cast your eye to the stars; tell ye their numbers if ye can. Astronomy has enlarged our vision and made us look upon this world as a mere speck compared with innumerable other worlds that God has made; and it has told us that, probably, all the myriads of worlds that we can see with the telescope are a mere fraction of the countless orbs which tenant infinite space.

Vast are God's riches in nature. It needs a Milton to sing, as he sang in *Paradise Lost,* the riches of the creating God.

The riches of God in providence are equally without bound. He saith to this creature, "Go," and he goeth; to another, "Do this," and he doeth it, for all things do His bidding.

Think of *the wealth of God in grace.* There nature and providence stand eclipsed, for we have the fountain of eternal love, the gift of an infinite sacrifice, the pouring out of the blood of His own dear Son, and the covenant of grace in which the smallest blessing is infinite in value. The riches of His grace! "God is rich in mercy"—rich in patience, love, power, kindness, rich beyond all conception.

Now your needs shall be supplied according to the riches of nature and the riches of providence and the riches of grace, but this is not all; the apostle chooses a higher style and writes "according to *his riches in glory.*"

Ah, we have never seen God in glory! That were a sight our eyes could not at present behold. Christ in His glory, when transfigured upon earth, was too resplendent a spectacle even for the tutored eyes of Peter and James and John. "At the too-transporting light," darkness rushed upon them, and they were as men that slept.

What God is in His glory do ye know, ye angels? Does He not veil His face even from you lest, in the excessive brightness of His essence, even you should be consumed? Who amongst all His creatures can tell the riches of His glory, when even the heavens are not pure in His sight, and He charges His angels with folly?

"His riches in glory." It means not only the riches of what He has done, but the riches of what He could do; for if He has made hosts of worlds, He could make as many myriads more, and then have but begun. The possibilities of God omnipotent, who shall reckon? But the Lord shall supply all your need according to such glorious possibilities.

When a great king gives according to his riches, then he does not measure out stinted alms to beggars, but he gives *like a king*, as we say; and if it be some grand festival day and the king is in his state array, his largesse is on a noble scale.

Now, when God is in His glory, bethink you, if you can, what must be the largesse that He distributes, what the treasures that He brings forth for His own beloved! Now, "according to his riches in glory," He will supply all your needs. After that, dare you despond?

O soul, what insanity is unbelief! What flagrant blasphemy is doubt of the love of God! He must bless us; and, blessed by Him, we must be blest indeed. If He is to supply our needs "according to his riches in glory," they will be supplied to the full.

Now let us close our meditation by considering

The Glorious Channel by Which These Needs Are to Be Supplied

". . . according to his riches in glory *by Christ Jesus.*"

You shall have all your soul's wants satisfied, but you must go to Christ for everything. "By Christ Jesus"—that is the fountain-head where the living waters well up. You are not to keep your wants supplied by your own care and fretfulness. "Consider the lilies, how they grow." You are to be enriched "by Christ Jesus."

You are not to have your spiritual wants supplied by going to Moses and working and toiling as if you were your own saviour, but by faith in Christ Jesus. Those who will not go to Christ Jesus must go without grace, for God will give them nothing in the way of grace except through His Son. Those who go to Jesus the most shall oftenest taste of His abundance, for through Him all blessings come. My advice to myself and to you is that we abide in Him; for, since that is the way by which the blessing comes, we had better abide in it.

We read of Ishmael, that he was sent into the wilderness with a bottle; but Isaac dwelt by the well Lahai-roi. And it is wise for us to dwell by the well Christ Jesus, and never trust to the bottles of our own strength. If you wander from Christ Jesus, brother, you depart from the center of bliss.

All this year I pray that you may abide by the well of this text. Draw from it. Are you very thirsty? Draw from it, for it is full; and when you plead this promise, the Lord will supply all your need. Do not cease receiving from God for a minute. Let not your unbelief hinder the Lord's bounty, but cling to this promise, "My God shall supply all your need, according to his riches in glory by Christ Jesus." I know not how to wish you a greater blessing.

III.

A New Year's Benediction: God Completes What He Begins

CHARLES SPURGEON

"But the God of all grace, who hath called us unto his eternal glory by Christ Jesus, after that ye have suffered a while, make you perfect, stablish, strengthen, settle you."—I Pet. 5:10.

I have taken this text as a new year's blessing. In discoursing upon it, I shall have to remark: first, what the apostle asks of Heaven; then, second, why he expects to receive it. The reason of his expecting to be answered is contained in the title by which he addresses the Lord his God—"The God OF ALL GRACE, who hath called us unto his eternal glory by Christ Jesus. . . ."

I. WHAT PETER ASKS FOR ALL TO WHOM THIS EPISTLE WAS WRITTEN

He asks for them four sparkling jewels set in a black foil. The four jewels are these: Perfection, Establishment, Strengthening, Settling. The jet-black setting is this: "After that ye have suffered a while." Worldly compliments are of little worth; for as Chesterfield observes, "They cost nothing but ink and paper."

I must confess, I think even that little expense is often thrown away. Worldly compliments generally omit all idea of sorrow. "A merry Christmas! A happy New Year." There is no supposition of anything like suffering. But Christian benedictions look at the truth of matters. We must not discard the sufferings. We must take them from the same hand from which we receive the mercy; and the blessing bears date "after that ye have suffered a while."

1. Perfection

The first sparkling jewel in this ring is perfection. The apostle prays that God would make us perfect. Indeed, though this be a large prayer and the jewel is a diamond of the first water and of the finest size, yet it is absolutely necessary to be a Christian that he should ultimately arrive at perfection.

Have ye never on your bed dreamed a dream, when stretching all your wings, your soul floated through the Infinite, grouping strange and marvelous things together, so that the dream rolled on in something like supernatural splendor? But all of you were awakened, and you have regretted hours afterwards that the dream was never concluded.

And what is a Christian, if he does not arrive at perfection, but an unfinished dream? A majestic dream it is true, full of things that earth had never known if it had not been that they were revealed to flesh and blood by the Spirit. But suppose the voice of sin should startle us ere that dream be concluded, and if, as when one awaketh, we should despise the image which began to be formed in our minds, what were we then? Everlasting regrets, a multiplication of eternal torment must be the result of our having begun to be Christians, if we do not arrive at perfection.

If there could be such a thing as a man in whom sanctification began, but in whom God the Spirit ceased to work, if there could be a being so unhappy as to be called by grace and to be deserted before he was perfected, there would not be among the damned in Hell a more unhappy wretch.

But such a thing shall never be. Whom once He hath chosen, He doth not reject. We know that where He hath done a good work, He will carry it on, and He will complete it until the day of Christ.

God perfects that which He begins. Grand is the prayer, then, when the apostle asks that we may be perfected. What were a Christian if he were not perfected? Have you never seen a canvas upon which the hand of the painter has sketched with daring pencil some marvelous scene of grandeur? You see where the living color has been laid on with an almost superhuman skill. But the artist was suddenly struck dead, and the hand that worked miracles of art was palsied. Is it not a source of regret to the world that ever the painting was commenced, since it was never finished? Do you think that the hand of divine wisdom will sketch the Christian and not fill up the details?

Shall God fail? Shall He leave His works imperfect? Point, if you can, my hearers, to a world which God has cast away unfinished. Is there one speck in His creation where God hath begun to build but was not able to complete? Shall it be said over the creature twice made—"The Spirit began to work in this man's heart, but the man was mightier than the Spirit, and sin conquered grace"? Oh, my dear brethren, the prayer shall be fulfilled.

But, beloved, it must be after ye have suffered awhile. Ye cannot be perfected except by fire. There is no way of ridding you of your dross and your tin but by the flames of the furnace of affliction.

2. Establishment

Let us now proceed to the second blessing of the benediction—establishment. It is not enough even if the Christian had received in himself a proportional perfection, if he were not established.

You have seen the arch of Heaven as it spans the plain: glorious are its colors and rare its hues. Though we have seen it many and many a time, it never ceases to be "a thing of beauty and a joy forever."

But, alas for the rainbow, it is not established. It passes away, and lo it is not. A thing that is made of transitory sunbeams and passing raindrops; how can it abide? And mark, the more beautiful the vision, the more sorrowful the reflection when that vision vanishes, and there is nothing left but darkness.

It is, then, a very necessary wish for the Christian, that he should be established. Of all God's known conceptions, next to His incarnate Son, I do not hesitate to pronounce a Christian man the noblest conception of God. But if this conception is to be but as the rainbow painted on the cloud, and is to pass away forever, woe worth the day that ever our eyes were tantalized with a sublime conception that is so soon to melt away.

Rooted and grounded in love. Is a Christian man better than the flower of the field, which is here today and which withers when the sun is risen with fervent heat, unless God establish him? Oh, may God fulfill to you this rich benediction. May your character be not a writing upon the sand, but an inscription upon the rock. May your desires be earnest. May your whole life be so settled, fixed and established that all the blasts of Hell and all the storms of earth shall never be able to remove you.

An appeal for maturity and progress. The benediction, however, of the apostle is one which I pray may be fulfilled in us, whether we be young or old, but especially in those of you who have long known your

Lord and Saviour. You ought not now to be the subject of those doubts which vex the babe in grace. Those first principles should not always be laid again by you; but you should be going forward to something higher.

How is it that some of the sunlight does not gleam from your eyes? We who are young look up to you older, established Christians; and if we see you doubting and hear you speaking with a trembling lip, then we are exceedingly cast down. We pray for our sakes as well as yours, that this blessing may be fulfilled in you, that you may be established: that you may no longer be exercised with doubt; that you may know your interest in Christ; that you may feel that you are secure in Him; that, resting upon the Rock of Ages, you may know that you cannot perish while your feet are fixed there.

3. Strengthening

Now for a third blessing, which is strengthening. Ah, brethren, this is a very necessary blessing, too, for all Christians. There be some whose characters seem to be fixed and established. But they still lack force and vigor.

Shall I give you a picture of a Christian without strength? There he is. He has espoused the cause of King Jesus; he hath put on his armor; he hath enlisted in the heavenly host. Do you observe him? He is perfectly panoplied from head to foot, and he carries with him the shield of faith. Do you notice, too, how firmly he is established? He keeps his ground, and he will not be removed.

Yet when he uses his sword, it falls with feeble force. His shield, though he grasps it as firmly as his weakness will allow him, trembles in his grasp. There he stands; he will not move, but still tottering is his position. His knees knock together with affright when he heareth the sound and the noise of war and tumult.

What doth this man need? His will is right, his intention is right, and his heart is fully set upon good things. Why, he needeth strength. The poor man is weak and childlike. Either because he has been fed on unsavory and unsubstantial meat or because of some sin which has straitened him, he has not that force and strength which ought to dwell in the Christian man. But once let the prayer of Peter be fulfilled to him, and how strong the Christian becomes!

There is not in all the world a creature so strong as a Christian when God is with him. He smelleth the battle afar off, and he cries in the midst of the tumult, "Aha! aha! aha!" He laugheth at all the hosts of his enemies. Or if you compare him to the Leviathan—if he be cast into the sea of trouble, he lashes about him and makes the deep hoary with benedictions.

He is not overwhelmed by the depth, nor is he afraid of the rocks; he has the protection of God about him, and the floods cannot drown him; nay, they become an element of delight to him, while by the grace of God he rejoiceth in the midst of the billows.

Here and there we hear of one who seems to work all but miracles in these modern times, and we are astonished. Oh, that ye had faith like these men!

I do not think there is much more piety in England now than there used to be in the days of the Puritans. I believe there are far more pious men; but while the quantity has been multiplied, I fear the quality has been depreciated. And this may account for the fact that, while our piety has become shallow, our strength has become weak.

Oh, may God strengthen you this year! But remember, if He does so, you will then have to suffer. "After that ye have suffered a while," may He strengthen you.

4. Settling

And now I come to the last blessing of the four—which is "settling." I will not say that this last blessing is greater than the other three, but it is a steppingstone to each; and strange to say, it is often the result of a gradual attainment of the three preceding ones. "Settle you"!

Oh, how many there are that are never settled! The tree which should be transplanted every week should soon die. How many Christians there be that are transplanting themselves constantly, even as to their doctrinal sentiments. There be some who generally believe according to the last speaker; and there be others that do not know what they do believe, but they believe almost anything that is told them. Men have come to believe that it does not matter what they do believe; that although one minister says it is so, and the other says it is not so, yet we are both right; though we contradict each other flatly, yet we are both correct.

I can never understand how contrary sentiments can both be in accordance with the Word of God, which is the standard of truth. But yet there be some who are like the weathercock upon the church steeple: they turn just as the wind blows.

Now, I pray that this may be taken away from any of you, if this be your weakness, and that you may be settled. Far from us be bigotry removed; yet would I have the Christian know what he believes to be true and then stand to it.

Take your time in weighing the controversy, but when you have once decided, be not easily moved. What is according to God's Word one day cannot be contrary to it another day; what was true in Luther's day and Calvin's day must be true now; that falsehoods may shift, for they have a Protean shape; but the truth is one and indivisible and evermore the same.

If, however, I wished you to be firm in your doctrines, my prayer would be that you may be especially settled in your faith. You believe in Jesus Christ, the Son of God, and you rest in Him. But sometimes your faith wavers; then you lose your joy and comfort.

I pray that your faith may become so settled that it may never be a matter of question with you whether Christ is yours or not, but that you may say confidently, "I know whom I have believed, and I am persuaded that he is able to keep that which I have committed unto him . . . ."

Then I pray that you may be settled in your aims and designs. There are many Christian people who get a good idea into their heads, but they never carry it out, because they ask some friend what he thinks of it. "Not much," says he. Of course, he does not. Who ever did think much of anybody else's idea? And at once the person who conceived it gave it up, and the work is never accomplished.

Now, I pray you, be settled in your aims. See what niche it is that God would have you occupy. Stand in it, and don't be out of it by all the laughter that comes upon you. If you believe that God has called you to a work, do it. If men will help you, thank them to stand out of your road or be run over. Let nothing daunt you. He who will serve his God must expect sometimes to serve Him alone.

But you will not be settled unless you suffer. You will become settled in your faith and settled in your aims by suffering.

Men are soft molluscan animals in these days. We have not the tough men who know they are right and stand to it. When a man is right, the worst thing he can have is inconstancy, vacillation, the fear of men. Hurl it from thee, O knight of the holy cross, and be firm if thou wouldst be victorious.

II. REASONS WHY PETER EXPECTED HIS
PRAYER WOULD BE HEARD

He asked that they might be made perfect, established, strengthened, settled. Did not Unbelief whisper in Peter's ear, "Peter, thou askest too much. Thou wast always headstrong. Thou didst say, 'Bid me come upon the water'; surely this is another instance of thy presumption. If thou hadst said, 'Lord, make them holy'—had it not been a sufficient prayer? Hast thou not asked too much?"

"No," saith Peter; and he replies to Unbelief, "I am sure I shall receive what I have asked for; for I am in the first place asking it of the God of all grace."

Surely, when we come to Him we cannot come for too much.

Believer, when you are on your knees, remember you are going to a King. Let your petitions be large. Imitate the example of Alexander's courtier who, when he was told he might have whatever he chose to ask as a reward for his valor, asked a sum of money so large that Alexander's treasurer refused to pay it until he had first seen the monarch. When he saw the monarch, he smiled and said, "It is true it is much for him to ask, but it is not much for Alexander to give. I admire him for his faith in me; let him have all he asks for."

And dare I ask that I may be perfect, that my angry temper may be taken away, my stubbornness removed, my imperfections covered? Yes, I may ask it; and I shall have it, for He is the God of all grace.

1. Think of Thy Calling

Look again at the text, and you see another reason why Peter expected that his prayer would be heard: "The God of all grace who hath called us." Unbelief might have said to Peter, "Peter, it is true that God is the God of all grace, but He is as a fountain shut up, as waters sealed."

"Ah," saith Peter, "get thee hence, Satan; thou savorest not the things that be of God. It is not a sealed fountain of all grace, for it has begun to flow."

"The God of all grace hath called us."

Now mark, if God has called me, I may ask Him to stablish and keep me; I may ask that as year rolls after year my piety may not die out; I may pray that the bush may burn, but not be consumed; that the barrel of meal may not waste, and the cruse of oil may not fail. Dare I ask that to life's latest hour I may be faithful to God, because God is faithful to me?

Yes, I may ask it, and I shall have it, too, because the God who calls will give the rest. 'For whom he did foreknow them did he predestinate, and whom he did predestinate, them he also called; and whom he called, them he also justified; and whom he justified them he also glorified.'

2. His Eternal Glory

But I think there is a stronger reason coming yet: "The God of all grace, who hath called us unto his eternal glory. . . . " Hath God called thee, my hearer? Dost thou know to what He has called thee? He called thee first into the house of conviction where He made thee to feel thy sin. Again He called thee to Calvary's summit where thou didst see thy sin atoned for and thy pardon sealed with precious blood.

And now He calls thee again. And whither away? The voice comes from the eternal glory. There where Jehovah sits resplendent on His throne, surrounded by cherubim and seraphim, from that brightness into which angels dare not gaze, I hear a voice, "Come unto Me, thou bloodwashed sinner; come unto My eternal glory."

Has God called me to Heaven, and is there anything on earth He will deny me?

3. Everything Comes Through Christ

The last reason why the apostle expected that his benediction would be fulfilled was this: "Who hath called us to his eternal glory by Christ Jesus. . . . " It is a singular fact that no promise is ever so sweet to the believer than those in which the name of Christ is mentioned. If I have to preach a comforting sermon to desponding Christians, I would never select a text which did not enable me to lead the desponding one to the cross.

Does it not seem too much to you, brethren and sisters, that the God of all grace should be your God? Does it not surpass your faith that He should actually have called you? Do you not sometimes doubt as to whether you were called at all? And when you think of eternal glory, does not the question arise, "Shall I ever enjoy it? Shall I ever see the face of God with acceptance?"

O beloved, when ye hear of Christ, when you know that this grace comes through Christ and the calling through Christ and the glory through Christ, then you say, "Lord, I can believe it now, if it is through Christ." It is not a hard thing to believe that Christ's blood was sufficient to purchase every blessing for me.

I would, in concluding, make this remark. I wish, my brothers and sisters, that during this year you may live nearer to Christ than you have ever done before. Depend upon it, it is when we think much of Christ that we think little of ourselves, little of our troubles and little of the doubts and fears that surround us. Begin from this day, and may God help you. Never let a single day pass over your heads without a visit to the Garden of Gethsemane and the cross on Calvary.

And as for some of you who are not saved and know not the Redeemer, I would to God that this very day you would come to Christ. You may come boldly. There is no fee required; there is no preparation necessary. You may come just as you are.

It was a brave saying of Luther's: "I would run into Christ's arms even if He had a drawn sword, but He has His wounds in His hands."

Run into His arms, poor sinner. "Oh," you say, "may I come?" How can you ask the question? You are commanded to come. The great command of the Gospel is, "Believe on the Lord Jesus." Those who disobey this command disobey God.

IV.

A New Year's Discourse

T. DeWITT TALMAGE

"This year thou shalt die."—Jer. 28:16.

Jeremiah, accustomed to saying bold things, addresses Hananiah in these words. They prove true. In sixty days Hananiah had departed this life.

This is the first Sunday of the year. It is a time for review and for anticipation. A man must be a genius at stupidity who does not think now. The old year died in giving birth to the new, as the life of Jane Seymour, the English queen, departed when that of her son, Edward VI, dawned.

The old year was a queen. The new shall be a king. The grave of the one and the cradle of the other are side by side.

We can hardly guess what the child will be. It is only two days old, but I prophesy for it an eventful future. Year of mirth and madness! Year of pageant and conflagration! It will laugh; it will sing; it will groan; it will die.

Is it not a time for earnest thought? The congratulations have been given. The Christmas trees have been taken down or have well nigh cast their fruit. The vacation ended, the children are at school. The friends who came for the holidays are gone.

While we are looking forward to another twelve months of intense activities, the text breaks upon us like a bursting thunderbolt: "This year thou shalt die!"

On the coast of England, three men entered a house of worship with stones in their pockets, intending to interrupt the services and assault the preacher. As the preacher began, one of the men said, "Let us throw." The other said, "Let us wait until he has made out this point." At the close of that, the first man said, "Now, let us throw." The third suggested, "I think we had better not throw these stones at all, but listen."

The first two, in disgust, left the building. Both were afterward executed for great crimes. The third remained and accepted the truth of the Gospel. Afterward he proclaimed it to many thousands.

So some may come to God's house armed with the weapons of criticism, but I think you had better drop your weapons. It makes but little difference to the preacher what you think of him, as it makes but little difference to you what he may think of you. But what think ye of Christ, of death, of the judgment, of eternity?

I. THE TEXT WILL BE TRUE OF SOME OF US

The text will probably prove true of some of us: "This year thou shalt die." The probability is augmented by the fact that all of us who are over thirty-five have gone beyond the average of human life. The note is more than due. It is only by sufferance that it is not collected. We are like a debtor who is taking the "three days' grace" of the banks. Our race started with 900 years for a lifetime.

We read of but one antediluvian youth whose early death disappointed the hopes of his parents by his dying at 777 years of age. The world then may have been ahead of what it is now, for men had so long a time in which to study and invent and plan. If an artist or a philosopher has forty years for work, he makes great achievements; but what must the artists and philosophers have done who had 900 years before them!

In the nearly two thousand years before the Flood, considering the longevity of the inhabitants, there may have been nearly as many people as there are now. The Flood was not a freshet that washed a few people off a plank, but a disaster that may have swept away a thousand million.

At that time God started the race with a shorter allowance of life. The 900 years were hewn down, until, in the time of Vespasian, a census was taken, and only 124 persons were found 100 years old, and three or four persons 120 years old.

Now a man who has come to 100 years of age is a curiosity, and we go miles to see him. The vast majority of the race pass off twenty years before.

To every apple there are five blossoms that never get to be apples. In the country church, the sexton rings the bell rapidly until almost through, and then tolls it. For awhile the bell of our life rings right merrily; but with some of you the bell has begun to toll, and the adaptedness of the text to you is more and more probable: "This year thou shalt die."

The character of our occupation adds to the probability. Those who are in the professions are undergoing a sapping of the brain and nerve foundations. Literary men in this country are driven with whip and spur to their topmost speed. Not one brain-worker out of a hundred observes any moderation.

There is something so stimulating in our climate that, if John Brown, the essayist of Edinburgh, had lived here, he would have broken down at thirty-five instead of fifty-five, and Charles Dickens would have dropped at forty.

There is something in all our occupations which predisposes to disease. If we be stout, to disorders ranging from fevers to apoplexy. If we be frail, to diseases ranging from consumption to paralysis.

Printers rarely reach fifty years. Watchmakers, in marking the time for others, shorten their own. Chemists breathe death in their laboratories, and potters absorb paralysis. Painters fall under their own brush. Foundrymen take death in with the filings. Shoemakers pound away their own lives on the last. Overdriven merchants measure off their own lives with the yardstick. Millers grind their own lives with the grist. Masons dig their graves with the trowel. And in all our occupations and professions there are the elements of peril.

Rapid climatic changes threaten our lives. By reason of the violent fits of the thermometer, within two days we live both in the arctic and the tropic. The warm south wind finds us with our furs on. The wintry blast cuts through our thin apparel. The hoof, the wheel, the firearms, the assassin, with their chance to put upon us their quietus.

I announce it as an impossibility that 365 days should pass and leave us all as we now are. In what direction to shoot the arrow I know not, and so I shoot it at a venture: "This year thou shalt die."

II. ADVICE TO ALL

In view of this, I advise that you have your temporal matters adjusted. Do not leave your worldly affairs at the mercy of administrators. Have your receipts properly posted, your letters filed, your books balanced. If you have "trust funds," see that they are rightly deposited and accounted for.

Let no widow or orphan scratch on your tombstone: THIS MAN WRONGED ME OF MY INHERITANCE. Many a man has died leaving a competency, whose property has, through his own carelessness, afterward been divided between the administrators, the surrogate, the lawyers and the sheriffs. I charge you, before many days have gone, as far as possible, have all your worldly matters made straight, for "this year thou shalt die."

I advise also that you be busy in Christian work. How many Sundays in the year? Fifty-two. If the text be true of you, it does not say at what time you may go; therefore, it is unsafe to count on all of the fifty-two Sundays. And since you are as likely to go in the first half of the year as in the last half, I think we had better divide the fifty-two halves and calculate only twenty-six Sundays.

Come, Christian men, Christian women, what can you do in twenty-six Sundays? Divide the 365 days into two parts: what can you do in 182 days? What, by the way of saving your family, the church and the world? You will not, through all the ages of eternity in Heaven, get over the dishonor and the outrage of going into Glory and having helped none up to the same place.

It will be found that many a Sunday school teacher has taken into Heaven her whole class; that Daniel Baker, the evangelist, took thousands into Heaven; that Doddridge has taken in hundreds of thousands; that Paul took in a hundred million. How many will you take in?

If you get into Heaven and find none there you sent and that there are none to come through your instrumentality, I beg of you to crawl under some seat in the back corner and never come out, lest the redeemed get their eyes on you and someone cry out, "That is the man who never lifted hand or voice for the redemption of his fellows! Look at him, all Heaven!"

Better be busy. Better pick the gunlock and bite the cartridge and be sure the caps are good. Better put the plow in deep. Better say what you have to say quickly. Better cry the alarm. Better fall on your knees. Better lay hold with both hands. What you now leave undone for Christ will forever be undone. "This year thou shalt die"!

III. IN VIEW OF PROBABILITIES, GET
READY FOR ETERNITY

In view of the probabilities mentioned, I advise all the men and women not ready for eternity to get ready. If the text be true, you have no time to talk about nonessentials, asking why God let sin come into the world; or whether the book of Jonah is inspired; or who Melchizedek was, or what about the eternal decrees. If you are as near eternity as some of you seem to be, there is no time for anything but the question, "What must I do to be saved?"

The drowning man, when a plank is thrown him, stops not to ask what sawmill made it or whether it is oak or cedar or who threw it. The moment it is thrown, he clutches it.

If this year you are to die, there is no time for anything but immediately laying hold on God. It is high time to get out of your sins.

You say, "I have committed no great transgressions." But are you not aware that your life has been sinful? The snow comes down on the Alps flake by flake, and it is so light that you may hold it on the tip of your finger without feeling any weight; but the flakes gather; they compact until someday a traveler's foot starts to slide, and it goes down in an avalanche, crushing to death the villagers.

So the sins of your youth, the sins of your manhood, the sins of your womanhood may have seemed only slight inaccuracies or trifling divergences from the right—so slight that they are hardly worth mentioning, but they have been piling up and piling up, packing together and packing together, until they make a mountain of sin, and one more step of your foot in the wrong direction may slide down upon you an avalanche of ruin and condemnation.

A man was crossing a desolate and lonely plateau when a hungry wolf took after him. He brought his gun to his shoulder and took aim. The wolf howled with pain. The cry woke up a pack of wolves. They came ravening out of the forest from all sides and horribly devoured him.

Thou art the man! Some one sin of thy life summoning on all the rest, they surround thy soul and make the night of thy sin terrible with the assault of their bloody muzzles.

Oh, the unpardoned, clamoring, ravening, all-devouring sins of thy lifetime! No time to lose if you want to escape your sins, for "this year thou shalt die."

IV. CHRIST STANDS READY TO SAVE

Let me announce that Christ the Lord stands ready to save any man who wants to be saved. He waited for you all last year and all the year before, and He has waited all your life. He has waited for you with blood on His brow, tears in His eyes and two outstretched, mangled hands of love. You come from your store and find your house has been on fire and your neighbor put it out. You thank him. You say, "I shall never forget this. When you want anything, come to me."

But when my Lord makes an attempt to put out the eternal consuming of your soul, you give Him no thanks and wish Him off the premises.

You come home some night and find the mark of muddy feet on your front steps. You hasten in and find an excited group around your child. He fell into a pond, and had it not been for a brave lad who plunged in, brought him out and carried him home to be resuscitated, you would have been childless. You feel that you cannot do enough for the rescuer. You throw your arms around him. You offer him large compensation. You say to him, "Anything that you want shall be yours. I will never cease to be grateful."

But my Lord Jesus sees your soul drowning in waves of death, and when He attempts to bring it ashore, you not only refuse Him thanks but stand on the beach and say, "Drop that soul! If I want it saved, I will save it myself."

I wish you might know what a task Jesus undertook when He carried your case to Calvary. They crowded Him to the wall. They struck Him. They spat on Him. They kicked Him. They cuffed Him. They scoffed at Him. They scourged Him. They murdered Him. Blood! blood! As He stoops down to lift you up, the crimson drops upon you from His brow, from His side, from His hands.

Do you not feel the warm current on your face? For thee the hunger, the thirst, the thorn-sting, the suffocation, the darkness, the groan, the sweat, the struggle, the death!

A great plague came in Marseilles. The doctors held a consultation and decided that a corpse must be dissected, or they would never know how to stop the plague.

A Dr. Guyon said, "Tomorrow morning I will proceed to a dissection." He made his will, prepared for death, went into the hospital, dissected a body, wrote out the results of the dissection—and died in twelve hours.

Beautiful self-sacrifice, you say. Our Lord Jesus looked out from Heaven and saw a plague-stricken race.

Sin must be dissected. He made His will, giving everything to His people. He comes down into the reeking hospital of earth. He lays down His hands to the work. Under our plague, He dies—the healthy for the sick, the pure for the polluted, the innocent for the guilty.

Behold the love! Behold the sacrifice! Behold the rescue! Decide, on this first Sunday of the year, whether or not you will have Jesus. He will not stand forever begging for your love. With some here His plea ends right speedily. "This year thou shalt die."

This great salvation of the Gospel I offer to every man, woman and child. You cannot buy it. You cannot earn it.

A Scotch writer says that a poor woman one cold winter's day looked through the window of a king's conservatory and saw a bunch of grapes hanging against the glass. She thought, *Oh, if I only had that bunch of grapes for my sick child at home!*

At her spinning-wheel she earned a few shillings and went to buy the grapes. The king's gardener thrust her out very roughly, saying he had no grapes to sell. She went off and sold a blanket, got some more shillings, came back and tried to buy the grapes. But the gardener roughly assaulted her, telling her to be off.

The king's daughter, walking in the garden at the time, heard the excitement and, seeing the poor woman, said to her, "My father is not a merchant, to sell, but he is a king, and gives." Then she reached up and plucked the grapes and dropped them into the poor woman's apron.

So Christ is a King, and all the fruits of His pardon He freely gives. They may not be bought. Without money and without price, take this sweet cluster from the vineyards of God.

When I sought for a text appropriate for the occasion, I thought of taking one in Job: "My days fly as a weaver's shuttle"; of a text in the Psalms: "So teach us to number our days, that we may apply our hearts unto wisdom"; of the prayer of the vinedresser: "Lord, let it alone this year also"; but pressed upon my attention, first of all and last of all and above all, were the words, "This year thou shalt die."

Perhaps it may mean me. Though in perfect health now, it does not take God one week to bring down the strongest physical constitution. I do not want to die this year. We have plans and projects on foot that I want to see completed; but God knows best, and He has a thousand better men than I to do the work yet undone. I have a hope that, notwithstanding all my sins and wanderings, I shall, through the infinite mercy of my Saviour, come out at the right place. I have nothing to brag of by way of Christian experience; but two things I have learned— my utter helplessness before God and the all-abounding grace of the Lord Jesus.

V. IF THE TEXT SHOULD MEAN YOU...

If the text means some of you, my hearers, I do not want you to be caught unprepared. I would like to have you, either through money you have laid up or a "life insurance," be able to leave the world feeling that your family need not become paupers. But if you have done your best and you leave not one dollar's worth of estate, you may confidently trust the Lord who hath promised to care for the widow and the fatherless.

I would like to have your soul fitted out for eternity so that, if any morning or noon or evening or night of these 365 days, death should look in and ask, "Are you ready?" you might, with an outburst of Christian triumph, answer, "Ay, ay! all ready."

I know not what our last words may be. Lord Chesterfield prided himself on his politeness and said in his last moment, "Give Dayrolles a chair."

Dr. Adam, a dying schoolmaster, said, "It grows dark. The boys may dismiss."

Lord Tenterden, supposing himself on the bench of a courtroom, said in his last moment, "Gentlemen of the jury, you will now consider your verdict."

A dying play-actor said, "Drop the curtain. The farce is played out."

I would rather have for my dying words those of one greater than Chesterfield or Dr. Adam or Lord Tenterden: "I am now ready to be offered, and the time of my departure is at hand. I have fought a good fight, I have finished my course, I have kept the faith; henceforth there is laid up for me a crown of righteousness, which the Lord, the righteous Judge, shall give me . . . ."

The sooner the last hour comes, the better if we are fitted for entrance into the celestial world. There is no clock in Heaven because it is an everlasting day; yet they keep an account of the passing years because they are all the time hearing from our world.

The angels flying through Heaven report how many times the earth has turned on its axis, and in that way the angels can keep a diary. And they say it is almost time now for Father to come up or for Mother to come up. Some days when they see a cohort leaving Heaven, they say, "Whither bound?" The answer is, "To bring up a soul from earth." The question is asked, "What soul?" And a family circle in Heaven find that it is one of their own number who is to be brought up. They come out to watch, as on the beach we now watch for a ship that is to bring our friends home. After awhile the cohort will heave in sight, flying nearer and nearer, until with a great clang the gates hoist, and with an embrace, wild with the ecstasy of Heaven, old friends meet again.

Away with your stiff, formal Heaven! I want none of it. Give me a place of infinite and eternal sociality. My feet free from the clods of earth shall bound the hills with gladness and break forth in a laugh of triumph. Aha! aha! We weep now, but then we shall laugh.

"Abraham's bosom" means that Heaven has open arms to take us in. Now we fold our arms over our heart and tell the world to stand back, as though our bosom were a two-barred gate to keep the world out. Heaven stands not with folded arms but with heart open. It is "Abraham's bosom."

Mother and the child in Heaven there meet. "How changed you are, my darling!" says the mother.

"Yes," says the child, "this is such a happy place, and Jesus has taken such care of me. Heaven is so kind. I got right over the fever with which I died. The skies are so fair, Mother! The flowers are so sweet, Mother! The temple is so beautiful, Mother! Come, take me up in your arms as you used to."

Oh, I do not know how we shall stand the first day in Heaven. Do you not think we will break down in the song from over delight?

I once gave out in church the hymn,

There is a land of pure delight,
Where saints immortal reign,

and an aged man standing in front of the pulpit sang heartily the first verse. Then he sat down weeping. I said to him afterward, "Father Linton, what made you cry over that hymn?"

He said, "I could not stand it—the joys that are coming!"

When Heaven rises for the doxology, I cannot see how we can rise with it if all these waves of everlasting delight come upon the soul, billow of joy after billow of joy. Methinks Jesus would be enough for the first day in Heaven, yet here He approaches with all Heaven at His back.

This is the last January to some of us. You have entered the year, but you will not close it. Within these twelve months your eyes will shut for the last sleep. Other hands will plant the Christmas tree and give the New Year's congratulations.

As a proclamation of joy to some and as a matter of warning to others, I leave in your ears these five words of one syllable each, "This year thou shalt die"!

V.

Spared for Another Year

HARVEY H. SPRINGER

(Delivered December 31, 1962, at Mobile Gospel Tabernacle, Mobile, Alabama)

"He spake also this parable; A certain man had a fig tree planted in his vineyard; and he came and sought fruit thereon, and found none. Then said he unto the dresser of his vineyard, Behold, these three years I come seeking fruit on this fig tree, and find none: cut it down; why cumbereth it the ground? And he answering said unto him, Lord, let it alone this year also, till I shall dig about it, and dung it: And if it bear fruit, well: and if not, then after that thou shalt cut it down." —Luke 13:6-9.

Here we have a story of a fig tree. One day the master of the vineyard came along and, noticing that it was not bearing fruit, said to the caretaker, "Cut it down!" The caretaker answered, "Wait a minute, Master. Let's give it another chance; let's spare it another year. Then if it does not bear fruit, we will cut it down."

Jesus always used simple illustrations to bring out some of the greatest truths. The very fact that you are sitting here tonight is because God has spared you. Even if the Lord should tarry, you may not be here for the next New Year's Eve service because you may not be spared another year.

God cursed the fig tree because it was not bearing fruit.

Most of us here tonight are Christians. Think back—haven't you neglected the work of the Lord this past year? As I look back, I think of many things I should have done but did not.

But last year is now history. I cannot redeem the time that is gone—any second of it, any opportunity. There is nothing I can do to change the past.

But what am I going to do about the future? What am I going to do about this year ahead of me? What are you going to do about it? Are we going to do any better this year?

I. SOME THINGS TO FORGET

Paul said, 'Forget those things which are behind.' One of the things we should forget is our past sins. If your sins are under the blood of Christ and Satan comes around to condemn you, ignore him; they are of the past. For example, when I came to church tonight, somebody whispered to me, "That man used to run a honky-tonk. He has just been converted." That new Christian can ruin his life if he continually thinks about the past, the souls he is responsible for sending to Hell. He must forget that.

Paul's life could have been ineffective had he continually worried about his past. Jesus Christ will not remember our sins if we have accepted Him as Saviour. Rather, He has blotted them out. So you should likewise forget them. He promises, "I will bury them in the depths of the sea. I will separate them as far as the east is from the west." So you forget them, too—or use them as steppingstones to success.

1. Let Us Forget Our Failures

Would you consider Thomas Edison a failure? Do you know how many experiments he made before his light bulb was a success? He failed 999 times. He tried to find a wire that would stand the heat from the electricity, but it would burn only a few seconds, then go out.

Thomas Edison never slept when he was on a special project, just dozed occasionally. When he became so tired he could no longer work, he would sit down in a chair in his lab with a bell in his hand. He would doze until the bell fell out of his hand. This would awaken him. He was then ready to go back to work. Sometimes he worked this way from six to eight weeks.

He failed time after time. When his assistant said, "Mr. Edison, let's give up," he responded, "No, we'll not give up. That's 999 ways I know it won't work."

Finally, he decided he had been working on the wrong principle. It didn't matter what kind of wire he used in the light bulb; as long as the air got to it, it burned up. He discovered that nothing will burn without oxygen. So he put wire in the bulb and then removed the air by suction. This proved to be successful.

We have electric lights tonight because Thomas Edison did not become discouraged because of his many failures.

I have seen people try something and, when it didn't work, quit. People like that get so sour, they look as if they were born in crab apple time, weaned on a dill pickle, put up in sour vinegar, and had had nothing to drink but buttermilk. All they think of is their failures. You can't get them to do anything because they are afraid they will make a mistake.

Well, who hasn't made mistakes!

We need to forget our failures, except to make them steppingstones to success.

Nobody looks upon Babe Ruth as a failure; yet think how many times he struck out. All the sports fans know is how many homeruns he made—701.

How many times do you guess he struck out? Over a thousand. But you do not hear anybody saying, "Babe Ruth fanned out over a thousand times." All they are concerned with is how many times he knocked the ball over the fence.

So why worry about the many times you struck out? Begin to think about how many times you have hit the ball.

2. We Need to Forget Our Grievances

Did you ever see a person with a grievance? He goes around with his lip stuck away out here. He gets hurt, and then he grieves. "So-and-so didn't treat me right." He can't get along with the cat, the dog, the chickens, his wife or the children, let alone with the church members. "Somebody hurt my feelings."

And do you know what? That very thing you are grieving over which is giving you a sour disposition and hurting the work of the Almighty God will not amount to anything in a few years.

A Christian should not have feelings—just accept what comes as a matter of course.

There was an article in the Reader's Digest years ago entitled, "Christmas in August." It was a story about a young man in World War II who had been called into the service. He had to leave his pregnant wife for the battlefront.

The baby was born. His wife loved him, but she was lonesome. Her husband had been gone for over two years, so she started going out with a young man whom she had met.

Soon she became convicted and thought she had better write her husband telling him what she had done.

In her letter she also expressed her love to him, told him how their little boy reminded her of him. She tried to explain why she did what she did.

Then she mailed the letter.

In six months her husband was discharged. They picked up right where they left off. He got acquainted with his little three-year-old boy, and they were as happy as they could be.

To her surprise, he never mentioned the letter. It had gone astray. After following him all over Europe, finally it was returned home.

The wife was gone when the letter came. Her husband read it. He had now been home for six months. Do you know what he did? He went out and bought a gift he knew she would appreciate and gave it to her. Of course, she was surprised. She said, "What is this— Christmas in August?"

Then he told her about the returned letter which he had just read for the first time.

You see, had he received it while he was overseas, their home would have probably been broken up and he would have never returned to her. But since he was back home and they were so happy and he knew he now had the love and fidelity of his wife, he forgave her for what had happened while he was gone. It made no difference now.

Some of the things that have hurt me the worst and that I thought I could not bear, now make no difference.

If you are grieving about something tonight, forget it. It probably won't matter two or three years from now. Let us forget our grievances.

3. Forget Ourselves

Too many of us have too much ego. I have been pastor of one church for twenty-seven years. I don't know how my members have put up with me, and I sometimes wonder how I have put up with them! I have seen many die. I have seen men and women who graciously accepted it as the Lord's will when a loved one was taken because they believed His promise, "All things work together for good to them that love God." They do not question God.

But I have also seen men and women destroy their effectiveness for God because they are so selfish. They are not willing to let a loved one go to be with the Lord. Don't you realize they are better off than we are? Did you ever think about it? You say, "Preacher, you are just talking." No, I know what I'm talking about. I lost my mother, and my father died instantly.

It is amazing what the Lord can do for us who follow His leadership. I seldom mentioned my father in church or paid him public tribute. I didn't want people thinking I was bragging. But this one Sunday morning I was going through one of the most trying times of my ministry. My father was aware of this. Suddenly, in the middle of my sermon, I looked down and saw my dad. I had him stand, and I told the people how he prayed for me, fought for me, stood by me. I praised him to the sky.

As he left the church that morning, he said, "Son, I won't be home for dinner."

He used to get in his car and drive out in the country where he could get alone with God. I knew he was going out there to pray for his son. He was living with us at that time. My mother had already gone on to Glory.

That afternoon about five o'clock, I was in my study when the telephone rang.

Someone said, "Harvey Springer?"

"Yes."

"Harvey, I hate to tell you this, but I have your brother down here." (It was the coroner of Douglas County calling.)

"My brother?"

"Isn't your brother's name Otto?"

"No, that's my daddy."

"Well, then, I've got your daddy. They just brought him in."

"Where did it happen?"

"On a little country road between Parker and Elizabeth."

It is about 28 miles from my house to Castle Rock. I drove down there, walked in, looked at my daddy and asked how it happened.

"He was standing by his car. A fellow driving by thought he needed help and got out to help him. He just dropped over backwards and was dead before he hit the ground, Harvey."

My mother and daddy are both in Glory now. I would not want either of them back. They are both so much better off.

I am reminded of a star football player whose name I cannot now recall. His father was born blind. This star player played game after game, but his father never saw how well his son played.

The father had a sudden heart attack and went to be with the Lord.

Now it was game time again. This day on the field the son played his heart out, knowing his daddy was watching him for the first time from the grandstands in Heaven.

Knowing our loved ones are watching makes Heaven more precious.

II. RESOLUTIONS

This time of year everyone is making resolutions. A great number of pipes are going into the ash can tonight. Packages and cartons of cigarettes will be thrown away. Do you know how long this will last? Probably until the day after tomorrow. Resolutions are all right if you keep them. But if you do not expect to keep them, don't make them.

1. To Pray More

As we look ahead, there are some things that we as Christians should resolve to do.

We should resolve to pray more during the coming year. Satan is becoming more powerful every day, and it is not easy to live for God.

A lot of people talk as though all our young people are going to Hell. I don't agree with them. I work with young people all the time. We had over three thousand boys and girls at our youth camp this summer. Don't tell me that young people can't live Christian lives anymore. I know they can. I do not think a fellow has to have one foot in the grave and be so old he can hardly get around before he can live a victorious life. I know a lot of young people who live for Christ. Don't tell me they can't.

I will say this, though: a young person today has a more difficult time living for Christ than at the time I was converted twenty-two years ago. The temptations are greater, and Satan is working harder. So I admonish you young people to pray.

2. To Preach Better

There is another thing: the preaching is weaker than it ever was. Brother, if we would preach like Jonathan Edwards and Whitefield and other such men of God, we would have their results. Let me give you an illustration.

I had a man call on me one day not long ago. He said, "Harvey, your preaching is too personal. We think you should preach as you are led, but we think you should preach a more positive Gospel."

I listened, and when he had finished, I thanked him and said, "There is a great deal of merit in what you say. I'll give it consideration."

When I got home that night my wife said, "Honey, I have been asked to bring a devotional at a bridal shower, and I want something on marriage. Have you something I can use?"

I found one of Talmage's books and gave it to her. When I read some of the messages in that book, they really got under my hide. I realized that I had been a little weak-kneed, thin-skinned, spineless-backboned, yellow-backed, white-livered, thumb-sucking, toe-kissing, pusillanimous, pin-headed, pie-rootin' biscuit hunter. I hadn't been preaching. You should go back and read some of the sermons those preachers who lived a hundred years ago preached. They make us look like a bunch of pussyfooters.

Then I studied the revivals. Do you know what Jonathan Edwards did? If he saw one of his church members go into a beer parlor, he called his name in church the next Sunday morning. Now, instead of preaching a man under conviction, we coddle him. When Jonathan Edwards preached his famous sermon, "Sinners in the Hands of an Angry God," he had men leave their seats and run down the aisle crying to God for mercy.

We ought to pray more for our pastors, that God would give them a backbone made out of cement and an iron rail up their shirttails instead of a sweet potato vine.

3. To Have Concern for the Lost

How few tears have you shed over a lost man or woman this year! You know, people used to shed tears for those who were unsaved.

Years ago I held a meeting in a community made up of hard-shelled Baptists. They believe what will be will be, whether it happens or not. You are predestinated for Hell, so there is no hope for you, no chance of your being saved.

Well, I went into this little community to hold a meeting. I poured out my heart, I begged, I pleaded, I bawled and squalled. I preached with all the fire I had. We came to the end of the meeting, and not a soul had been saved.

The last night I gave the usual invitation, as the Lord led. Nobody walked the aisle. I got mad. Maybe I should have gotten mad the week before, but I really got mad. I jumped down off the platform and began to shake my old boots. I ranted: "The Bible says when you preach the

Gospel and people won't hear it, then shake the dust off your feet. You are a bunch of Hell-bound sinners. Now you go on to Hell if you want to, for I'm done with you."

Before I got through, a little old mother got up out of her seat and came down the aisle. I can still see her yet. She paid no attention to me. She fell on her face, and I never heard such bawling and squalling! Every once in awhile she would cry out, "God, save my daughters!" Then she would cry some more. The tears were rolling down her cheeks.

Soon a girl came down the aisle and knelt by her mother. Soon the other daughter came.

I had already dismissed the service, so most of the people had left. The word got out, and the people started back to the church. We had dismissed the service at 9:30, but do you know what time we went home? Five o'clock the next morning! Scores of people got saved between those hours. Do you know why? One little mother could stand it no longer. She shed tears out of a broken heart.

Paul preached with tears. Jesus was called "a man of sorrows." Jeremiah, known as the weeping prophet, said, "O that my head were waters and mine eyes a fountain of tears, that I might weep day and night for the slain of the daughter of my people."

Let us shed a few tears over the lost and see if it doesn't make a difference.

You are spared for another year. How long do you think God is going to let you stick around?

4. Let Us Give More

Somebody is always saying, "The preacher is all the time talking about money." You are right. I won't argue. But who isn't? You think it odd because I talk about money! Every time I listen to the radio, I hear about the government borrowing a million or giving a million or doing something else which costs millions.

(My employees are either wanting a raise or hollering about the income tax!)

Oh, we ought to give more for the Lord's cause. Do you realize the American people only give one-tenth to the church of what is spent for cigarettes alone? No wonder God is not blessing us.

In Corinthians, we read, "They gave themselves willingly." I am not boasting, but a great part of my work is done with volunteer labor. A volunteer crew of men and women have been coming into my office two days a week to put out *The Western Voice.* They have never drawn one penny of salary, and I seldom thank them for their labor. They put the paper in the mail every week, and I don't even have to worry about it. Mrs. Springer and I used to prepare the paper for mailing on our front-room table. We had about 200 subscribers then. But now it is a big job. So these people come in and volunteer their services, their service to God.

When I started in evangelistic work, we would go into a town and build a tabernacle in three days that would seat two to three thousand people. We didn't know anyone in the town, so I would go downtown, approach someone on the street and say, "I am a preacher. I want to hold a revival and would like to build a mule barn. (That is what they were then called.) I am going to have some lumber out here in an hour or two, and I would like you fellows, if you are not doing anything today, to come and give me a hand."

I never saw it fail; we would have that thing built in three days!

But you walk into a church today, and you can beg people to do just the least little thing; but they'll say, "Well, I'll tell you, Preacher, I'm going to be busy tonight." What are they going to be busy doing? Watching "Gunsmoke"!

Spare that tree. Give it another chance! If it does not have any fruit on it next year, cut it down.

In World War I, King Emmanuel of Italy was called on to view the troops. A caravan of five automobiles came to a mine that blew up four of the cars. The car that King Emmanuel was riding in stopped just before they got to the mine.

The captain and one lieutenant were badly hurt—the lieutenant more than the captain. The captain went over to the lieutenant. Thinking that there might be another explosion, he begged the captain to go away and just let him die. But the captain refused. He stayed there and cradled the boy's head in his arms.

While he was holding him, he heard the car drive away. There he was, out on the battlefield, near the frontline trenches, and no car.

Shortly, the lieutenant died in his arms. The captain fell across his body and said, "My God! The king has left me to die on the battlefield! The king has left me to die on the battlefield! The car has gone, and there is no hope!"

About that time he heard a quiet voice behind him saying, "The car is gone, but the king is here."

Beloved, this year has gone, and another year is at hand. The King is here. He is watching to see what we are going to do with the treasures with which He has entrusted us.

We have this blessed Book. Let us resolve to pray more, give more, work more and read our Bibles more.

Some of you have read our tract that gives the story of Mr. McPherson, the man who in a northern Colorado mine had both eyes blown out and both arms blown off at the shoulder in an explosion.

They told him he was going to die, but he lived. Having no fingers or arms with which to read Braille, he had a special table made, and he learned to read Braille with his tongue, spending all night learning to read one letter.

The Braille Bible consists of twenty volumes, and they stand six feet high. That man has read the Bible through four times with his tongue. It becomes so tender at times that it bleeds.

Many of you say you are a child of God. You believe in the Lord, yet you have not read the Bible through even once. You should resolve, by the grace of Almighty God, to read your Bible through this year. You have twenty-twenty vision, so why can't you!

Why should you read your Bible? Because "faith cometh by hearing, and hearing by the word of God." Mrs. Springer and I read our Bibles through every year aloud to one another—three chapters a day and five on Sundays or the equivalent thereof.

God has spared you for another year, so He wants to use you for His honor and glory. Are you going to meet the challenge, or are you going to pass it by?

Beloved, no labor done for God is in vain. Those of you who were with me laying tile today were not doing it for Harvey Springer or for the school, but for the honor and glory of Christ. You are going to share in the reward for every boy and girl who finds Christ as a result of this building; and twenty years from now, if I'm in Glory and people are still being saved, I will still have a part in the reward. So will you. Nothing done for God is in vain.

Every teacher who sacrifices by teaching at a lower salary in this school, when you could be teaching in a public school for more money, will be rewarded. Some justify themselves by saying, "I can make more money in the public schools, and I still have the same opportunity to witness for Jesus." No, you don't, and you know you don't. When you make a sacrifice by putting God first, your earthly wages may not be too much; but you are sure stacking up treasures on the other side.

O beloved, let us resolve in our hearts to work for God and win souls and bear fruit this year, that we might be spared another year.

T. T. SHIELDS
1873-1955

ABOUT THE MAN:

Dr. Shields was born in Bristol, England, 1873, the son of a Baptist minister.

Converted in his youth.

Received early education in England.

Ordained to the Baptist ministry in 1897.

Held Ontario pastorates in Florence, Delhi, Hamilton and London.

In 1910 was called to Jarvis Street Baptist Church, Toronto.

Elected to the Board of Governors of McMaster University 1920-28.

Received Doctor of Divinity degrees from Temple and McMaster Universities.

Founded THE GOSPEL WITNESS, a weekly magazine, in 1922.

Was author of several books and booklets.

Was president of Baptist Bible Union from 1923-1930.

Founded Toronto Baptist Seminary in 1927.

For many years was president of Union of Regular Baptist Churches of Ontario and Quebec.

In 1948 was elected vice-president of International Council of Christian Churches.

Passed on to be with Christ April 4, 1955.

VI.

Songs in the House of My Pilgrimage

T. T. SHIELDS

(Preached January 1, 1899)

"Thy statutes have been my songs in the house of my pilgrimage." —
Ps. 119:54.

However old or young we may be, this coming year to us is new.
The very word *new* is significantly suggestive. That which is new is
necessarily untried. Some of you have seen the beginnings of many
years, but this year is as untried to you as to the infant of days.

Have you a tried staff, a tried Friend upon which to lean, with whom
to live this new and untried year? A new path, unless we have for our
guide one who has traveled it before, must necessarily be unknown.
We have not passed this way heretofore. "It is not in man that walketh
to direct his steps."

Have we a Guide—there is only one Guide who has walked life's
path before us without stumbling, and He is Jesus—have we put our
hand in His to walk with Him this new and unknown way?

This coming year will bring to all new experiences. We shall find the
new year a teacher of a higher and more advanced knowledge than
last year. We have not learned our hardest lessons yet. We shall have
new experiences, and we shall have to learn how to meet them. There
will be new difficulties, new trials, new sorrows. There may be new
deliverances, new triumphs and new joys. There will be new oppor-
tunities, too. There will be a wider horizon, a larger field to sow with
the good seed, a more extensive plain from which to gather golden
sheaves. There is possible for all an infinite enlargement of heart and
life. There will be new privileges, new gifts from His hand whose mercies are new every morning and fresh every evening.

And all this will entail new and increasingly heavy responsibilities.

New leaves will be turned over and written in God's book of accounts.

And so it is ours, whether we will or no, to cross soon the threshold of a new year. But this morning I would have you pause on the threshold and rejoicingly remember that, amid the light and the shadow, the joy and the sorrow, the life and the death, amid the many new, untried and changing things, we shall have no new or untried Bible, no new or untried Gospel, no new or untried God!

"Jesus Christ, the same yesterday and to day, and for ever." So David, who is said to have "served his own generation by the will of God and fallen on sleep," found Him. It is written of David, "He died in a good old age, full of days, riches and honour."

Let us learn the art of living from him whose life was so well lived that it pleased God and brought blessing to men. Let us try to find the secret of his sweet contentment, the source of his unequalled power. "I find the earthly life a pilgrimage," says David. "I was not different from others in this. I was a stranger and a pilgrim as all my fathers were. But," he continued, "I did not go my way with weeping. I wanted not for songs in the house of my pilgrimage." There was but one reliable subject for unceasing song; therefore, he says, "Thy statutes have been my songs in the house of my pilgrimage."

I. THE EARTHLY LIFE IS A PILGRIMAGE

David here speaks of "the house of my pilgrimage." I do not know that I need make any distinction here between the Christian and the unconverted soul; whatever your name, you are a pilgrim passing through the world. There is this difference, however, that the Christian pilgrim is wending his weary way upward into the light, while the unsaved sinner stumbles downward into the darkness. The conditions under which they journey are quite different, too. One is "in Christ" and the other "without Christ." But in this one particular we are all alike—pilgrims in a journey.

A pilgrimage suggests a *changeful life*. I have met with people who have lived in one place for twenty or thirty years and sometimes more than that. For all those years they have lived in the same house, walked the same street, known—except those who have died—the same people.

How different their lives to that of the man who has lived in both hemispheres, who has had residences in many towns, who all his life long has been meeting with strangers, breaking up old acquaintances

and forming new friendships. Two people having lived life so different-
ly could hardly understand each other. But even the man who has lived
on one little patch of earth all his life finds that his soul is on a pilgrimage.

I have been on a railway train when it moved so smoothly and quiet-
ly that I would not have known I was moving at all had it not been that
looking out of the window I saw that things were changing all around
me. And there are some whom God suffers to live in such long un-
disturbed quietness that they forget they are pilgrims.

If you doubt the truth that you are pilgrims in the earth, look out from
your window and you will see that things are moving, changing, passing away. And then you will pray:

> **Swift to its close ebbs out life's little day;**
> **Earth's joys grow dim, its glories pass away;**
> **Change and decay in all around I see:**
> **O Thou, who changest not, abide with me!**

A pilgrim's life must necessarily be an *impermanent,* unsettled one.
A pilgrim is away from home, and until his journey is ended, he calls
no place his home. He sees a fine landscape; he has an artist's eye;
his soul is enraptured; he would like to stay; but he is anxious to get
on his way; and with a passing grateful glance, he continues his journey.

He meets many pleasant people; but unless they are going the same
way, he has no time to enjoy their society: he is a pilgrim and must
move on. He does not—if he remembers that he is a pilgrim—think
within himself that his house shall continue forever or his dwellingplace
to all generations. He calls not his land after his own name. He does
not dig deep in the earth and lay a strong foundation for a princely dwelling as though he had reached the journey's end. "What were the use?"
he says. "I might never live in it; certainly I could not remain in it for
long. I must move on tomorrow." And so, like Abraham, he pitches
a tent.

So the Christian lives, setting not his affections upon things which
are upon the earth, but upon things in Heaven. "I am a pilgrim," he
says, "a sojourner in a strange country. I desire a better country—that
is, an heavenly. I look for a city which hath foundations, whose builder
and maker is God."

My dear friends, have we forgotten that we are pilgrims? Do we call
the earth our home? If our hearts are wedded to earthly things, there
will be bleeding, broken hearts when God calls us hence.

I fear there is too much truth in Whittier's lamentation:

> **The church, to place and power the door,**
> **Rebukes the sin of the world no more,**
> **Nor seeks its Lord in the homeless poor.**
> **Everywhere is the grasping hand,**
> **The eager adding of land to land,**
> **And earth, which seemed to the Father meant**
> **But as a pilgrim's wayside tent,**
> **A nightly shelter to fold away,**
> **When the Lord should call at the break of day,**
> **Solid and steadfast seems to be,**
> **And Time has forgotten Eternity.**

Let us remember that we came from eternity and are on the way back; therefore, the earth should have but a very little place in our affections—we are strangers and sojourners, only pilgrims here.

A pilgrim's life will necessarily be one of *much weariness,* and remember the life of the godly is a pilgrimage. I have read of some calling themselves pilgrims making their way in a railway train—that is not the pilgrimage of which my text speaks. How many would make the Christian course other than a pilgrimage! Over a prepared road they would go by bicycle or ride in a pneumatic-tired carriage or travel in a train, resting upon comfortable reclining chairs. They would "be carried to the skies on flowery beds of ease, while others fought to win the prize or sailed o'er bloody seas."

But God has made no railway to Heaven. We must go as Abraham went, as Paul went. "Walk before me," saith the Lord. "As ye have received Christ Jesus the Lord, so walk ye in him."

The Christian life is a pilgrimage, and there is no way to the Eternal City but the way is trodden by pilgrim feet; that means downhill and uphill, as well as the level plain, rough roads, stony and thorny, and bleeding, tired feet. It means facing contrary winds and pressing one's way against many who are going the opposite way.

See what words the psalmist presses into his service to describe his pilgrimage: "affliction," "derision," "comfort," "horrors," and in the verse following the text: "I have remembered thy name, O Lord, in the night." So must we pass through darkness to dwell in eternal light.

Progress is implied in the word *pilgrimage.* The Christian life is progressive; we do not stand still.

As I have traveled by train, I have noticed the boards at the stations: so many miles from one place, so many miles to another. The number of miles became less and less in the one case and more and more in the other.

So is it with us. We are leaving behind us the visible temporal things; swiftly we are passing them by, while we draw hourly nearer to the eternal verities. We are a day's march, a year's march nearer home.

Nearer our Father's house
Where the many mansions be;
Nearer the great white throne,
Nearer the crystal sea.
Nearer the bound of life
Where we lay our burdens down;
Nearer leaving the cross,
Nearer gaining the crown.

Therefore be not weary, pilgrim; though you move but slowly, you are getting nearer Home.

For life shall on and upward go;
The eternal step of Progress beats
To that great anthem calm, and slow,
Which God repeats.
God works in all things, all obey
His first propulsion from the night:
Wake thou, and watch! the world is grey
With morning light!

II. THE CHRISTIAN'S IS A PILGRIMAGE OF SONG

The psalmist sang in the house of his pilgrimage. *Christianity is distinctively a religion of music and song.* If you would know what it is to sing, you must hear a Christian heart pour forth its treasures in song. I would like you to get the plain teaching of the text that the godly soul should rejoice instead of mourn, and sing instead of weep.

So many people like to pose as martyrs. They are always talking about their trials and difficulties. One would almost need to be clad in waterproof clothing in their company, so profusely do they weep. With what melancholy emphasis do they drag out that word *cross*; one would think that Jesus had not yet accomplished His mission.

If there are any of these Christian wailers here this morning, I have a word for you. You are not a martyr. God never yet made a martyr or allowed one to be made of that material which might fittingly be called *grumblestuff.* Many of them, though they could have quenched the flames with their bending, never shed a tear.

Jerome of Prague came to the martyr's stake in his pilgrimage and, like Elijah, finished his journey in a chariot of fire. Ere he left, even when the house of his pilgrimage was wrapped in flame, he burst forth into

song; and to the accompaniment of the music of the crackling of fag-
gots, he sang that resurrection hymn:

Welcome, happy morning!
Age to age shall say:
Hell today is vanquished,
Heaven is won today!

If we sing no songs in the house of our pilgrimage, I fear we are scarcely deserving of the name of pilgrims. The songless Christian is the disobedient, lame, halting, wobbling, creeping, crawling soul who does not
"walk before God."

Many sing *love songs*. And why should we not join with Isaiah and
say, "Now will I sing to my well beloved a song"? Are there no charms
in Jesus to inspire our heart and tongue? There are *songs of hope*, and
shall we not sing who have a "blessed hope" which cannot fail of realization? And there are *songs of trust*. Have we no Rock Divine, no Refuge
sweet, of which to sing?

The psalmist had a house in which to sing. That is, he had times of
rest and periods of quietness in which he had leisure to think and to
sing. And so have we. We are allowed to rest in the night sometimes
and wait in the journey till the storm is overpast. Then it may be ours
to say: "My meditation of him shall be sweet: I will be glad in the Lord."

III. THE ONLY THEME OF THE PILGRIM'S SONG

"Thy statutes have been my song in the house of my pilgrimage."
We must sing, but we must be careful what we sing about.

If you sing about your friends and loved ones, your singing will end
in a funeral dirge by and by.

Sing of your wealth today, and tomorrow you will lament its loss.

Make health the subject of your song; and ere you have sung the
second bar, grim pain will cut the music short.

If you sing of summer, winter will soon mock your melody; and the
song that is begun in praise of light and life soon dies away into the
silence of darkness and death.

So in this pilgrimage we all have proved that that which is a fitting
theme for song today will become a subject for sighs tomorrow. What
therefore shall we sing about? This pilgrim seems to have said to himself,
*I would have a song that will not wear out. Therefore, thy statutes shall
be my songs in the house of my pilgrimage.*

This word translated "statutes" does not mean simply the written Word of God. It does include that, but it means very much more. It means that which is decreed and unalterably established and settled, whether revealed or unrevealed. In other words, it means the revealed and the unrevealed will of God. We might put the text thus: "Thy will, O God, has been the subject of my songs in the house of my pilgrimage."

It is a well-known fact that *everyone cannot sing*. Most people can make a noise, but noise and music are not synonymous terms. Singing is not the exercise of the voice merely; it is rather the utterance of the heart. To sing of God's statutes is not to sing, "Thy will be done."

You remember John tells us:

"And I heard the voice of harpers harping with their harps. And they sung as it were a new song before the throne . . . and no man could learn that song but the hundred and forty-four thousand, which were redeemed from the earth."

"No man could learn that song": the song of the text is equally hard to sing. Indeed, we might none of us learn to sing it were it not that our Teacher's skill is great.

Can you sing of God's will? Have you learned to sing of His revealed will? For if you sing not of revelation, how shall you ever sing of mystery? God's will is revealed in Jesus, and that which is hid from the wise and prudent is revealed unto babes.

You must know Jesus first if you would sing at all, for the mystery of God's dealings with men can only be understood in the light of the revelation of His love in the cross of Jesus Christ.

You must know Jesus, or otherwise for many a day and year—and if you know Him not at all—forever your harp shall hang upon the willows and you shall never learn to sing even one of the Lord's songs.

Some people would need a new voice and a new ear to make them singers; we all need new hearts and new spiritual ears before we can make God's statutes our songs in the house of our pilgrimage. We must be born again.

And yet, while I have said this song is hard to learn, *there are parts of it that to those who have been taught to sing at all are comparatively easy*. The will of God the subject of our song? How easy at times to sing of that: "It is your Father's good pleasure to give you the kingdom"; can you not sing of that? "Come unto me"; "God so loved the world"; "If heirs, heirs of God"; "The last enemy that shall be destroyed is death";

"In my Father's house are many mansions." How easy to sing these songs!

But there are difficult passages in this song, passages which only the few can sing. You know that, while most people can enjoy a simple, merry melody, it is only a few of rare, cultivated musical taste who can fully appreciate the minor strain. To the many, such notes are a jarring discord; but to the true musician these minor strains produce the sweetest harmony.

And so, they must have learned the sweetest of the minor key who are able to say, "Thy statutes have been my songs in the house of my pilgrimage." It is not always easy to gladly and joyously sing the will of God. Does not the divine will seem at times to strike a note of discord in your life? It is not discord. It is one of God's minors, making music which angels love to hear. There is no discord in the believer's life— "All things work together for good."

> **All discord is but harmony not understood,**
> **All partial evil, universal good.**

Those seemingly discordant notes are sweetest harmony if but our ears were trained to appreciate them. And what I want you to remember is this: that grace makes it possible for the child of God to sing even when God writes life's music in a minor key. "Thy statutes have been my songs."

Grace taught the psalmist to find pleasure in singing God's minors. Hear him in this Psalm: "Before I was afflicted I went astray: but now I have kept thy word." "It is good for me that I have been afflicted that I might learn thy statutes." And listen: "I know, O Lord, that thy judgments are right, and that thou in faithfulness hast afflicted me."

Can you sing that? Make His statutes your song; and if you cannot sing them all with joy, submit yourself to Jesus that He may teach you how sweet His will is and pray:

> **Strike, Thou the Master, all Thy keys,**
> **The anthem of the destinies!**
> **The minor of Thy loftier strain,**
> **Our hearts shall breathe the old refrain,**
> **Thy will be done.**

VII.

New Year's Resolutions

BOB GRAY

"When thou vowest a vow unto God, defer not to pay it; for he hath no pleasure in fools: pay that which thou hast vowed. Better it is that thou shouldest not vow, than that thou shouldest vow and not pay." — Eccles. 5:4,5.

At this particular time of year we are especially conscious of vows or resolutions which we have made toward a better life. A "vow" is a promise or an express desire of our determination to do better for the Lord.

Every Christian ought to know the joy of moving forward in Christian growth by making solemn and sacred vows. If we are to grow and mature in our Christian faith, then we must be willing to commit ourselves, in solemn promise, to God.

We have a commandment in II Peter 3:18 which tells us to ". . . grow in grace, and in the knowledge of our Lord and Saviour Jesus Christ." The Christian who never makes any conscious dedication to Christ is the believer who does not mature in our most holy faith.

The making of holy vows unto the Lord is scriptural. In Psalm 76:11 we read, "Vow and pay unto the Lord your God." There is obviously a very close relationship between the making of sacred vows and the rendering of effective praise unto God. In Psalm 61, verse 8, the Bible tells us that David testified "unto thy name for ever, that I may daily perform my vows."

Many Bible characters in both the Old and New Testaments made holy vows. The Apostle Paul made sacred vows during his tremendous and inspiring ministry.

Personally, I believe in vows. Every Christian ought to know the joy of making some promises or commitment, a yielding of his life, to the

Lord. Only an uninformed or backslidden Christian would refuse to make solemn vows.

Perhaps all of us have, at one time or another, heard someone say that it is better to make a vow than not to affirm any truth or intention in one's heart, even if we do not intend to carry out the vow! But the words of our text indicate that just the opposite is true. It is wicked to make a vow to God and not fulfill it. The Christian who has no intention of fulfilling his vow should never have made it in the first place. The plain commandment of God in verse 5 is, "Better it is that thou shouldest not vow, than that thou shouldest vow and not pay."

Of course, many faithless saints will never venture forward for Christ for fear of not being able to fulfill their stated intentions for Him. However, Christian growth and the Lord's blessings are withheld from those who never make any step forward by faith. If we truly believe the promises of God, then we will be willing to stand upon them and move forward, trusting completely in His power to sustain us as we determine to walk by faith.

It is wrong to make a vow and not do your best to fulfill your obligation to God. Most Christians would not think of taking the Lord's name in vain or swearing; yet it is just as much a sin to express an intention to serve Christ with some degree of loyalty and dedication and not intend to do so.

During my long ministry I have united many a couple in the bonds of holy matrimony. Solemn vows have been taken before God and an assembly of Christian witnesses regarding their marital relationship to each other. Unfortunately, some of these vows must have been taken with tongue in cheek since they did not remain married for very long. Flaunting the marriage vows which we make before God is a sin.

Every young couple coming to the altar of marriage should be reminded of the importance of the vows to which they are about to commit themselves. Very few young people these days realize that they have pledged themselves before God to remain together until "death do them part." The phrase "for better or worse" is generally not thought of as comprising a part of the marriage contract whenever troubles and difficulties arise later on.

For you who look lightly upon the marriage contract and are thinking of abandoning your pledge to remain together, I would quote a portion of our text in verse 4: ". . .pay that which thou has vowed"!

Another wicked sin of profanity is when Christians sometimes rededicate their lives or make some promise to God which they make no serious effort to fulfill. Some Christians have spent so much time running up and down the aisles of the church to "rededicate" that they have just about worn out their "dedicator." Please do not misunderstand. I believe that there is a definite place for rededication and reconsecration of a Christian's life to God. Realizing the weakness of the flesh, I would be among the very first to urge every believer to reaffirm his vows to Christ as often as is necessary.

On the other hand, I want to impress upon every saved person the vital importance of not making a mockery out of your rededication. In practically every revival meeting that I have conducted or have participated in as pastor, scores of Christians have walked forward and taken solemn vows to the Lord for the upbuilding of their Christian faith. My heart is always grieved to see such dedication wear off in a few weeks.

Many of you who read this message have doubtless been guilty of profaning a vow in the name of Christ. Scores of you have walked the aisles of your churches and promised the Lord and your pastor that you would be faithful in attending all the services; however, it wasn't long after the revival meeting closed until you missed your first Sunday. Now the habit has been established so that you are irregular once again in attendance.

Others of you have pledged yourselves to be faithful in the giving of your tithes and offerings for the support of the Lord's work; however, now that the pressure of the campaign is over, you no longer feel obligated to be faithful and consistent in your giving.

My heart literally aches when I think of the host of brothers and sisters in Christ who have pledged themselves to be faithful in soul-winning visitation and witnessing in days past but who cannot be found to go out and speak a word for our Saviour at the present time!

Listen, beloved, when you promise God that you are going to do something for Him, you had better keep that vow. It is easy to try to excuse ourselves on the failure of the flesh, but I want to remind you that you are guilty of sin whenever you make a vow and do not fulfill it.

Have you made promises to God that you have not faithfully kept? Have you made promises to your church and pastor which you have not been faithful in carrying out? May God give us the grace to confess our sins and the humility to resolve that we will be faithful in carrying out our determinations which will bring glory and honor to His name.

Let us consider some vows which some have already made and others of us need to make for the coming year. Do not be faithless but believing. The old adage, "Nothing ventured, nothing gained," is certainly true in this case. Determine in your heart that the coming year will be the greatest of your Christian life. By faith, step forward on the promises of God and make solemn vows which will bring you joy and happiness as well as render praise to Christ.

From the Word of God, let us notice some solemn vows which God would have us to make.

I. A VOW OF SEPARATION

After we are saved, we are commanded to separate from the world. Separation from sin is a Bible doctrine. No Christian can be obedient to Christ who does not live a separated life.

Let me mention right here that I am not speaking about a mere negative separation. Those believers who abstain from worldly practices and habits with no intention of doing anything positive for Christ have completely missed the point. It is unfortunate that so many church members are proud of the fact that they do absolutely nothing—including nothing for the Lord.

Just as a young lover separates himself from former companions in order to give himself completely to the bride of his choice, even so must the believer in Christ separate himself from worldly attractions in order to give himself to Christ in love and complete devotion.

Now that you have become a Christian, have you begun to separate yourself from the world?

In the Old Testament we have a wonderful story about a noble servant of God—Daniel. The young man was a separated Christian and was not ashamed to take a vow of separation to God. Notice what the Scripture tells us about his separation in Daniel 1, verse 8:

"But Daniel purposed in his heart that he would not defile himself with the portion of the king's meat, nor with the wine which he drank: therefore he requested of the prince of the eunuchs that he might not defile himself."

May God grant that none of us shall defile ourselves with the "wine" and "meat" of this world. These elements are symbolic of worldly ease and sinful pleasure.

The pressure of modern social life is tremendous. Many well-meaning young people have been led into gross sin because they have not purposed in their hearts to remain aloof from the contaminating sins of this generation. We are now living in a time when not many church members are living separated lives. Those who are separated from the sins of this world will always be a minority. Daniel was not the only Israelite in captivity at this particular time, but he was among the few who purposed in his heart that he would not defile himself with the worldliness and sin of Babylon.

Separation from the world is clearly taught for all Christians. In II Corinthians 6:17, 18, God says,

"Wherefore come out from among them, and be ye separate, saith the Lord, and touch not the unclean thing; and I will receive you, And will be a Father unto you, and ye shall be my sons and daughters, saith the Lord Almighty."

Too many Christians want to get to Heaven without any reward or expecting anyone else to meet them there as a result of their soul-winning labors. Our eternal destination is not determined by our behavior or conduct but by whether or not we have received the Lord Jesus Christ as our personal Saviour.

It is possible to smoke and go to Heaven. We know that it is also possible for a Christian to dance and go to Heaven. However, no Christian can engage in these worldly practices and please the Lord. Victorious Christians realize that separation is a must. Let us desire to be filled with the Holy Spirit in order that we might be effective witnesses for the Saviour.

Separation closes out the world and secludes us alone with God. A separated Christian is a happy Christian. If you are not separated from the world, then make a holy vow to do so now. With Daniel of old, purpose in your heart that you will not defile yourself with the "wine" and "meat" of this world.

If the majority of members in any New Testament church will practice the Bible doctrine of separation, then that church will soon have a testimony for Christ that will be distinctive and bring glory to His name.

May this new year see our church take a more separated stand for Christ than ever before. The line of demarcation between the children of God and the children of this world must be clear.

There must never be any doubt as to where we stand concerning our loyalty to Christ. Lot is a typical example of what happens to a worldly church member. He lost his influence, his character and the spiritual lives of his own children. You and I are no better than Lot. We will also vex our righteous souls if we try to live in Sodom and pursue the ways of the world.

If the Christian life does not indicate daily improvement in the moral and spiritual quality of your relationship to the Lord, then you certainly have not experienced any growth in grace since you were saved. Every day that we live for Christ should bring us closer to Him.

Nothing thrills me more than to see some of my sheep come down the aisle to take a further step of separation for Christ. God deliver me from a church in whose services there is no manifestation of the power of God to lift the level of daily living in the lives of His people.

This is an especially good time to take spiritual inventory for the coming year. Are you closer to the Lord today than you were at this time last year? If you cannot definitely observe a growth in grace and a separation to a greater extent on your part from sinful pleasures of this world, then by all means make a vow of dedication today! Nothing more completely delights the heart of God than to see His children walk in truth and grow in grace. Be a separated Christian.

II. A VOW OF SERVICE

For all of our duties to God, there is a definite pattern clearly laid out in Holy Scripture. This is true about salvation, consecration, giving and service. Since some of you are getting a reputation with God for being "shirkers" rather than "workers," this admonition is especially timely.

This is the day of spectator Christianity. So many are willing to attend church regularly but expect all of the work for Christ to be done by a group of professionals who are commonly referred to by most church members as the "staff."

Do not misunderstand. I believe that God can use a dedicated, consecrated staff of Christian workers. However, no member of the church staff can ever substitute for you in service of our Christ. Every Christian is called on to render faithful service to God. This is a task for which God will accept no substitute.

Are you faithful to serve the Lord? Can you look back and see that this has been a fruitful year of Christian service in your life? Let this year be a time of special dedication as you take a holy vow for God in Christian service.

God's plan for effective service is through the head of the home—

the husband and father. This is plainly laid out for us in Joshua 24, verses 14 and 15. Here we observe a time of crisis in the life of this great prophet of God. He said:

"Now therefore fear the Lord, and serve him in sincerity and in truth: and put away the gods which your fathers served on the other side of the flood, and in Egypt; and serve ye the Lord. And if it seem evil unto you to serve the Lord, choose you this day whom ye will serve; whether the gods which your fathers served that were on the other side of the flood, or the gods of the Amorites, in whose land ye dwell: but as for me and my house, we will serve the Lord."

How I pray that every husband and father in our churches will take his stand for Christ and vow to God that during the coming year he will seek faithfully to serve the Lord and lead his family to do the same. When the head of the home is faithful to serve God, you may rest assured that, in most cases, the wife and children will follow suit.

On the other hand, I have known many Christian women and young people who were negligent in their service for Christ because of the slothful example of an unfaithful husband and father.

Upon every one of us men is a very solemn and sacred responsibility—a vow of Christian service. Instead of the wife or the children taking the initiative for family altar and faithfulness to all of the services of the church, every one of you husbands and dads should lead the way. It should be the responsibility of the man to see that all of his family serve the Lord.

If the membership of a church is to engage in faithful service for Christ, then the leadership of that church must set the example. Every preacher should be faithful to all the services, along with each member of his family.

It has broken my heart to conduct some revival meetings in churches where preachers' wives and children did not attend. No pastor can expect his people to be faithful if his own family is negligent in this matter. Pastors should not just tell their people what to do but should lead them in doing.

Some preachers wonder why their visitation programs do not accomplish the job for God when they themselves never attend or participate. A church congregation never rises any higher than the leadership.

Every deacon should be faithful in performing his service to God.

Many deacons have not seen the inside of a widow's home in years! The office of a deacon requires that a man be filled with the Holy Spirit; however, it is a tragedy to observe that many have never led a soul to Jesus Christ!

The deacons of any church and their families should be faithful to all of the services of the church and should never miss soul-winning visitation unless providentially hindered. If the proper example for soul winning is not set by the pastor and deacons, how can we expect others to follow? May we all be able to say with our families, "As for me and my house, we will serve the Lord."

All over the nation churches are failing in their cause for existence. Sunday night services are rapidly being abandoned. Wednesday night prayer meeting services are rarely held in many churches. For the most part, our duties and activities for Christ are relegated to some position of unimportance and insignificance.

Church members have time for social events and recreational activities but no time for the service of God. May the coming year see every one of us more faithful in service than we have ever been. May every service see each member in his place manifesting a godly concern for the lost.

My heart is especially concerned for the many people who have walked the aisles of our churches in revival campaigns to pledge themselves for soul-winning visitation and who never come anymore. Beloved, that is a sin! Make a vow to God that you are going to put first things first and be a soul winner during the new year.

Real Christian fellowship in the church is best promoted in soul-winning activities. Some people have the mistaken idea that fellowship can best be had over a cup of coffee and with a doughnut in hand. This is not true. Our fellowship is in the Lord Jesus Christ and the blessed task to which He has called each one of us. May God give us grace and determination to serve Him acceptably.

III. A VOW OF STEWARDSHIP

No person is a good Christian who fails God in the matter of stewardship. The Bible tells us that "God loveth a cheerful giver." Church members who are sensitive about the word *giving* are usually out of the will of God. The faithful Christian is one who realizes that stewardship is a vital part of our Christian life. Jesus made the issues quite clear when He said that those who loved Him would obey Him and keep His commandments. It is not so much what we profess but what we practice that determines our real devotion to Jesus Christ.

If you are not a tither, then may God give you the grace to make your vow to do so at this time. The word *tithe* means a "tenth." As a principle of ownership, we learn from God's Word that the tithe is the Lord's. No Christian has given an offering unto the Lord who has not first of all given a tenth of his income to God before the offering is made. Our offerings are those gifts which we bring to the Lord above our tithes. The tithe is God's plan for carrying out the Great Commission.

It is a shame that a small minority in most every church must bear the financial load. People have money for lodges, civic clubs, recreation, P.T.A. and the March of Dimes, but none for the greatest cause on the face of God's earth! It is an insult to Jesus Christ to belong to His church and not be a tither.

In Genesis, chapter 28, Jacob made a holy vow unto God concerning the tithe.

"And Jacob vowed a vow, saying, If God will be with me, and will keep me in this way that I go, and will give me bread to eat, and raiment to put on, So that I come again to my father's house in peace; then shall the Lord be my God: And this stone, which I have set for a pillar, shall be God's house: and of all that thou shalt give me I will surely give the tenth unto thee."

Christian friend, if you have not yet made your vow to tithe, then make it today. If you wait until you are able to afford to tithe or until it pleases the flesh, you will never be a victorious Christian. Our tithes and offerings represent a portion of our lives; consequently, we cannot be good stewards of the grace of God unless we recognize our responsibility to give our complete selves to God.

Those who do not tithe are guilty of possessing a covetous heart before the Lord. Make a vow today that you will be honest with God and honor Him with your tithes and offerings. Do not wait until the Lord causes you to pass through some trial or crisis before you are willing to be honest with Him in the matter of stewardship. Never forget that Jonah spent three days and three nights in "Whale College" before he was willing to pay his vows unto the Lord. Stewardship is serious business for the Christian. If you resent a preacher mentioning anything about giving, then it is the best sign in the world that you need it more than anybody else!

Preaching the Gospel to every creature is our worldwide task. Souls are perishing and going to Hell! Sinners need to be reached with the Gospel!

May the Heavenly Father cause each one of us who is not already doing so to join with Jacob in making a vow of stewardship to the Lord.

Not only is the giving of our tithes and offerings the obedient pathway for every Christian to follow, but it is also the pathway of prosperity and unlimited blessing. The Lord has promised to open the windows of Heaven and pour out a material blessing upon all who are faithful in stewardship.

IV. A VOW OF SALVATION

A literal burning Hell is filled today with people who said they were going to take care of the matter of their soul's salvation last year. It is tragic to realize that they died without repenting and receiving the Lord Jesus Christ as personal Saviour.

To simply talk about your lost condition avails nothing. Many of you have been speculating for years as to the exact time and occasion when you will be saved. But as of this hour, you are still lost and in your sins.

Can you not realize that this contemplation without decision is a deceitful trick of Satan? The Devil will even consent to your realizing your need of Christ as long as you do not determine in your heart to be saved at a particular time. No one in his right mind intends to be lost and go to Hell. Only a fool would know what the Bible teaches concerning Heaven and Hell, sin and salvation, Christ and Satan, and determine that he will die lost! I find that most people plan to get saved someday, but they just never seem to get around to making that decision for the Lord.

If someone had asked you several years previously whether or not you would be lost by 1988, most of you would have said, "Why, of course not. I plan to get saved long before that time." But idle talk and good intentions will not save your soul.

Why don't you say now, "Yes, Brother Gray, I realize that I am a lost sinner and have delayed about making my decision for Christ. Right now I do repent and accept the Lord Jesus Christ as my personal Saviour. On this day, I make a solemn vow unto God to receive His Son and depend wholly upon Him for my salvation."

V. RAYMOND EDMAN
1900-1967

ABOUT THE MAN:

V. Raymond Edman was born on May 9, 1900, in Chicago, where he received his early education. While attending Columbia University, service in the U.S Army interrupted. He later earned his B.A. degree from Boston University.

A missionary effort to the Quichua Indians in Ecuador drew Edman's energies from 1923-1928. His forced retirement due to climactic illness brought him back to the States.

While serving as a pastor and conducting a radio ministry in New England, he earned the M.A. and Ph.D. degrees in history from Clark University.

Sworn in as president of Wheaton College, Wheaton, Illinois, on May 9, 1940, Edman guided the college through 25 years of growth and advancement, until 1965 when he became Chancellor, the office he held until his death. Under Edman's tenure was the acquisition of a western campus in South Dakota, a modern science field station in the heart of the Black Hills; a northern campus for leadership training at Honey Rock Camp, a 400-acre woodland tract in Wisconsin; the Graduate School of Theology; and a cooperative nursing program with West Suburban Hospital, Oak Park, Illinois. Fourteen major buildings were erected on Wheaton Campus during his administration.

Always eager to represent the college, Edman traveled extensively in the States and abroad, and spoke on six of the seven continents. He was also a prolific writer, having authored 18 books.

He served on the Cooperating Board of the Sword of the Lord Foundation and was a Sword Book Club judge for many years.

His philosophy of living all of life "not somehow, but triumphantly" showed up in everything he did.

Some "Edmanisms" were: "It's always too soon to quit"; "Keep chin up and knees down"; "Never doubt in the dark what God told you in the light."

Dr. Edman died September 22, 1967, while speaking in chapel at the college.

VIII.

Nothing Like Being Sure!

V. RAYMOND EDMAN

"For I know whom I have believed...."—II Tim. 1:12.

This is a new year. We have not passed this way before. Many things will face us, many situations, many affairs will confront us.

But can any situation be more dreadful than that of uncertainty?

We can face any circumstance, however difficult or dangerous, if we just know the facts; but uncertainty destroys any possibility of hopefulness or courage. To be uncertain is to be filled with apprehension, anxiety and fear.

Some time ago I was visiting missionaries in the jungles of interior Liberia. I had retired for the night alone in a little guest room. The generator on the mission station had stopped, and there would be no light until morning.

As I lay thinking and relaxing inside the mosquito netting which covered the bed, I was conscious all of a sudden that some living creature had come into the room. In the intense darkness I could not see it, but I could detect its movement on the mud floor. The missionaries had been telling me of the dreaded *mamba,* as deadly as the cobra, and which hunts at night. Of course, my thought was, *If I just had a light, then I would know the extent of my danger.* But there was no light, only fear manufactured and magnified by uncertainty.

And if that situation is dreadful, how much more terrible for a human soul to be in close proximity with death and not have the Light of the world, the Lord Jesus Christ!

If I were an artist, and I am not, and were called upon to paint a picture of uncertainty, the result would be much as follows: a lovely day in late spring, blue sky with some white cumulus clouds, some sturdy oak trees, and in the foreground a lovely lassie of sixteen or seventeen sitting upon a carpet of daisies. In her hand she holds a daisy and is deliberately removing one petal after another in order to ascertain the answer to her heart's question, *He loves me; he loves me not?*

Why is she asking a daisy which cannot give her the answer? Just because of uncertainty!

That situation may not seem serious to you, but it really is to her; but how dreadful for you to sit here, and deep in your own heart not to know the love of God, the reality of that word, "God so loved the world, that he gave his only begotten Son, that whosoever believeth in him should not perish, but have everlasting life."

In my classes I frequently see evidences of extreme uncertainty. I announce to the students at the beginning of the semester that they should buy a textbook and read its contents, that they should listen to the lectures, especially that they be prepared for certain "golden days" when it will be their privilege to write history as they understand it. (Some people call such an opportunity an "examination"; actually, it is an opportunity to show what one has learned. One could paraphrase James 1:2 by saying, "My brethren, count it all joy when ye fall into divers quizzes," for that is what "temptations" or "testings" really mean.)

When a "golden day" arrives, immediately I see responses of uncertainty. The young folks look at the questions; then some look out the window, perhaps with the vain hope that some aviator will write the answers against the sky with his plane. Some study the floor very steadily, perhaps with the vain hope that the grain in the wood will be food for thought. I recall one little freshman girl who would look steadily at me, as though I were the answer to some maiden's prayer. (I was, but that's medieval history, for Friend Wife and I are grandparents by now!)

Uncertainty! And why are they uncertain? Uncertain because they do not know what is written in the textbook.

If that is a sad situation, how much more dreadful for you to be uncertain about your soul's salvation when all the while you could find the answers in the Book of God! Hear, then, what the Book says. By the inspiration of God's Spirit we have the testimony of the Apostle Paul, written in the very shadow of death: ". . . for I know whom I have believed, and am persuaded that he is able to keep that which I have committed unto him against that day" (II Tim. 1:12).

No uncertainty here; rather, the strongest possible assurance when one is facing the greatest test of all—death itself!

Paul was entirely unafraid because he was perfectly sure of his salvation. Nothing in all the world can compare with that assurance—no wealth, no achievement, no honor, no reward, absolutely nothing can compare with certainty about one's salvation.

How could Paul be so sure of being saved? And how can we have that same certainty? What answer does the Book of God give?

I. TO BE SAVED, ONE MUST FIRST REALIZE
THAT HE IS LOST

The first step toward assurance of salvation is to realize beyond any shadow of doubt that *apart from the Lord Jesus Christ one is lost.* No one is ever really saved without knowing first that he is lost and needs the Saviour. Until one is convinced that he is actually lost and bound for Hell, he will trust in his religion, in his own righteousness and in his relative superiority to other people to make him worthy of God's favor; but when he *knows* he is lost, he will flee to the Saviour for salvation.

1. The Strictest Religious Pharisee, Paul,
Was a Lost Sinner

For a long time Paul did not think he was lost. Why should he? In his own words, he was "an Hebrew of the Hebrews; as touching the law, a Pharisee; Concerning zeal, persecuting the church; touching the righteousness which is in the law, blameless" (Phil. 3:5,6).

The Pharisees were much more religious than we could ever pretend to be. The Lord Jesus described one praying in his smug self-sufficiency, "God, I thank thee, that I am not as other men are, extortioners, unjust, adulterers, or even as this publican. I fast twice in the week, I give tithes of all that I possess" (Luke 18:11,12). Religious to the extreme, but lost; the Lord Jesus said so.

It was to a leader of the Pharisees, Nicodemus, that the Lord Jesus said, "Verily, verily, I say unto thee, Except a man be born again, he cannot see the kingdom of God" (John 3:3).

If any human being could have been saved by religious zeal and righteousness of life and conduct, that would have been Paul or Martin Luther. Both took their religion most seriously, applied themselves to its requirement with unabated zeal and desperate earnestness. If religion and morality could give assurance of salvation, they would have found it; but what is their testimony? Paul said,

"But what things are gain to me, those I counted loss for Christ. Yea

doubtless, and I count all things but loss for the excellency of the knowledge of Christ Jesus my Lord: for whom I have suffered the loss of all things, and do count them but dung, that I may win Christ, And be found in him, not having mine own righteousness, which is of the law, but that which is through the faith of Christ, the righteousness which is of God by faith: That I may know him. . . ." —Phil. 3:7-9.

"That I may know him"—no religious observance, no sacrament nor ceremony, no abstinence or good works, no developing of character could achieve that assurance—but faith in Christ did!

2. Luther, Most Zealous Monk, Was a Lost Sinner

Martin Luther followed much the same procedure and with precisely the same results. Hear his testimony:

> I tortured myself almost to death in order to procure peace with God for my troubled heart and agitated conscience, but surrounded with thick darkness, I found peace nowhere. . . . While I was yet a monk, I no sooner felt assailed by any temptation than I cried out "I am lost!" Immediately I had recourse to a thousand methods to stifle the cries of my conscience. I went every day to confession, but that was of no use to me. Then, bowed down by sorrow, I tortured myself by the multitude of my thoughts. . . . I was indeed a pious monk and followed the rules of my order more strictly than I can express.
>
> If ever a monk could obtain Heaven by his monkish works, I should certainly have been entitled to it. Of this, all the friars who have known me can testify. If it had continued longer I should have carried my mortifications even to death, by means of my watchings, prayers, reading and other labours.

D'Aubigne, one of Luther's biographers, declares:

> Luther did not find in the tranquility of the cloister and in monkish perfection that peace of mind which he had looked for there. He wished to have the endurance of his salvation; this was the great desire of his soul. Without it, there was no repose for him.
>
> But the fears that had agitated him in the world pursued him to his cell. Nay, they were increased. The faintest cry of his heart reechoed loud beneath the silent arches of the cloister. God had led him there that he might learn to know himself and to despair of his own strength and virtue. His conscience, enlightened by the divine Word, told him what it was to be holy; but he was filled with terror at finding, neither in his heart nor in his life, that image of

holiness which he had thoughtfully considered with admiration in the Word of God.

A sad discovery, and one that is made by every sincere man! No righteousness within, no righteousness without! All was omission, sin, impurity!

If you have thought about your soul's salvation you have reasoned, "There is something that I must do about it." That is the natural, human response, the same that is made the world over; yet you have begun to realize that nothing you have tried as yet has brought you to this knowledge of the Lord Jesus as personal Saviour such as Paul knew.

3. All Are Sinners Alike

Without doubt, the greatest handicap to one's realizing that he is lost apart from the salvation provided in the Lord Jesus is the persuasion that one is not as bad as other people. Because I am not a thief nor a murderer, I have therefore better chances in eternity than does one guilty of such crimes.

What is the answer in God's Book to such rationalization? It is found in Paul's own testimony, "For all have sinned, and come short of the glory of God" (Rom. 3:23).

All have sinned; there is no exception! The Bible does not teach that all men are equally sinful but that all are equally sinners. Says the Word: "Some men's sins are open beforehand, going before to judgment; and some men they follow after" (I Tim. 5:24). Some are guilty of very heinous crimes against humanity and against God; some have lived far better lives; but "all have sinned, and come short of the glory of God."

Let me illustrate.

Suppose all of us have gone to a park beside some lovely lake. We have enjoyed the activities of the afternoon—three-legged races, sack races; and have come to the last scheduled event before the picnic supper is to be served. And what is it?

A running broad jump across the lake!

How ridiculous, you say—a running broad jump across the lake. But we are good sports; we line up for the whistle that announces our effort. We get up as much momentum as we can and make the best jump we have accomplished in years.

Some of you who are younger and very athletic will jump sixteen or eighteen feet, perhaps even twenty feet, in the general direction of the opposite shore. Some of us whose athletic days have disappeared in added weight and slower movements will make more splash than distance, just sort of fall over the edge into the lake.

You made a long jump, and I a very little one; but both of us fell into the lake.

What advantage is it to you that you jumped twenty feet and I, two, for in reality we are both alike—we have come short of landing on the other shore! It is the other shore that counts, not the distance of your jump.

We remember it is written, "Not by works of righteousness which we have done, but according to his mercy he saved us." Actually, it would be far easier to jump over the Pacific Ocean by our own effort than to get into Heaven by our own good works, and our being better than others. Then, too, we remember that the Scriptures speak of a lake of fire into which fall all those who come short of the glory of God.

Lost apart from the Lord Jesus Christ. That is our true condition; and when that fact is fully realized, then we are ready to run to the Saviour for salvation. I trust you will do just that at the beginning of a new year.

II. REQUIRED NEXT: A DEFINITE ACCEPTANCE
OF CHRIST AS SAVIOUR

The second and final step to assurance of salvation is definitely to receive the Lord Jesus Christ as one's personal Saviour. We find that, on the authority and basis of God's Word, "As many as received him, to them gave he power to become the sons of God, even to them that believe on his name" (John 1:12). We are ". . . born again, not of corruptible seed [that is, the opinion of men], but of incorruptible, by the word of God, which liveth and abideth for ever" (I Pet. 1:23).

1. Paul Came to See Only God's Grace
Could Save Any Sinner

Paul's own testimony is contained in Romans 3:23 and 24. Immediately after stating that "all have sinned, and come short of the glory of God," he adds triumphantly: "Being justified freely by his grace through the redemption that is in Christ Jesus."

God saves sinners by grace through faith. Hear what He says: "Now to him that worketh is the reward not reckoned of grace, but of debt; But to him that worketh not, but believeth on him that justifieth the ungodly, his faith is counted for righteousness" (Rom. 4:4,5). We are redeemed ". . . with the precious blood of Christ, as of a lamb without blemish and without spot" (I Pet. 1:19).

On the road to Damascus, Paul met the risen and glorified Lord Jesus; and seeing how unworthy was his own righteousness in contrast with the worthiness of the Lord Jesus, he acknowledged himself to be lost and immediately accepted the Lord Jesus as his own Saviour. Thereafter, whatever might be the circumstances of his life, even into the valley of the shadow of death, he could say with complete confidence, "I know whom I have believed"!

He had the answer from the Book of God wrought in his life by actual experience, so that for him to live was Christ and to die was gain.

That is the certainty you should have, and can have.

2. How a Sixteen-Year-Old Ecuadorian Faced a Firing Squad With Assurance

Let me illustrate.

Years ago there had come to the Republic of Ecuador, in which for some years we labored as missionaries, an attempted overthrow of the government by revolution. The effort failed; and after a number of the rebels were taken captive, peace was restored.

Several days later a sergeant of the Ecuadorian army called for Mr. Will Reed, chairman of our mission, to go to the great prison that overlooks the seaport of Guayaquil. On arrival, Mr. Reed was taken into a subterranean chamber where there were many prisoners. Among them was a lad of sixteen who had sent for Mr. Reed. His name was Philip, a boy who had drifted into the Sunday school to hear the singing and the story of the Gospel. He came just a few times and then drifted away without our knowing where he had gone.

"I am very sorry, Philip, to see you here," said Mr. Reed. "What has happened?"

"I was inveigled to join the revolutionary forces. We were promised a large reward. Our officers betrayed us, and we were captured. We have been condemned to be shot at sunrise. Mr. Reed, do tell me again about the Lord Jesus Christ. I need Him now."

The missionary drew his New Testament from his pocket and read the promises such as John 1:12, 3:16, 6:37, ("Him that cometh unto me I will in no wise cast out,") and Romans 10:13, ("Whosoever shall call upon the name of the Lord shall be saved.")

The sergeant of the guard interrupted the conversation to say it was time for Mr. Reed to go. The missionary pushed the New Testament into Philip's hand saying, "Lad, believe on the Lord Jesus and thou shalt be saved."

At the gate Mr. Reed inquired for permission to be with Philip at the execution on the morrow. With that permission he returned early the next morning, only to learn that the execution had been postponed until the following day.

Again he came, very early it seemed to him; but as he came close to the prison, he heard a volley of shots ring out. Fear gripped his heart that possibly Philip might be among the first prisoners to be executed.

On turning in his pass at the gate, he learned to his dismay that Philip was already dead. Not another chance in which to tell him about salvation in the Lord Jesus.

Two nights later the sergeant of the guard returned the New Testament to Mr. Reed with these words, "Philip asked me to give this to you. You will note that he has written something therein for you."

On the fly leaf Mr. Reed read the penciled word from Philip: "I have believed on the Lord Jesus Christ. I shall be waiting for you in Heaven. Good-by! Philip."

When Mr. Reed had finished reading that testimony, he looked up to see the sergeant still standing before him. The latter then said,

> Sir, let me tell you about Philip. The other morning when we went into the prison to take out the condemned men, we had to bind them and blindfold them—all of them except Philip. He came to the doorway and inquired of me if he might not walk unbound to the place of execution. He said he was not afraid to die, that he was a Christian, that Christ had forgiven his sins, that when he would die out there in the field, he would go at once to Heaven. When I gave him that permission, he walked erect to his appointed place. He turned. With eyes open and hands unbound he faced the firing squad. Then he died. He was a brave Ecuadorian and a true Christian!

A sixteen-year-old boy unafraid to die! Why? Because Philip, like the Apostle Paul and like countless others who have come to saving knowledge of the Lord Jesus, could say, "I know whom I have believed, and am persuaded that he is able to keep that which I have committed unto him against that day."

Such is the simplicity and wonderful reality of assurance of faith in Christ—recognizing that apart from Him one is a lost sinner, and then receiving Him as Saviour on the authority of His Word.

There is nothing like being sure of salvation. That is the moment for you to step out of uncertainty with all its anxiety, apprehension and fear into full certainty of faith in Christ, for time and for eternity.

Will you do it now, at the start of a new year? This is how to have a happy new year!

Now

> **God be with you in the coming days—**
> **In the dark as in the sunny ways—**
> **With you in your hours of joy and pain;**
> **With you in your loss and in your gain;**
> **Ever near, your Helper and your Friend,**
> **From the year's beginning to its end.**

CURTIS HUTSON
1934-

ABOUT THE MAN:

In 1961 a mail carrier and pastor of a very small church attended a Sword of the Lord conference, got on fire, gave up his route and set out to build a great soul-winning work for God. Forrest Hills Baptist Church of Decatur, Georgia, grew from 40 people into a membership of 7,900. The last four years of his pastorate there, the Sunday school was recognized as the largest one in Georgia.

After pastoring for 21 years, Dr. Hutson—the great soul winner that he is—became so burdened for the whole nation that he entered full-time evangelism, holding great citywide-areawide-cooperative revivals in some of America's greatest churches. As many as 625 precious souls have trusted Christ in a single service. In one eight-day meeting, 1,502 salvation decisions were recorded.

As an evangelist, he is in great demand.

At the request of Dr. John R. Rice, Dr. Hutson became Associate Editor of THE SWORD OF THE LORD in 1978, serving in that capacity until the death of Dr. Rice before becoming Editor, President of Sword of the Lord Foundation, and Director of Sword of the Lord Conferences.

All these ministries are literally changing the lives of thousands of preachers and laymen alike, as well as winning many more thousands to Christ.

Dr. Hutson is the author of many fine books and booklets.

IX.

What I Want for the New Year

CURTIS HUTSON

More than twenty years ago I read a short essay entitled, "What I Want for Christmas." The author said he had just taken his four little girls for their annual visit with Santa Claus. One by one the man playing Santa sat each girl on his knee and then asked, "What do you want for Christmas?" Each child had memorized her list of requests and carefully explained to him exactly what she wanted.

When the last little girl finished, the father took her and left. As he walked away, Santa chuckled and asked him, "And what do you want for Christmas?" The man jokingly replied, "A fortune!"

But afterwards he thought, *If I could have anything and everything I requested, what would I really want for Christmas?*

Thinking on the theme, "What I Want for Christmas," I jotted down six things that I would like to have if I could have anything I asked for. But really they are things I want for the coming year.

I. FAITH ENOUGH TO ACCEPT WHATEVER GOD DESIGNS

The man who surrenders his life to the Lord does not live accidentally. Romans 8:28 says, "And we know that all things work together for good to them that love God, to them who are the called according to his purpose." If that be true, then Christ designs *everything* that comes into my life.

The poet was right who said,

> **My life is but a weaving**
> **Between my Lord and me.**
> **I cannot choose the colors,**
> **He worketh steadily.**
> **Oftimes He weaveth sorrow,**
> **And I in foolish pride**

Forget He sees the upper,
    And I the underside.
Not till the loom is silent
    And the shuttles cease to fly
Shall God unroll the canvas
    And explain the reason why.
The dark threads are as needful
    In the weaver's skillful hand
As the threads of gold and silver
    In the pattern He has planned.

I have lived long enough to know by experience that Romans 8:28 is true. I now look back and see that some things that I thought were bad were really good for me.

Somewhere I read of the farmer who cut down some trees and brush and stacked the limbs in a large pile to be burned after they had dried out. One morning when he noticed a bird building a nest in the brush pile, he took his hands and destroyed the nest. A few days later the same bird had begun construction of another nest. Again the farmer destroyed it. This happened several times. Finally the discouraged bird moved and began building its nest in a tree near the house.

Several weeks later when the little eggs had hatched and the wee birds were in the nest chirping, the farmer set fire to the brush pile. He knew what his plan was and, not wanting the birds to be burned, he interrupted the little bird's plans for its own good.

How often God interrupts our plans! And though we don't understand it for the moment, it is always for our good.

Before we built the Forrest Hills Baptist Church on Valley Brook Road in Decatur, Georgia, we had plans to build on another site. But God interrupted our plans by having someone buy the property. Our plans were already complete. We were at the lawyer's office for the closing when he discovered that someone else had an option on the property. He called the individual, thinking he would release his option so that we could buy the property. But to his surprise and ours, the man insisted that he was going to exercise his option; so we lost what I thought was an ideal location for a church.

Later that same day I spotted another piece of property, which we bought and where the church is now located. A few months later the street in front of the church was widened, and the Stone Mountain Expressway was built just down the street from our location. Everyone who sees the present site and knows where we intended to build, realizes that we got the best location for the church. I didn't know it then, but God was working things out for our good.

If I understand the Scriptures, even trials are designed by God. The Bible says in I Corinthians 10:13:

"There hath no temptation taken you but such as is common to man: but God is faithful, who will not suffer you to be tempted above that ye are able; but will with the temptation also make a way to escape, that ye may be able to bear it."

In other words, the Bible says that God knows how much we can bear, and He has promised never to overload us.

I sometimes visualize all my trials and temptations as coming across God's huge desk. He in turn checks out every trial and says about a certain one, "Curtis will not be able to bear that one. We won't let it through." Then He looks at another and says, "He can bear that one, and it's for his good. We'll let that one through." God okays every test and trial that comes to our lives.

If I enjoy this next year to its maximum, then I must have faith to accept whatever God designs for me.

Ephesians 2:10 says, "For we are his workmanship, created in Christ Jesus unto good works, which God hath before ordained that we should walk in them." This says we are His own handiwork.

Recently when I visited my father in North Carolina, he very proudly showed me a number of things which he had made—tables, chairs, picture frames, even some beautiful precision-made knives, including a pocketknife which was an expert piece of craftsmanship.

I said, "Daddy, did you make this?"

Very proudly he held out his hands and said, "With my own hands."

That knife was my father's workmanship. And every born-again believer who surrenders his life to Christ is God's workmanship. Philippians 1:6 says, "Being confident of this very thing, that he which hath begun a good work in you will perform it until the day of Jesus Christ." This says God is working on each of us. He brings just the right trial into our life that will work out for our good. He brings just the right blessings into our life that will make us into the vessel He intends us to be.

In Jeremiah 18:6 God says, "As the clay is in the potter's hand, so are ye in mine hand, O house of Israel." Just as Israel is in God's hands, so is every child of God.

It is not always easy to accept all things that come to us. It is not always easy to follow the admonition in Ephesians 5:20, "Giving thanks always for all things unto God and the Father in the name of our Lord Jesus Christ." But if we couple the "all things" of Ephesians with the "all things" of Romans, then we can thank God for everything no matter how bad it may be for the moment.

It is exciting to know, as we set out on our adventure, that everything which comes our way is screened by a loving God and designed for our good.

I want faith enough to accept whatever God designs for me this year!

II. A LIFE SO YIELDED TO GOD THAT I WILL REALIZE HIS COMPLETE PURPOSE FOR MY LIFE

God Almighty has a will and purpose for every believer. And it is His desire "that ye may prove what is that good, and acceptable, and perfect, will of God."

God is not a purposeless God. There is no loose motion with the Divine Potter's hand. Even the smallest insect has a divine purpose. God has something He wants to do with my life, and I'm excited about cooperating with Him that I may realize His complete purpose.

When I was pastor of a small country church, I knew that God had something else in store for me. When I was a full-time mail carrier and part-time pastor, I knew He had something else in store for me. The best I knew how, I yielded my life to Christ in full surrender.

We saw the tiny Forrest Hills Baptist Church of Decatur, Georgia grow to over 8,000 members and become the largest in the state and the fastest-growing Sunday school in America. But even then, I sensed that God had something else in store for me. And in His own good time, He put it on Dr. John R. Rice's heart to invite me to Murfreesboro to become the editor of THE SWORD OF THE LORD when the Lord called him Home.

I am thoroughly convinced that none of these things would have happened had not my life been yielded. Romans 6:13 says, ". . . yield yourselves unto God, as those that are alive from the dead, and your members as instruments of righteousness unto God."

Dwight L. Moody heard a man say, "The world has yet to see what God can do with a man who is fully surrendered to Him." Moody said, "I'll be that man."

With no education and no ordination papers, D. L. Moody surrendered his life to Christ; and the rest is history. He took England in one hand and America in the other and shook them both for God. The

Moody Bible Institute has been a pattern for most others who followed, and Moody's methods in building Sunday schools are still used today with great success.

We have read that before his death Mr. Moody said, "The world has *yet* to see what God can do with a man who is totally surrendered to Him." We suppose by that statement Moody meant that, even though he tried, he was not fully surrendered.

It is amazing what God could do with any of us if we were totally yielded to Him. I have often said that we are valuable to God only as we are available to God. The best ability is availability. God doesn't always use the most educated man, but He always, without exception, uses the available man. This has been proven over and over again, not only in the Bible, but throughout history.

He used a stammering, stuttering Moses because he was available.

He used a Gideon, the least in his father's household, because he was available.

He used David, overlooked by his own father as a prospect for king, because he was available.

He used a little boy with five loaves and two fishes because he was available.

He used the jawbone of an ass to slay a thousand Philistines because it was available.

And it's amazing what He will do with us if we'll make ourselves totally available to Him. He has plenty to do if He can find available instruments.

III. GRATITUDE ENOUGH TO BE THANKFUL FOR GOD'S EVERY MERCY AND BLESSING

In Psalm 103:2 the psalmist said, "Bless the Lord, O my soul, and forget not all his benefits." And in 68:19 he said, "Blessed be the Lord, who **daily** loadeth us with benefits, even the God of our salvation."

One of the greatest of all Christian graces is gratitude. Dr. Bob Jones, Sr., said, "Gratitude is the loveliest flower that grows in the garden of a man's soul; and when gratitude dies on the altar of a man's heart, he is well nigh gone." How true!

Jesus told the story of the ten lepers who were healed, and how only one turned back to give Him thanks.

Thank God for His mercies! Lamentations 3:22 tells us, "It is of the Lord's mercies that we are not consumed, because his compassions fail not." Verse 32 declares, ". . . yet will he have compassion according to the multitude of his mercies." Regarding God's mercies, the Bible says they are new every morning. They are higher than the heavens, and they endure forever.

Psalm 86:5 says, "For thou, Lord, art good, and ready to forgive; and plenteous in mercy unto all them that call upon thee."

Grace is God giving to us something that we do not deserve, and mercy is God withholding from us something which we do deserve. If it were not for God's mercies, we would all be lost forever. May the dear Lord help me not to be unmindful of His plenteous mercies. Thank God for every mercy and blessing!

Many things we take for granted are great blessings, and some things we consider as drudgery are really blessings. We sometimes complain about work and the drudgery of having to get up at the same time every morning, drive through traffic, spend eight hours in the office, and then drive back. But did you ever think how you would feel if you had no work? Suppose you had to sit around all day every day for months with nothing to do. You would then realize what a blessing work is.

Mothers sometimes complain about the children, about the dirt they track into the house, the clothes they leave lying around, and on and on. But when the children are gone and the house is quiet again, we realize what a blessing they were.

During the holidays we spent two nights in Atlanta with our daughter Donna. In the bedroom where we slept, I noticed a plaque on the wall:

A child is someone who passes through your life and then disappears into an adult.

It is an old adage but nonetheless true: "You don't miss the water until the well runs dry."

Yes, this year I want gratitude enough to be thankful for every mercy and blessing of God.

Somewhere I read that our word *thankfulness* comes from an Anglo-Saxon word which means "*think*-fulness." The more one *thinks*, the more *thankful* he is.

At this time of the year, it would be wise to take an inventory of what we have and express our gratitude again to God for His many mercies and blessings.

A man wanted to sell his home because he was dissatisfied with it. He called in a realtor who asked the seller to describe the home so that he could write an ad for the newspaper.

The man began: "Well, it's a three-bedroom house with two baths. We just replaced the roof last year. We just put a new water heater in recently. And this summer we landscaped both the back and front yards." He went on to describe exactly the kind of shrubbery he had planted.

When he had finished describing his home, the realtor said, "Let me read it back and see if we have it correct." When he read the description the man had given, the owner smiled and said, "That's the very kind of home I've wanted all my life! I'm not about to sell it! Forget the ad in the paper."

He didn't realize what he had until he began to describe it.

I'm afraid that's true of most of us.

May the dear Lord help me to be a grateful person.

Ingratitude leads to other sins. Romans 1:21 tells us, "Because that, when they knew God, they glorified him not as God, neither were thankful; but became vain in their imaginations, and their foolish heart was darkened." That passage goes on to describe how they gave themselves over to do those things which were not convenient, and adds, "God also gave them up to uncleanness through the lusts of their own hearts, to dishonour their own bodies between themselves" (vs. 24). Now look at verse 25: "Who changed the truth of God into a lie, and worshipped and served the creature more than the Creator, who is blessed for ever. Amen."

Why did God give them up to uncleanness? Why did they worship and serve the creature more than the Creator? Well, in part, because they were not thankful.

In the coming year, I would like to have enough gratitude to be thankful for every mercy and blessing of God.

IV. ENOUGH PATIENCE TO BUILD SWORD OF THE LORD FOUNDATION INTO AN EVEN GREATER MINISTRY

Before his death, Dr. John R. Rice said to me, "Curt, you ought to take what I have done and build on it a far greater ministry."

God has blessed us, and this year more people wrote to say they were saved after reading a sermon in THE SWORD OF THE LORD than in any previous year. And according to our circulation manager, we now have the highest paid circulation ever. The conferences are better attended now, and God is blessing in every respect. This year we have had more people saved in our meetings than in any previous year.

But we are not satisfied. We want to see Sword of the Lord Foundation grow into an even greater ministry. If we are to realize our desire, then we must have patience. The dictionary defines *patience* as "capable of bearing delay and waiting for the right moment." A friend of mine said, "Patience is the ability to put up with what you want to put down."

The word *patience* is found 33 times in the New Testament, and most times it appears as an exhortation. We read in II Corinthians 6:4, "But in all things approving ourselves as the ministers of God, in much patience, in afflictions, in necessities, in distresses."

Patience is the child of tribulation, says James 1:3—"the trying of your faith worketh patience." Romans 5:3 says "tribulation worketh patience." I know from experience that no one can pastor an aggressive, soul-winning church without patience; and I am convinced that no great ministries are built without it.

One Sunday school teacher, wanting to explain the dangers of alcohol to her class of small boys, took a glass of clear water, placed it on a desk and then took a glass of alcohol and placed it next to the glass of water. She then dropped earthworms into the water. They were not harmed. But when she dropped earthworms into the alcohol, they died immediately.

Holding the glass of alcohol in one hand and the glass of water in the other, she asked, "Now, boys, what does this teach us?"

One small boy spoke up. "If you've got worms, drink a lot of alcohol."

Anyone who has taught a class of small children or is rearing children, knows it takes patience. It is common to hear a mother or father say, "If I have told Billy one time to pick up his clothes, I have told him a thousand times. When will he ever learn?"

An oriental fable tells of a Chinaman who wanted a needle. When one could not be found, someone said, "I have a crowbar and a file." The Chinaman took the crowbar in one hand and the file in the other and said, "It is just a matter of time, and I will have a needle."

If we preachers had that kind of patience, we could build great churches.

A farmer bought a calf and was leading it home on the end of a rope. To make sure the calf didn't get away, he tied the other end of the rope around his own waist. The calf got frightened, ran away and dragged the farmer through several fences, a briar patch and several other objects of scenery. When the calf finally stopped, some sympathetic bystanders walked over and started to untie the rope from the farmer's waist. "Never mind me," said the farmer. "Untie the calf. I'll stand!"

God give us patience to stand in the New Year! Many things will come to try our patience, and, if we are not careful, we will lose our temper and hinder our own ministry. I would like to have patience enough to continue building Sword of the Lord Foundation into a greater ministry.

V. GOD'S SMILE AND APPROVAL ON ALL I SAY AND DO

Paul said in II Corinthians 5:9, "Wherefore we labour, that, whether present or absent, we may be accepted of him." The marginal rendering in the Scofield Bible is that we may be "well pleasing to" Him.

I pray for the approval of respected fundamental leaders, but I would far rather have the approval of God, wouldn't you?

When Abraham was ninety, the Lord instructed him in Genesis 17:1,2, "Walk before me, and be thou perfect. And I will make my covenant between me and thee, and will multiply thee exceedingly." The expression "walk before me" means "live your life to Me."

I fear we sometimes get too concerned about what people think and forget that the important thing is what God thinks about us.

Several years ago I read of a man whose duty it was to collect passes from those who rode a commuter train. On this particular morning there was a long line waiting to board the train. When one in the line reached the ticket-collector, he suddenly realized he didn't have his ticket.

The collector said, "I'm sorry, but I can't let you board the train without a ticket."

The angry man exclaimed, "But I have a ticket. I've just lost it."

"I'm sorry," said the man, "I can't let you board without a ticket."

The fellow who had lost his ticket literally cursed the man. Finally a police officer carried him away.

The next man in line smiled at the ticket-collector and said, "You're not a very popular man this morning, are you?"

At that remark, he pointed to a glass booth where his supervisor was sitting and said, "As long as he is pleased, I really don't care what others think about me."

It is our job to please the Lord; and, if in so doing we please others, well and fine. But if not, we must still please the Lord.

The greatest words anyone will ever hear will be when the Master says, "Well done, thou good and faithful servant."

In the coming year I'd like to have God's smile of approval on all that I do and say. That will not be easy. If it comes to pass, I'll have to work at it.

A young preacher accepted a church with 700 members. After a few weeks, the members gave a reception for him.

During the reception, one lady remarked, "Young man, I marvel at your courage in coming here and attempting to please 700 people."

The young preacher smiled as he said, "I didn't come here to please 700 people. I came here to please one Person; and if I please Him, that's really all that matters."

How true!

VI. GRACE ENOUGH TO BE SWEET UNDER ALL CONDITIONS

Preachers face temptations that I am not sure others understand. For instance, the Bible says in II Timothy 4:2 that we are to "reprove, rebuke, exhort with all longsuffering and doctrine." The verse literally means that we are to show people in what ways their lives are wrong. We are to convince them, rebuking, correcting, warning and urging; and we are to do it with inexhaustible patience—that is, with all longsuffering.

It is difficult for a preacher to deliver a hard sermon rebuking the congregation and at the same time maintain a sweet spirit. I discovered early in my ministry that I was going to have to learn how to change gears quickly. There were occasions when I had to rebuke the congregation. It was not always easy to have a sweet, happy attitude during Sunday lunch after having delivered such a message.

It's not always easy for a father or mother to have a sweet, happy attitude after having spanked a child. It is difficult to change gears that fast.

Then, too, it is difficult to stay sweet when people say unkind and untrue things about you. I suppose every living soul has been falsely accused at one time or another.

Just this week I received a letter informing me that a preacher had told his congregation some untrue things about me. My initial reaction was the desire to go and beat the daylights out of the fellow. But that certainly wouldn't be proper. It is easy to become angry in such a situation and harbor bitterness and anger, but that's a foolish thing to do. Anger and bitterness only destroy the vessel in which it is kept, and

I don't want to let anyone harm me by causing me to hate him or be bitter towards him.

Blessed is the man who can be sweet under all conditions.

Even the direst catastrophes may be softened by our attitude to them. Charles II said to those who had gathered about his deathbed: "You'll pardon any little lapses, gentlemen. I've never done this thing before."

KEEP SWEET

Don't be foolish and get sour when things don't just come your way—
Don't you be a pampered baby and declare, "Now I won't play!"
    Just go grinning on and bear it;
    Have you heartache? Millions share it,
    If you earn a crown, you'll wear it—
      Keep sweet.

Don't go handing out your troubles to your busy fellowmen—
If you whine around they'll try to keep from meeting you again;
    Don't declare the world's "agin" you,
    Don't let pessimism win you,
    Prove there's lots of good stuff in you—
      Keep sweet.

If your dearest hopes seem blighted and despair looms into view,
Set your jaw and whisper grimly, "Though they're false, yet I'll be true."
    Never let your heart grow bitter;
    With your lips to Hope's transmitter,
    Hear Love's songbirds bravely twitter,
      "Keep sweet."

Bless your heart, this world's a good one, and will always help a man;
Hate, misanthropy and malice have no place in Nature's plan.
    Help your brother there who's sighing,
    Keep his flag of courage flying;
    Help him try—'twill keep you trying—
      Keep sweet.

—Strickland W. Gillilan

To be sure, I am not claiming that I am able to do it, but I would like to have grace enough to be sweet under all conditions. We are reminded in I Corinthians 13:4, "Love suffereth long, and is kind." It's one thing to endure long; it's another thing to be kind. Blessed is the man who can do both!

Years ago there was a group of people we referred to as tramps. These had no home. They roamed from one town to another sleeping anywhere they could and living off the generosity of others. When it came time for a meal, these seldom went to a restaurant. They would stop at the nearest house and ask for something to eat.

I remember seeing them when I was a little boy. They would usually have a stick across one shoulder and all their belongings tied in a small bag on the end of the stick.

One day such a tramp stopped at a lady's home and asked for food. She gave him a biscuit with ham. As he walked back toward the street, he looked to see what she had given him. And when he saw it, he threw it into the ditch and kept walking.

The lady, who had seen his ungrateful gesture, screamed out to others in the home, "I wish I had never given him a bite! You'll never see the next time I give another tramp something to eat!" Kind—yes, but she wasn't very longsuffering.

There are few things more wonderful than sweet, dedicated Christians. Just recently I spoke in a church in Florida; and before I was introduced, a beautiful Christian lady old enough to be my mother was called on to sing. The presence of Christ was very evident in her life. Her smile said it all. As she sang, I found myself saying, *Dear Lord, make me as sweet a Christian as this lady obviously is.*

God, help us not to fly off the handle and say things we can never retract and do things we can never undo.

Not every Christian has grace enough to be sweet under all conditions, but what a joy when we find someone who does! Someone explained the difference between prejudice and conviction by saying, "The difference between prejudice and conviction is that you can explain conviction without getting mad." In other words, you can stay sweet while explaining your stand.

If I could have anything I wanted this year, I would like to have faith enough to accept whatever God designs for me; a life so yielded to God that I could realize His complete purpose for me; gratitude enough to be thankful for His every blessing and mercy; God's smile of approval on all I do and say; patience enough to continue building Sword of the Lord Foundation into an even greater ministry; and grace enough to be sweet under all conditions.

Dear reader, what do you want for this coming year?

X.

The Eyes of the Lord Are Always Upon You

JACK HYLES

"The eyes of the Lord thy God are always upon it, from the beginning of the year even unto the end of the year."—Deut. 11:12.

The Israelites were about to go into the Promised Land. The year 1451 B.C. was one of the most eventful and contrasting years of all in the life of the Israelites. Moses speaks to them at the first of the year. He knows what they will face during the year.

He knows that in 1451 B.C. the Jews will begin the year in the wilderness in wandering and suffering. But during this year they will cross the Jordan River. They will fight and win the battle of Jericho. In 1451 B.C.—this same year—they will lose the battle of Ai because of the secret sin of Achan.

In 1451 B.C. they will conquer the land of Canaan. They will wander in the wilderness, cross the Jordan, be victorious at Jericho, get defeated at Ai, and conquer the land all in one year.

So Moses is saying, "Folks, don't forget this. From the beginning until the end of the year, the eyes of the Lord are always upon you."

Moses is telling them, "Folks, you have a busy year. You will have to start it in the wilderness. The eyes of the Lord will be upon you from the beginning unto the end of the year."

He reminds them, "You are going to have to cross the Jordan River sometime this year. Don't forget—the eyes of the Lord will be upon you from the beginning unto the ending of the year."

Then he says, "You are going to have to fight the battle of Jericho. You are going to live up on top of the mountain, but don't forget—the eyes of the Lord will be upon you from the beginning unto the end of the year."

He said, "You are going to have some sin this year in your life, that secret sin of stealing that coat and that gold from the city of Jericho; defeat will come, but don't forget—while you sin, the eyes of the Lord are upon you from the beginning unto the end of the year."

Then he adds, "You will conquer the land. You will know what it is to languish in defeat, yet you will know what it is to rejoice in victory. You will know what it is to scrape the bottom, yet overflow the top. You will know what it is to go down the darkest of midnight valleys, but you will also know what it is to rise to the most beautiful sunlit peaks of all. On the mountaintop, in the valley, in victory, in defeat, in good days, in bad days, in righteousness and in sin, the eyes of the Lord will be upon you from the beginning of the year unto the end of the year."

It is a simple truth we teach our little boys and girls:

> O be careful, little hands, what you do!
> O be careful, little hands, what you do!
> For the Father up above is looking down in love;
> O be careful, little hands, what you do!
>
> O be careful, little feet, where you go!
> O be careful, little feet, where you go!
> For the Father up above is looking down in love;
> O be careful, little feet, where you go!
>
> O be careful, little tongue, what you say!
> O be careful, little tongue, what you say!
> For the Father up above is looking down in love;
> O be careful, little tongue, what you say!
>
> O be careful, little ears, what you hear!
> O be careful, little ears, what you hear!
> For the Father up above is looking down in love;
> O be careful, little ears, what you hear!

A simple truth, but God *does* hear everything you say; be careful what you say. God does know what you hear; be careful what you hear. God does see where you go; be careful where you go. God does know what you do; be careful what you do.

Moses, the meekest man and, I think, the greatest man who ever lived on earth apart from our Saviour, gathered all the Israelites and reminded them, "This year, 1451 B.C., will be a year of victory and defeat, a year of mountaintops and valleys, a year of shadows and sunshine; but don't forget—whether in the mountaintop or in the valley, every year, every month, every day, every moment, from the beginning of the year until the ending of the year, the eyes of the Lord are upon you!"

I wish you would get that at school. The eyes of the Lord will be upon you at school when you take the test, when you say what you shouldn't say—the eyes of the Lord will be upon you from the beginning unto the ending of the year.

I wish you could get that idea while you work. God will see and scrutinize everything you do at work. Every curse word you use, every dirty joke you listen to, every suggestive thought you have, every dirty book you read, every lewd calendar you see, every dirty story you read or tell—He knows it all. You may stay up at night and watch some dirty, sexy movie on television while your children and wife are asleep, but the eyes of the Lord are upon you from the beginning of the year until the ending of the year.

God's eyes will see everything you do this year. What a truth! We teach this to our boys and girls, but let every adult hear it. Let every teenager hear it. Let every aged saint hear it. Let us live this year with a consciousness that what we do, what we hear, what we say, where we go, what we read, where our feet lead us and what our hands do, are under the constant inspection of Almighty God who knows all we know, hears all we hear, sees all we see, sees all we do.

"The eyes of the Lord are upon thee from the beginning of the year unto the ending of the year." The key word is *always*. God doesn't make spot checks on His children. He **always** watches. While I'm preaching, for example, I look around the building and spot check the teenagers and see how they are listening; but God **always** has His eyes upon you. Always! God doesn't check occasionally to see how you are doing; He **always** watches.

I. IN THE WILDERNESS

Now listen carefully. They start the year off in the wilderness, and Moses says God will see them in the wilderness in the new year. A wonderful thought.

In the funeral home when you are sitting beside a loved one with your heart crushed, you think the sun will never again shine through the clouds. The eyes of the Lord are upon you.

In the hospital room, God will see you. Your surgery is about an hour away, and the nurse comes with the needle. You know what is going to happen. Your eyes will get a little bleary, and soon you will be rolled off to have surgery, and you wonder if it will be malignant.

The eyes of the Lord will be upon you. God knows every sacrifice, every pain, every heartache. He sees every tear. The eyes of the Lord will be upon you.

By the way, you *will* have some wilderness this year. You *will* shed some tears this year. You may face the surgeon's knife this year. The new year may hold for you the bedside of a dying loved one. It may hold for you the sorrow of standing beside Babyland in the cemetery. It may hold for you the heartbreak of standing by the casket of your beloved father or mother, husband or wife, brother or sister. It may hold for you a dark wilderness valley of shadow. But, blessed be God, the eyes of the Lord are always upon those who love Him!

II. IN CANAAN

Another thing about the Israelites: they not only spent time in the wilderness, but they spent time in Canaan where the victories are. Do you know that God beholds you when you do things for Him? In fact, Zechariah 4:10 teaches us that the eyes of the Lord search to and fro to see the little things.

One year I was in my office on a Saturday morning. There was a knock on my office door. One of our dear bus ladies was there. It was about 14 degrees outside. That dear lady had been visiting all morning and was going to visit the rest of the afternoon. She had some little problem which needed my help.

I shook her hand, and it was cold. Her eyes were a little red. As she and another partner went out to spend the rest of the day in the cold going from house to house trying to get some poor little bus kids to come to Sunday school the next day, I thought, *Few know she is out there. But the dear Lord knows!*

One of the young single ladies in our church came to one of our staff ladies who had worked so very long and said, "You work so hard. Why don't you let me keep your house clean for you?"

I happened to find out that that young lady goes to that staff lady's home where there is a family and a rather large house; and she washes, irons, does the dishes, sweeps, mops and vacuums. Nobody knew about it. The eyes of the Lord are upon her.

Last night my mother and I took two of our fine girls out soul winning. It was raining and cold. It was Christmas night. At the first place, they got out of the car and in the cold rain bowed their heads and asked God to bless them on this visit. These two went up and knocked on the door, but nobody was at home. We went to another place, and they again prayed in the rain.

How would you like to go to a strange house on Christmas night, knock on the door and say, "How do you do? I'm from First Baptist Church. It's nice to know you." Many of our kids did that last night!

The girls came back to the car and reported that one mother said, "You can't talk to my daughter! I'll answer all the questions. We have had enough visits from your church!" While Mother and I were talking, they were in the back seat having a prayer meeting. "O God, help So-and-So to get saved tonight. Please help us."

We made twelve calls. Not many were at home, and the ones who were, weren't very nice. They were not glad to have visitors from the church on Christmas night.

Finally one of the girls said, "I wonder where everybody is. I thought folks stayed at home on Christmas night."

I said, "They are all together in somebody's home. The family is gathered all together somewhere." One of them said, "I wish we could find out where that is so we could win them all."

We went to another house. It was getting late. I prayed for the Lord to give these girls at least one soul. "Lord, these girls got out in the rain and prayed before they went to every house. They have made twelve calls. It just wouldn't be fair, Lord; it just isn't like You not to answer their prayer."

They were gone this time about thirty minutes. Finally when the door opened to the car, one of them happily said, "Praise the Lord! All the teenagers in one family were together—seven of them! We won all seven in one house!"

The newspaper said nothing about those two fine girls this morning, but the eyes of the Lord were upon them! The dear Lord looked down from Heaven and saw those girls and many others like them as they served Him last night.

A couple in our church entered the Hammond Baptist Schools contest for free tuition. The fellow holds down two and three jobs at a time so he can send his children to school. They entered the contest so the husband could quit his extra jobs and hold just one job in order to have more time as a family. They worked and worked and worked and won the top prize in the contest so as to have the tuition of the kids paid at school.

I went to my office and found the lady waiting. "Pastor, we have been praying, and God has burdened us to do something. My husband has been holding down two and three jobs so our kids can go to the school. We won the top prize in the contest, but we have decided to take that prize and pay some poor kid's tuition to Hammond Baptist Schools."

Now that husband still works three jobs. Late at night when he is working and tired, the eyes of the Lord run to and fro and watch him.

Nothing is hid from His eyes, and nothing is hushed from His ears. No footprints are covered up, and no fingerprints are disguised. God knows what you do.

Hear me, college student away from home—the eyes of the Lord are upon you.

Hear me, serviceman in the service in some city where you have never been before and where no one knows you—the eyes of the Lord are upon you.

Hear me, young person on vacation—the eyes of the Lord are upon you.

Hear me, children—the eyes of the Lord are upon you.

While shopping the other day in downtown Hammond, I saw one of our girls in a mini-skirt. It was cold. She saw me and quickly pulled everything down and almost tore off the top. She pulled hard on her coat. Then she got behind somebody next to her. She didn't want the preacher to see her! But God's eyes saw her.

I was out making a visit in Hessville. One of our members came to the door smoking a cigarette. She didn't know it was me. She put it behind her, but the smoke was coming out of the top of her head! The eyes of the Lord are upon you!

Do you know what is wrong with this old sin-cursed generation, this generation that defies God, laughs at punishment, decency and honor? We have forgotten there is a holy, righteous, vengeful and wrathful God.

Listen, I believe in love, but I believe that the God who loves good also hates bad! The God who loves Heaven hates Hell. The God who loves righteousness hates sin. God is a vengeful God, a wrathful God, a furious God; and He pours out His wrath upon those who reject the Gospel and the Word and truth of God.

I get a little weary of this new "Jesus-freak" kind of religion. God is sick of a religion that says, "I don't care what you say about being clean; I'll be dirty if I want to be dirty." He is sick of rebellion against authority. He is sick of refusal to accept His truth. America needs a revival of the preaching of the holiness and righteousness and the justice of an omnipotent God whose eyes always behold His people.

God sees you. Yes, God sees you! Nothing is hid from Him. Remember that dark night on a lonely road? The eyes of God were there. Remember that time you smoked just one marijuana cigarette to see what it was like? The eyes of God were there.

I say to you as we point toward a new year: if I could give you one word of admonition as your pastor, I would say, "For twelve months, 52 weeks, 365 days, live every moment of every hour of every day of every week of every month of the year realizing the eyes of the Lord are upon you from the beginning to the end of the year."

By the way, His eyes were upon you this past year!

Young people, are there any decisions you ought to make today? Is there anything you have been doing that has not pleased God when His eyes focused upon your activities? Ladies and gentlemen, are there any shady deals, critical natures, bitterness, gossip, unkindness, dishonesty, lewdness, unholy literature? What is it that you would not do if Jesus Christ lived in your house? The eyes of the Lord are upon you from the beginning of the year unto the end of the year. Don't forget it!

When you rise in the morning, don't forget—the eyes of God are upon you. When you go to bed at night, don't forget—the eyes of God are upon you. When you go to school, don't forget—the eyes of God are upon you. The eyes of God are upon you from the beginning of the year to the ending of the year. This could change your year and your life.

(From the book, *From Vapor to Floods*.)

XI.

If This Were My Last Year on Earth

JOHN LINTON

"Therefore thus saith the Lord. . .this year thou shalt die." —Jer. 28:16.

Like a thunder clap from a clear sky came Jeremiah's warning upon the ears of Hananiah. He was not more likely to die that year than you or I this year. But Jeremiah's word was God's Word. For Hananiah it came true. In sixty days he was a dead man!

Death is an avoided subject. References to death have become unpopular. Although people know they must die, they banish the thought of it. Even when a man is on his deathbed and is facing his inevitable exit, it seems as if the doctors, nurses and relatives enter into a conspiracy of deceit. While they are planning in their minds for the interment, they are telling the patient his condition is improved.

Is that wise? Is it best?

That dying man is either saved or unsaved. If saved, he is either an obedient or a disobedient Christian.

Now if a man is ready to die because he is both saved and in happy fellowship with God, why should he not go consciously and triumphantly into the presence of Christ, leaving a testimony that will glorify God and inspire his loved ones?

If a man belongs to Christ but has lived a poor, ragged and shabby Christian life, let him use his last days to get into fellowship with the Saviour before he sees Him face to face.

And if a man is unsaved, do not deceive him as to his approaching end lest you find the blood of his soul upon your hands.

Now some of the readers of this message will tell me the text does not fit them. They will say, "The text may be true of someone else but it is not true personally of me. It is not true that this year I will die."

Let me ask you, are you quite sure of that? Do you have it in writing? Will you swear to the truth of it? Is there one single person reading this word of mine—man, woman, boy or girl, youth or maiden—who is ready to say deliberately, "For me that text is not true. I know that this year I shall not die"?

The fact is, the text may be true of any of us. This year someone now reading this sermon may die. Indeed I need change only one word and the text is true of every one of us—"This year thou mayest die." No one will dispute that. You may die. Beyond contradiction this may be your last year on earth.

Now isn't it wise to get ready for what may be? For example, I do not look like a delicate man. The poor doctors would have a hard time if people needed them as seldom as I do. I do not look like a man who would die soon. But I may. I may! And because of that maybe, I have placed on my life sufficient insurance to provide a roof over my family's head if I go.

My Christian friend, this year you may die. Are you living the kind of Christian life you would want to live if you knew God would call you Home this year?

And, oh, man or woman unsaved, if this year you may die, don't you think it is good sense to get ready for the maybe?

Yes, this text as it stands may be true of some of us. This year someone reading this may die. Within five months some of my readers may be in the other world.

As I sit in my home typing this message, I feel fairly certain that this year I will not die. And as you sit reading this message, while you agree as to the truth of it, nevertheless you say to yourself, as I do to myself, *The text does not mean me: this year I will not die.* That is human nature. We are loath to face what may be. Yet the text is true in the sense of maybe. This year you or I may die.

I was praying at the close of a Youth Rally service one night, asking God to bless the unsaved who had heard the message, asking Him to help the unsaved present to make their decision that very hour, asking Him to make them see the danger of delay. There was a slight commotion in the pew before the pulpit where I prayed. Before the prayer had ended, a man had breathed his last.

Let us get ready then for what may be. Let us suppose this year were to be our last. It may be, and if so, what then? Are there not some things that would be different if we knew this year were our last?

First of all, as Christians,

What About Our Separation From the World?

A young farmer in the Canadian West was engaged to a girl in the East. This farmer had had an unusually prosperous harvest, so he decided to get married a year earlier than they had planned. Without informing his girl of his intention, he boarded a train and returned unexpectedly to take his bride to her new home.

When he arrived at her house, he found a dance was in progress and the farmhouse was full of young people. He went back of the house and looked through a window where the room was in semi-darkness. Two young people were sitting out the dance. They were locked in each other's arms. One was the girl to whom he was engaged!

He went away, and the girl never knew from him but only from others why she was allowed to pass out of his life. Had that young woman known her lover might have returned that night, it would have made a difference.

What about our contacts with the world and its sinful pleasures? Are you allowing things in your life that you would not allow if you knew you had only a few months to live?

A good man in a Toronto church where I was pastor came to me one day and said, "Pastor, I want to tell you of a decision I made the first Sunday you preached after vacation. God used that sermon to deliver me from a habit of years." When I reminded him that I had not mentioned that particular sin in that message, he said, "No, but God did, and in answer to prayer I have been fully delivered."

It may be God is showing you, my friend, something wrong in your life without my mentioning it; and because this year may be your last year on earth, you are going to surrender that thing to God this very hour.

What About Your Prayer Life...

if this were your last year on earth?

When you intend visiting relatives, you write them beforehand. You may have neglected your correspondence until then, you may have been out of touch with them for months—but since you are going to be with them soon, you feel you must renew fellowship and so prepare the way for your visit.

My friends, if shortly we may be with Christ, isn't it wise to immediately get on speaking terms with Him? If we do not know how to converse with the Lord Jesus here, how shall we know what to say when we meet Him up yonder?

Are you on speaking terms with the Lord? How long is it since you had a real face-to-face, heart-to-heart talk with the Saviour? Not how long since you said your prayers; not how long since you prayed in a meeting; not how long since you had family devotions; but how long since you and Jesus Christ were face to face? If you knew for certain that your days on earth were numbered, would you not want to spend more time in prayer? If this year were to be your last year here, would you not want to spend next Wednesday night with your Christian friends in the house of prayer?

Then, too,

What About Your Soul-Winning Service?

I began a new year in a certain pastorate by having one hundred people covenant to try to win one soul for Christ that year. By the end of September, between thirty and forty had been won for Christ through their efforts. Some of them had their first experience that year in soul winning. Some of them knew for the first time the unutterable joy of placing a jewel in the crown of the Lord Jesus Christ.

Well, the sands of the new year are fast running out. If you knew for certain it would be the last chance you would have, would you not put forth some special effort to win someone this year before God took you Home? Would it not add to the glory of Heaven to see some soul there won through your efforts? Up yonder there are no tears to dry, no burdens to lift, no souls to save. All that must be done here. Will you get ready for the maybe and win some soul for the Saviour this year?

Moreover,

What About Our Gifts for God's Work?

Would there not be a difference in our Christian giving if we knew this year were to be our last?

Some Christians give great sums to God's work, but they give in the future tense. You have settled in your minds to give so much to God's work—that is, after your car is paid for and when the mortgage is clear or when the children are educated and grown up and married and there is nobody to keep but themselves. You are good givers, wonderful givers;

but it is all in the future tense. It is all definitely and sincerely purposed but never actually done.

No thought will more quickly disillusion such a man as the thought that this year may be his last. Let a man believe that, and he will see that the time to give is now, that to give later may be too late, and that if he postpones his giving and the Lord should call him Home, he would receive a stern rebuke for robbing the Lord and feathering his own nest at God's expense.

Someone reading this may have been going to give something special to God's work for a long time. Inasmuch as this year thou mayest die, had you not better make that gift to God now? There are missionaries abroad, there are evangelists at home, there are radio ministries, TV ministries, Bible institutes and the printed page through which you could win souls for Christ's crown. Has not God told you again and again that you ought to give Him a special gift for such work? 'Whatsoever He saith unto you, do it.' And 'that thou doest, do quickly,' for time flies and the days of us all are numbered.

I am coming very close to some of you with my next point. It is this:

What About Our Personal Differences With Others...

if this were our last year on earth?

Christian, is there a brother or sister on earth against whom you have a grievance? Has someone wronged you or slighted you or displeased you in any way? Is there any man or woman on earth against whom you have a grain of hard feeling?

Well, if this year you knew you would die, would you not want to be reconciled to that brother before you went Home? If your joy is being limited and your testimony hindered because of personal differences between you and some other Christian, are you willing to live and die in that condition of soul?

If there is anything in your heart between you and another, I bid you in God's name let not the sun go down upon that difference. This year you and I may die. If anyone has ever wronged John Linton, let him know here and now that he is freely and fully forgiven. It would be a shame if death found us not reconciled to our brother. God can enable us to love those who have wronged us. Let us give Him a chance while yet there is time.

I have been speaking thus far to Christians. Let me close by asking, If this year were your last,

What Difference Would It Make to You Who Are Unsaved?

If you knew you had only one month or six months to get right with God, would you not begin now to get ready for His presence? Knowing "it is appointed unto man once to die and after that the judgment," would you be willing to face death unpardoned, unforgiven? You would not! You know you would not.

Well, my friend, you may not have until December 31. No man on earth, no angel in Heaven can give you that assurance. The only day you have is this day. Now is the accepted time. Now is the day of salvation.

Said an ancient preacher, "The time to turn to God is the day before you die."

"But," said one man, "I may die today."

"Very well," said the preacher; "therefore, the time to turn to God is today."

A friend of mine told me this story. He went to a young businessman and laid before him the need of life insurance. This thoughtful man admitted his need. "I am convinced but I would like to consult my wife. Call on me Wednesday, and I will give you my answer."

On Wednesday my friend called. The man said, "We have talked the matter over, my wife and I; and while we see the need of insurance, we have decided to wait until the fall."

My friend urged him for the sake of his young wife and family not to put off what his business sense told him was the right thing to do. But, no, he would wait until fall.

Eight short weeks later my friend received an urgent message asking him to go to that home and break the news to his loved ones that death had suddenly taken their loved one.

O man, O woman unsaved, one day you intend being saved. You know it is right to serve Jesus Christ. You know that you need, as we all do, to prepare to meet God. But hitherto you have postponed your decision; you have delayed your coming; you have said, "Tomorrow." And one of these days tomorrow will come and find you gone—unprepared, unforgiven, unsaved.

In every life, for every good resolve, for every decision to do right, God says, "Today." And in every life, for every good resolve and every noble decision, Satan whispers, "Tomorrow."

Is it conversion? "Today," says God; "Tomorrow," whispers Satan.

Is it breaking off that evil friendship? "Tomorrow."

Is it giving up that evil habit? "Tomorrow."

Is it making that public confession of faith? "Tomorrow."

"Tomorrow," "Tomorrow," always "Tomorrow," until by Tomorrow's road we are at Never, and the dream has vanished, the chance has gone, the hope is lost.

O my friend unsaved, it will never be easier for you to say yes to God than now. God is right with you wherever you sit reading this message. If you really want to be saved, you can be saved right this very moment. Let no fancied difficulty keep you back. You are a sinner just like the rest of us. You need a Saviour just like the rest of us. You are not prepared to meet God. This year you may die. Get ready to meet Him! Open your heart to God right now and tell Him you want to be saved. Tell Him you do now take Jesus Christ His Son as your Saviour.

Then believe what God has said about all such. "He that hath the Son hath life" (I John 5:12). Thank God for the gift of eternal life! Believe you have this gift from God. You will find you are saved by believing. Then it will matter little whether it is this year or some other year that you die, for you are ready to die; and, bless God, you are also ready to live.

WALTER ARTHUR MAIER
1893-1950

ABOUT THE MAN:

Called "Jeremiah of the 20th Century," Dr. Walter A. Maier was the preaching-est preacher in the world during the 1940s, operating through twelve hundred radio stations in a number of different languages.

The air sizzled and crackled when the high-strung, athletic-formed and youth-vigored Maier let go his flaming message for exactly 19 minutes every Sunday to an estimated 20 million people over the Mutual Broadcastiing System and independent stations around the world.

He hurled invective without quarter at modern adulterers, cheats, crooks, hypocrites and worldlings. "You are all sinners, unforgiven and without hope in this world or the world to come if you haven't taken Christ as your Saviour," Dr. Maier shouted into the microphone. A manuscript was before him but often he forgot it, as he hurled wide and far his thunderbolts of warning to a lost world.

He often received 25,000 letters a week. It took 70 women to handle all the mail.

The Lutheran Hour was a work of faith. Dr. Maier got not one dime for all his broadcasting. It was labor of love for lost souls. His only income was a professor's salary (of O.T. Exegesis) supplied him by Concordia Theological Seminary, the Missouri Synod Lutheran school at St. Louis for the training of ministers.

Walter Maier was a shining example of the influence of a truly Christian home. He was born in 1893 in Boston to devout Christian parents, who prayed daily for and with their children.

He was the author of fifteen volumes of radio sermons. Perhaps his best known book was the 598-page work on marriage and the Christian home, entitled, For Better, Not for Worse, and it is reported that his commentary on the Prophet Nahum is the most comprehensive and authoritative ever prepared on this relatively little known book of Scripture. Many of his sermons have appeared in THE SWORD OF THE LORD.

XII.

Lord, Lead Us Another Way

WALTER A. MAIER

(Preached on the Lutheran Hour Broadcast in January, 1946)

"Being warned of God in a dream that they should not return to Herod, they departed into their own country another way." —Matt. 2:12.

What would happen if all the Christians in the United States should cut themselves off from the rest of the world for twenty-four days and study the marvelous story of the Saviour's love?

Over two hundred years ago George Frederick Handel did just that. For three weeks and three days without interruption he studied the prophecies concerning Christ's coming as he set them to music. During this period he scarcely left his room. Although he was a heavy eater, mealtime often passed unnoticed, and his food remained untouched. When the twenty-four days were over, he had written the masterpiece of sacred song which this Christmas season again has thrilled millions throughout the world, *The Messiah*, the oratorio of our Redeemer's advent into the flesh, which many place among the greatest musical compositions of all times.

Uncounted multitudes have heard it in the past two centuries, but perhaps no one has been more affected by its study and its marvelous power than Handel himself. When he wrote the music to Isaiah's prediction of Jesus' suffering, *"He was despised and rejected,"* tears streamed down his face. He was so greatly moved by our Lord's self-sacrifice for sin-stricken mankind that often he had to pause and regain his composure. As he penned the last lines for his famous "Hallelujah Chorus," he cried out, "I think I did see all of Heaven before me and the great God Himself!"

By living closely with Christ those twenty-four days and studying Scripture, Handel was mightily strengthened in his faith. He stopped writing operas and secular compositions and devoted himself exclusively to sacred music. His hot temper left him, and he found a new serenity.

Because he had been near God's Son in *The Messiah*, he could overcome the crushing depression which seized him when later he became blind; indeed this affliction helped make him even more devout and considerate of others. Though he had lost his sight, the inner vision of his Redeemer became brighter. Influential friends tried to coax him away from his faith, but he had seen too much of Jesus to go that way.

In his last illness he expressed the hope that he might live one week longer, until Good Friday, and then, he prayed, "meet the good Lord, my sweet Lord and Saviour, on the day of His resurrection."

His plea was granted. He died on Good Friday; and what is more important, unlike many famed composers, Handel, to whose music kings arise, died in the Redeemer. His closeness to Jesus, particularly during those twenty-four triumphant days, had deepened his trust, changed his life and led him *another way*.

Similarly, if masses in our country could concentrate on Christ for two dozen days—and surely every American should find at least that much time for Him who had His lifetime for them—not only would their thoughts, lives and actions be directed *another way*, but the widest revolt against evil this wicked world has ever seen would be accompanied by the mightiest revival of all times.

Today, on the first Sunday of the new year, may you who are dissatisfied with your past—its sordid failures, its selfishness, its constant surrender to evil—resolve to come all the way to Jesus and serve Him so devotedly that under the Spirit's guidance your course for the days ahead will go *another way* than the road of reckless and ruinous refusal to follow the Son of God completely!

The Holy Spirit grant that, as the sinister, suicidal trend of world affairs in recent times flashes through your mind, as you review the murder and massacre of thousands, crime and lust, unbelief and brazen blasphemy, selfishness and self-worship—all on the increase—you may shudder at the specters of a third global conflict, and with a faith founded on Jesus plead, "Lord, lead us another way!" That is the prayer my message suggests to you on this first Sunday in January. The Wise Men learned this lesson of *another way*, for our text records, "Being warned of God in a dream that they should not return to Herod, they departed into their own country another way."

I. LEAD US FARTHER FROM THE ENEMIES OF CHRIST!

How magnificent is Jesus' mercy! It would have been marvelous grace had the Son of God been born to save only a few from a privileged, chosen group and redeem these for eternity. But thank God with me today, as you behold these Magi journeying to His manger from far Eastern pagan lands, that Jesus is the universal Saviour, the royal Redeemer of all who accept Him regardless of race, rank, region, color, class, condition. He came for you white people, you black people, you red men, you of the yellow race. He came for the Germans and Japanese. Never has the world witnessed a love as embracing and inclusive as that expressed in Scripture, *"He died for all."*

Even in democratic America, wealth, position and prominence often divide people into opposing classes. Can you believe that on one Christmas Eve two hospitals in the Saint Louis area refused to receive a penniless woman critically ill with pneumonia!

How I thank God, as letters of love for the Lord come to my desk from the Island of Tobago, the Island of Nevis, Northern Rhodesia, New Zealand, the Aleutians, almost all over South America, from Panama down toward the Straits of Magellan—and we have received mail from more than fifty different countries—the Gospel of Jesus Christ proves it is "the power of God unto salvation to EVERY ONE that believeth"!

1. Scientific Advances Do Not Cure the World's Ills

These Wise Men were of the scientists of their day, among the most learned scholars of the ancient world. Their desire to seek, find and worship Jesus is thus the more challenging to the intellectual leaders of our time.

Deeply we must deplore the tragedy that all the epochal achievements of twentieth-century scientists have not made the world better spiritually. Armies of experts have been mobilized and billions of dollars spent to perfect ways of killing more men quickly, killing them more surely, killing them in larger numbers, with greater ease, with deeper horror; but where in all the laboratories on earth can you find one discovery which helps men live more honest, sincere, devout and God-fearing lives? Where does a single invention hold out hope for a morally spiritual better tomorrow?

In his lecture entitled, "Decoration Day Oration," Robert Ingersoll, Number 1 scoffer of his generation, announced this "vision of the future," predicting:

I see a world without a slave. Man at last is free. Nature's forces have by science been enslaved. Lightning and light, wind and wave, frost and flame, and all the secret, subtle powers of earth and air are the tireless toilers for the human race.

I see a world at peace, adorned with every form of art, with music's myriad voices thrilled, while lips are rich with words of love and truth; a world in which no exile sighs, no prisoner mourns; a world on which the gibbet shadow does not fall; a world where labor reaps its full reward; where work and worth go hand in hand. . . .

I see a world without the beggar's outstretched palm, the miser's stony, heartless stare, the piteous wail of want, the livid lips of lies, the cruel eyes of scorn.

I see a race without disease of flesh or brain, shapely and fair, the married harmony of form and function, and, as I look, life lengthens; joy deepens; love canopies the earth; and over all, in the great dome, shines the eternal star of human hope.

He never saw this vision, nor will anyone ever see such peace and progress on an earth that rejects Jesus.

By contrast, however, at the height of scientific achievement, we do see the world drained of much of its wealth, multitudes impoverished and bankrupt, more exiles and prisoners than ever before, destruction and agony above the worst we have known.

Even scientists themselves are sometimes terrorized by the Frankenstein of frightfulness which men may yet produce. How horrifying beyond words will be the nuclear bomb under pressure of a future war! Disease bombs are said to also be in the offing.

Regrettably much of present-day scientific thought is atheistic, blind to the evidence of divine power in the world about us, in history behind us, in the ground beneath us, and in the skies above us. Men, whom even two world wars have not torn from their madness, are screaming, "There is no God!"

They ought to remember the Arab guide in the Sahara Desert who answered a French infidel's question, "How do you know there is a God?" with another question: "How would I know that a man and not a camel passed my tent last night in the darkness? Was it not by the print of his foot in the sand? Even so," he concluded, pointing to the rays of the sun flashing over the sandy waste, "that footprint is not a man's."

The Magi looked to the heavens with its myriad stars; and if ever you doubt that there is a God, go out to survey the star-spangled heavens! On a clear, cold winter night you can count hardly 2,500 stars; but, aided by telescopes, astronomers have listed multiplied millions. Their photographic plates made with high-powered lenses already show about a billion stars, leading to the conclusion that there may be as many as 30 billion, some certainly many millions times as large as this earth. When believing scientists consider the regular movements of the heavenly bodies, the definite law and the system which keep each in its pathway, like the great astronomer Keppler, they bow humbly before the Almighty because they know that He alone could produce this myriad of miracles. Even human reason tells us that the mathematical probability of these 30 billion stars coming into their present size, form, brightness, position and system by accident or evolution is one in a number so vast that it can be expressed in decillion times decillion. Yet all these stars, as Psalm 8 clearly states, are the work of only the Creator's fingers, not even of His hands, His arms, His whole strength.

What a glorious Lord of unlimited power He is for us in all our needs! Compared with a star of the first magnitude, you and I are truly less than one-millionth part of a grain of dust; yet how deeply the Lord loved us, insignificant specks in the universe that we are, when He gave His own Son into death for our redemption! Marvelous as these mightiest stars are, they do not mean as much to our Father as your soul. Jesus Himself declared, "What is a man profited if he shall gain the whole world and lose his own soul?"

2. Many Great Scientists Have Trusted Christ

The scientific research of these Magi, blessed by God, led them to discover the one star in this myriad which the Almighty had destined was to direct them; and when these Oriental sages, following the heavenly beacon, knelt at the Christ Child's cradle, gave Him gold, frankincense and myrrh, royal, precious tributes of their faith, you behold science serving the Saviour as it should today.

Thank God that even in our generation truly wise men worship Jesus! Don't be discouraged by the fact that certain prominent university teachers, physicists, chemists, geologists, physicians are unbelievers! Since these Magi knelt at the manger, the most eminent scientists have been humble disciples of our Lord.

Professor Taylor of Princeton asserts, "The farther a scientist goes, the humbler he becomes in regard to faith."

Sir Ambrose Fleming, noted British physicist, asks preachers who deny the possibilities of miracles to begin "resting on the Word of the increasingly verified, inspired Scriptures, which," he says, "are the utterance of the 'men of God who spake as they were moved by the Holy Ghost.'"

Dr. William Bell Dawson, son of Sir William and one of the Dominion's most distinguished scientists, wrote scores of important treatises which brought him honors from many learned societies; but he also wrote a booklet entitled *Forgiveness Through the Blood of the Lamb.*

Surveying the needs of this war-torn world, David Anderson, president of the Institution of Civil Engineers of Great Britain, states:

> As one who for many years in his private life sought to stress the importance of the great Christian doctrines . . . in the New Testament, I should like to plead for a definite application of these to our postwar problems. . . . As good engineers, our aim should be to plan the future on the solid foundation of the unchanging and beneficent laws of God.

I repeat: the most eminent scientists have been men of deep personal faith in Christ. Take only the physicians and leaders who have relieved human pain and advanced health! When the celebrated Dutch physician Boerhave once prepared to dissect the corpse of an executed criminal before his anatomy class, he suddenly turned pale and told the students, pointing to the lifeless form before him:

> I spent my boyhood with this man. Now I am the honored Boerhave, while he lies here. Let me tell you clearly that besides the grace of God I know of no reason why I do not lie there in his place.

Similarly Sir James Simpson, the renowned discoverer of chloroform, reported:

> When I was a student at the university, I saw . . . a man brought out to die. . . . Would any friend loose the rope and say, "Put it around my neck! I die instead"? No; he underwent the sentence of the law. For many offenses? No, for one offense. He had stolen a money parcel. . . . He broke the law in one point and died for it. . . .
>
> I saw another sight I shall never forget—myself a sinner, standing on the brink of ruin, condemned to eternal punishment in the lake of fire. For one sin? No; for many, many sins committed against the crushing laws of God.
>
> I looked again, and, behold, Jesus became my Substitute. He bore in His own body on the tree all the punishment of my sin.

He died on the cross that I might live in glory. He suffered, the Just for the unjust, that He might bring me to God.

Listen to Dr. Howard Kelly, world-famous physician and scientist, who declared:

> I am certain that Jesus Christ is the Son of God born of the Virgin Mary. I believe that all men by nature are sinners, alienated from the life that is in God and that... the Son of God Himself came down to earth to... shed His sacrificial blood on the cross to pay the infinite penalty of a lost world.

An assistant came into Pasteur's laboratory, found the scientist with bowed head, excused himself for intruding and said, "Pardon me! I thought you were praying." "I was," Pasteur answered.

This year I spent part of Christmas afternoon with black inmates of the Saint Louis City Infirmary. One of them had worked with Dr. George Carver, black scientist whose research helped save many lives in the South and in the Congo and whose memory the nation honored yesterday. With sparkling eyes this invalid told me, "Whenever a problem confronted Dr. Carver, he took it to God in prayer, in his laboratory or on long walks, alone with his Lord."

Some of the nation's outstanding surgeons are men who would not think of undertaking an operation without invoking divine help or, concluding it successfully, without giving the Master Physician thanks.

Now, if the march to the manger which these Magi started has continued ever since, as learned leaders have humbly found their way to Jesus, by what right can freshmen high school teachers, sophomore college professors, who have never contributed an original or constructive thought, sneer and jeer at Christianity as they do? The truly wise always worship the Saviour.

3. Obey God's Warning!

After they had bowed before Jesus, the Magi, we read, "being warned of God in a dream that they should not return to Herod," heeded the divine instruction.

Do you obey God? Have you followed the Almighty's repeated appeals to avoid evil and walk in His way? Some of you do not listen to the warnings even of human counselors. You are like Julius Caesar. The very day he was assassinated through a conspiracy of Roman senators, a friend handed him a paper revealing the whole plot against his life. Instead of reading it on the way to the Senate, Caesar thrust it into his pocket, together with other documents, and without glancing once at the facts and taking measures to save his life, he rode directly to the Senate house, where he was slain.

A capable doctor tells you, "If you value your life, stop drinking and carousing"; but you know better than your medical advisor and continue to dig your own alcoholic or drug grave.

A godly mother pleads with you young folks who are sowing to the flesh and begs you to stop living in sin, but you are too hardened to notice your own mother's tears and prayers.

A Christian pastor sees you on the road to spiritual and moral ruin. As your soul counselor, he raises his voice to warn you against your perilous, destructive ways; but rather than thank him, you often accuse him of meddling in your affairs.

Now, if you do not heed the warnings of men whom you can see, you will certainly not listen to God whom you cannot see, unless He employs special, drastic means of awakening your soul to the conspiracy which the Devil with his agents on earth and in Hell has formed against you.

If it takes sickness, remorse, loss, heavy affliction, to bring you to the realization that you must have Christ as your Saviour, then I say, "Oh, blessed pain and anguish which helps spare you the immeasurable agony of eternal rejection by your Heavenly Father!"

We do not know the road on which the Wise Men returned to their homes, but we do know that it was a route by which they could avoid Herod's murderous hatred.

Today, too, Christians must constantly strive to go *another way* from that which takes them back to their Saviour's enemies and farther from their faith.

What tragic losses have been caused by people who parade as believers, but whose words and conduct belie the blessed Redeemer and give offense to those outside the church!

At the Battle of Quebec, General Wolfe, urging his men onward, was mortally struck by a bullet. To prevent his soldiers from knowing that he was wounded, he directed the officers around him, "Hold me up! Don't let the men see me fall!"

Similarly, you who have been called to Jesus should realize that, as children of light, you should walk in the light, not in darkness. Your prayers should daily ask, "O Holy Spirit, don't let me fall," lest the example of your sin lead others to spurn their Saviour, point to you and say, "Well, if that is all Christianity means, then I want nothing of it."

Who can tell what might have happened had the Magi disobeyed God, returned to Herod, and told him where the Christ Child was? You do know, however, what has happened to many who have sold their Saviour to secure public favor. Judas went to Hell because of his unbelief; and if you are now turned away from Him, should you not be paralyzed by the fear of the fate which will overtake you unless you repent?

Therefore, on the first Sunday of this new year, Jesus, who loved you and gave Himself for you, stands before the ungrateful who have joined the twentieth-century crucifiers and, as He points to these learned men from the East, He pleads: "My beloved, for whom I shed My blood, go *another way* this year! Stop running away from grace! Come back, all the way, to Me! Why will you destroy yourself by your unbelief? Why, with your unforgiven sins, will you consign your soul to Hell, when here, with Me, there is overabundant mercy?"

And as He who never refused to welcome a contrite sinner stretches His arms toward you—the Holy Spirit grant it!—may you declare, not tonight when you go to bed, not tomorrow, not next Sunday, but now: "O precious Redeemer, forgive me my transgressions by Thine endless mercy and limitless love! Let Thy blood, shed for the sins of the whole world, cleanse me of my transgressions! Then, Thy Spirit helping me, I promise that I will live this year *another way*, forsaking iniquity, always walking with Thee."

II. LEAD US CLOSER TO THE LOVE OF CHRIST!

The Magi not only went *another way* and kept their distance from murderous Herod, as we should avoid the enemies of our Lord, their souls also began to go *another way*. They were different men, stronger in faith, after they knelt and worshiped, in the Christ Child, their God and Saviour, just as those who contritely come to Jesus, their sin-removing Redeemer, cannot behold and believe Him without having their whole lives changed, their entire conduct directed *another way*.

It is written,

"If any man be in Christ, he is a new creature: old things are passed away; behold, all things are become new."

When John Sunday, a converted Indian chief, spoke to a congregation in Plymouth, England, he said:

> I understand that many of you are disappointed that I have not
> brought my Indian dress with me. . . . When I was a pagan In-
> dian . . . my face was covered with red paint. I stuck feathers in my
> hair. . . . I had silver ornaments on my breast, a rifle on my shoulder,
> a tomahawk and scalping knife in my belt. That was my dress then.
> Now, do you wish to know why I wear it no longer? . . . When
> I became a Christian, feathers and paint *passed away*. I gave my
> silver ornaments to the mission cause. I have done away with the
> scalping knife. That is my tomahawk now,

he concluded, pointing to the Ten Commandments, translated into the
Indian language.

1. A New Person by Trusting Christ

Do you ask, "How can I have new life for the new year, a changed
heart and a reborn spirit for the years ahead?"

Follow the Magi as their mighty minds bow submissively before the
Son of God! With a sin-stricken but grace-gripped heart behold the Lord
Jesus! Let the Holy Spirit direct your life *another way* as you, outward-
ly dissatisfied and distracted through your ignorance of the Saviour's
love, delve into the treasures of the gospel truth!

Many of you feel that something definite is lacking in your lives. I
promise you that, if you will believe the Saviour, trust His promises,
read Scripture fairly, without raising any willful objections of unbelief,
you will see that the Almighty can grant you spiritual contentment and
real joy in life.

John von Muller, the eminent Swiss historian, had that experience.

> I do not know why two months ago I took it into my head to
> read the New Testament. . . . I had not read it for many years and
> was prejudiced against it before I took it in hand. . . . I have always
> felt the want of something, and it was not until I knew our Lord
> that it was all clear to me. With Him there is nothing which I am
> not able to solve. If this religion is not divine, I understand nothing
> at all.

Do you want this grace which takes you *another way*, past the
restlessness and disturbance seething within you, to peace of mind and
soul and heart—peace with God, peace with your neighbors, peace
in your own family, peace within your conscience?

More true even than that, I now speak to you is God's guarantee
that you can have this peace if only you are ready—and the Spirit grant
you will be—first of all, to confess, without the reservations some of

you have made, that in your repeated, unnumbered transgressions of the divine law, you are under God's wrath, headed for Hell, doomed to everlasting death, barred from the beauty of Heaven. Then you must acclaim Jesus, as these Magi did, your Saviour, your God, your King!

This tiny Babe in the manger, God's Son and the Virgin's, was born at Bethlehem so that on Golgotha's grim brow He could satisfy divine justice, pay the penalty for your iniquities, remove the curse of your transgressions, fulfill the Law in your stead, suffer the punishment to which you had been sentenced, die the death you had deserved and thus, by His atoning, substitutionary sacrifice of Himself in your behalf, take away your sins, free you from divine judgment, make you sinless, stainless, in God's sight, and guarantee you the glories of eternal blessedness, unending joy in His presence!

With this grace offered you freely in the Gospel—dare you, the half-convinced, the half-indifferent, refuse to come the whole way and, obeying the Spirit, kneel contritely but confidently before the Christ Child?

2. How Many Have Become New Creatures by Faith!

This, then, is the personal Epiphany appeal which, if you accept it, as I pray you will, leads you *another way*, a blessed way, the Gospel's way.

Do you want the Lord Jesus as your Saviour, your Friend in every need, your Guide in each dark perplexity, your interceding High Priest before His Father's throne, the Sovereign of your soul, indeed, your glorious God with whom "*nothing shall be impossible*"? Meet Christ in faith as the Magi did! Know in personal acquaintance who Jesus is and what He has done for you! If only you will take time to behold the Saviour face to face on the pages of His revealed record, you too can come to the greatest glory men are privileged to have on earth—the assurance through the Son of God that their sins are forgiven and Heaven is theirs.

Francis Junius was a distinguished British scholar but a prejudiced, poison-minded enemy of the Lord. His grief-stricken father, watching this infidelity increase, placed a New Testament in his son's library, hoping that the Holy Spirit would direct the young man to the saving truth. What happened? Francis Junius writes:

> One day I unwittingly opened the New Testament thus providentially laid before me. At the very first view, though I was deeply engaged in other thoughts, the grand chapter of the Evangelist and Apostle presented itself to me, "In the beginning was the Word,"

the passage many of you listeners recognize as the opening of Saint John's Gospel and his testimony to the eternal Christ.

Junius continues:

> I read a part of the chapter and was so affected that I instantly became struck with the divinity of the argument. . . . My body shuddered; my mind was all in amazement, and I was so agitated the whole day that I scarce knew who I was.
>
> From that day God wrought so mightily in me by the power of His Spirit that I began to have less relish for all other studies and pursuits, and bent myself with greater ardor and attention to everything which had relation to God.

Many of you unbelievers have Bibles in your homes. For the sake of your souls, for the blessings of forgiven sins, for the escape from Hell and for the benediction of Heaven, read this sacred Book, believe it and apply its sure promises to yourself!

For years William Cowper, the British poet, was seized by melancholy and driven to the depths of despair. He gave this account of the light Christ's Gospel brought in the darkest moments of his life:

> I flung myself into a chair near the window and, seeing the Bible there, ventured once more to apply to it for comfort and instruction. The first verse I saw was the twenty-fifth of the third chapter of Romans. Immediately I received the strength to believe, and the full beams of the Son of Righteousness shone upon me. I saw the sufficiency He had made for my pardon and justification.
>
> In a moment I believed and received the peace of the Gospel. . . . The happy pardon which was to shake off my fetters and afford me a clear discovery of God's mercy in Christ Jesus had now arrived.

From that time on Cowper went *another way*; the menace of melancholy was over.

In the Saviour's name I promise you, the distracted and depressed, that if you kneel before Bethlehem's Babe to receive Him as your Redeemer, your life will be directed *another way*. The morbid grief, the dark distrust, the unworthy suspicion will vanish from your soul as you find joy, light, help, comfort, courage, strength and radiance in the Saviour.

It was a mysterious process, following a star which led the Magi to the manger; and today God often uses mysterious means of bringing men to faith.

In Lyons, France, a brave gospel preacher, Adolph Monod, proclaimed Christ crucified and His promise of free grace through faith. Bigots reported these sermons as objectionable, and he was ordered to bring copies to the prefect of police, Count de Gasparin, who himself had never learned the full mercy of the Lord Jesus.

The Count had to investigate the sermons, irksome as this duty seemed to him. To make the task easier, his wife offered to read the objectionable scripts with him. Though they started to read in resentment, by the Spirit's guidance they actually continued with amazement and inner joy.

As each paragraph brought new interest, the work which had been an official chore now became a sacred privilege.

Past midnight they read on, finishing two sermons, with the result that Count de Gasparin and his wife were converted. From that moment they began to take *another way*, the path of love and life in the Lord.

We often speak of chance happenings, accidental occurrences by which men are brought to Jesus; in truth, however, the Holy Spirit definitely leads *every* believer to his Saviour.

Admiral Mahan, one of the great American authorities on sea power, recalls a notable visit to a Boston church. In the midst of the sermon, which was to direct the admiral's life *another way*, the preacher, whose name he never learned, quoted the Christmas promise, "Thou shalt call his name Jesus, for he shall save his people from their sins."

Admiral Mahan writes:

> Almost the first words of the Gospel! I had seen them for years, but at last perceived them. Scales seemed to fall from my eyes, and I began to see Jesus Christ and life as I had never seen them before.

Then, too, he recognized that the Holy Spirit had led him to the service.

Perhaps you think that chance or accident brought you to read this message of which until a few minutes ago you knew nothing; but you are wrong. The same God whose Spirit guided those Oriental leaders to Bethlehem has helped you find this so that, illumined by His Spirit, you too can confess the Lord Jesus your Saviour and, clasping His hand, go with Him, through Him and for Him *another way*, the way of faith, holiness and victory.

Do you want new life, new hope, new blessing through the assurance that your sins are washed away? Now, while the Holy Spirit urges you, decide for Christ! Let us help you learn the mind of the Magi as you worship Him, whom to know and believe is earth's highest joy and Heaven's greatest glory!

Even the best of you believers who say: "Amen," "It is true," to this pledge of a new life in the Saviour can come closer to Jesus and walk on *another*, a higher and holier *way*, as the Magi, who, leaving their costly gifts in Bethlehem, went back to their distant homes as different men, poorer in money but richer in reliance on their newfound Saviour.

When you read the life of Frances Ridley Havergal, author of many sacred songs, you will find that, despite her amazing devotion to the Lord, she too could direct her life *another way*, always closer to the Redeemer. After she had written the hymn:

**Take my life and let it be
Consecrated, Lord, to Thee!**

the poem remained unprinted for four years. Then, when she reread her own plea,

**Take my silver and my gold,
Not a mite would I withhold,**

she realized that she was asking others to do something she herself had not done. So she took all her jewels, except a few pieces her parents had given to her, put them into a box, sent it to a missionary society; and to be sure that she was not withholding "a mite," she included a check covering the value of the jewels she had retained. After the treasure chest was on its way, she exclaimed, "I never packed a box with such pleasure!"

Today in thanks to Jesus, give even more than Miss Havergal did; give yourself wholly to Christ who gave Himself for you. Then indeed you can go *another way*, the way to divine comfort and courage, the way to joy and strength, the way to help and hope, the way to pardon and peace, sometimes the way to the cross, but always the way to the crown, the way to Heaven—the way to Jesus. Lord, lead us all that way for His sake! Then you can have a happier year this new year, and many more!

(From the book, *Let Us Return Unto the Lord,* published by Concordia Publishing House.)

TOM MALONE
1915-

ABOUT THE MAN:

Tom Malone was converted and called to preach at the same moment! At an old-fashioned bench, the preacher took his tear-stained Bible and showed Tom Malone how to be saved. He accepted Christ then and there. Arising from his knees in the Isbell Methodist Church near Russellville, Alabama, he shook the circuit pastor's hand; and this bashful nineteen-year-old farm boy announced: "I know the Lord wants me to be a preacher."

Backward, bashful and broke, yet Tom borrowed five dollars, took what he could in a cardboard suitcase and left for Cleveland, Tennessee. Immediately upon arrival at Bob Jones College, Malone heard a truth that totally dominated his life and labors for the Lord ever after—soul winning!

That day he won his first soul! The green-as-grass Tom, a new convert himself, knew nothing of soul-winning approaches or techniques. He simply asked the sinner, "Are you a Christian?" No. In a few minutes that young man became Malone's first convert.

Since that day, countless have been his experiences in personal evangelism.

Mark it down: Malone began soul winning his first week in Bible college. And he has never lost *the thirst* for it, *the thrill* in it, nor *the task* of it since. Pastoring churches, administrating schools, preaching across the nation have not deterred Tom Malone from this mainline ministry.

It is doubtful if young Malone ever dreamed of becoming the man he is today. He is now Doctor Tom Malone, is renowned in fundamental circles for his wise leadership and great preaching, is pastor emeritus of the large Emmanuel Baptist Church of Pontiac, Michigan, Founder and President of Midwestern Baptist Schools, and is eagerly sought as speaker in large Bible conferences from coast to coast.

Dr. John R. Rice often said that Dr. Tom Malone may be the greatest gospel preacher in all the world today!

XIII.

"An End Is Come"

TOM MALONE

(Preached in 1965.)

"An end is come, the end is come: it watcheth for thee; behold, it is come."—Ezek. 7:6.

This is the last Sunday night, the last Lord's Day of the year. If the Lord tarries, the next Sunday will be in a new year altogether. I am speaking on "An End Is Come," and thinking of the end of another year in the lives of us all.

When I was small, a year seemed a long time. But all of us know that the older we grow, the quicker time passes. When we grow older, the years come and go so quickly.

I was thinking today about what is involved in a year. Three hundred and sixty-five days mean that there are 8,760 hours in every year. I was thinking also of some 31,536,000 seconds in every 365 days. And while you are sitting here tonight, from the time you left your home, if by the providence of God you get back to your home safe and sound and alive, 120 golden minutes will have gone into eternity, or 7,200 seconds of your life will be history when you reach your home again.

"An end is come." It is brought to my mind as a preacher almost every day of my life. Two young men are here tonight who were riding in a car. They picked up a sailor boy a day or two ago. One of those young men works at the hospital. He talked to the young man in the Navy about his soul and about Christ and about meeting God and about the need of being saved. But the sailor refused, as people often do. Then, a few hours later, when the ambulance pulled up to the hospital bringing two bodies, he recognized one of the men as the one he had talked to a few hours before. Both were dead on arrival.

This young Christian man at a hospital prepared the body of a young man whom he had talked to about his soul just a few hours previously, getting it ready for the undertaker. He had died in his sin and had gone out to meet God without hope and without salvation.

My friends, if tonight God could have His way in our hearts and lives, He would speak to us plainly about the end of some things.

When I think of the end of a year, two things come to mind. First, the future is absolutely certain. I don't believe that a Christian man or woman is groping in the dark. The Bible says, "I will guide thee with mine eye." So the future of a Christian, in one sense of the word, is just as certain as God Himself. It is absolutely certain tonight that, if we die, we will be with the Lord. If Jesus comes, we will be with the Lord. Our destiny is settled. Our future is certain.

Yet, there is a sense in which our future is uncertain. Who knows when the loss of health will come? Who knows when the greatest test of all your earthly existence will meet you face to face? Who knows what another twenty-four hours holds? I have known people to have, in a moment's time, a complete change in their life. Things come we never dream will come.

Our future is certain in a sense. Our future is uncertain, in a sense. The Bible says, "Boast not thyself of to morrow; for thou knowest not what a day may bring forth."

I studied four things the Bible says will come to an end. God, three times through His preacher to religious people, said, "An end is come."

I. THE END OF A NATION COMES

It was the prophesied end, the predicted end of a nation. If you are interested in the Bible, if you are interested in God's plan for the ages, if you are interested in God's great overall plan for redemption, there is one thing you must come face to face with in the Bible: God has dealt with a nation. Among other things in which you find the story of redemption and the beautiful story of salvation by grace, this Bible is the story of a nation as well as a body, a church, a bride, the Lord's people. That nation begins back in the book of Genesis.

I shall never forget the first time I read the Bible through as a Christian. What a revelation it was that all God has done, even what He is doing for me, started with one nation.

Back in Genesis 12 we read where God said unto Abraham:

"Get thee out of thy country, and from thy kindred, and from thy father's house, unto a land that I will shew thee: And I will make of

thee a great nation, and I will bless thee, and make thy name great, and thou shalt be a blessing: And I will bless them that bless thee, and curse him that curseth thee: and in thee shall all families of the earth be blessed." —Vss. 1-3.

God said, "What I am going to do with all the world, I am going to do through My plan with one nation."

Out of that nation came a tribe. Out of that tribe came a family. Out of that family came a man. From that man, we find the genealogy of the Son of God.

All that God has ever done for all this world, He has done through one nation. And how He loved that nation! Not only did He call her people out from all other people and say, "You are a peculiar people. I will favor you and love you," but He delivered them again and again.

Nothing ever happened in all the history of this world, with the exception of Calvary, that was any greater than the deliverance of Israel from the bondage of Egypt.

For 430 years they served under the cruel whips of the Egyptian taskmasters until God said, "These are MY people." God heard their cry and saw their tears, saw their bleeding backs, and one day said, "I am going to deliver them."

He said to that nation down in Egypt in servitude, "Get thee out of Egypt and into Canaan. I will give it to you, and it will belong to you forever, and I will give you that land."

All the sovereign purposes of God are wrapped up in that nation Israel. This Bible says, "To the Jew first, then to the Gentile." God's sovereign purpose has been working through a nation.

One day, God said to that nation out of whom our Saviour came, out of whose loins the Lord came, "An end is come."

For 2500 years there was no such thing as the nation of Israel, until it was recognized by the United Nations in 1948. Even now she is divided. There are guns, planes, tanks, swords and soldiers in readiness. They struggle with the Arabs for that land. The land of Israel and the land of Jordan are the Promised Land. But it is divided tonight, because God said 2500 years ago, "An end is come."

God brought an end to a nation He loved more than He has ever loved any other nation. Since that is true, God have mercy on our nation tonight. God have mercy on a nation that has ruled God and prayer out of its schools. God have mercy on a nation that is given over to modernism and the denial of the faith once delivered to the saints. An end is come. An end is come. And for 2500 years God has been saying, "See, I meant what I said." The predicted end. The end of a nation came.

II. THE END OF THE DISPENSATION
OF GRACE WILL COME

I read in the Bible that the most wonderful period the world has ever known will come to an end—the period in which you and I are living right now.

I don't want to be technical. This is a preaching, not a theological, service. There are seven different dispensations. A dispensation is a period of time in which God deals in a particular way with people. If you go through the Bible, you will find there are seven of them.

The first one was the dispensation of absolute innocence, when man in that garden was as naked as when God made him. But he was innocent and didn't know any shame.

It was followed by the dispensation of conscience.

That was followed by the dispensation of promise.

That was followed by the dispensation of human government.

That was followed by the dispensation of law, which ended with Calvary and the death of Jesus.

And you and I are living in the dispensation of the grace of God. And for two thousand years God, because of Christ and on the basis of Calvary, has dealt with men in grace. "The grace of God that bringeth salvation hath appeared to all men."

This is the dispensation of grace. This is the dispensation when God says, "And whosoever will, let him take the water of life freely." This is the dispensation when any man, any woman, any boy, any girl can come to Christ. He needs no mediator, save that One God provided, even His own Son.

But God said this dispensation is going to end with the rapture of the church. When that comes, something is going to take place in this old world that is more weighty and more significant than even the upcatching of the people of God. God is going to remove His Holy Ghost from this earth.

Way back in the book of Genesis God had said, "My spirit shall not always strive with man." And when the Lord takes up His church, He will take up Him who indwells that church, the Spirit of God, leaving this world without the ministry of the Holy Ghost. The Antichrist is going to reign. People are going to worship a false Christ. Men will not be able to repent.

People ask, "Preacher, after the Lord comes, will I have a chance to be saved?" No. Theologians say, "Well, doesn't the Bible say that out of the tribulation shall come a great host whom no man can number? Doesn't the Bible teach that the Jew during the tribulation shall preach the Gospel of the Kingdom and many people will be saved?" Yes. And the Bible teaches that a nation shall be born in a day.

But this Bible also teaches that there will be people in that day who will gnaw their tongues for pain. They will do everything except one— repent. That they cannot do because they have sinned away their chance of being saved. People will cry, 'Oh, mountains and rocks, fall on us, and hide us from the face of the Lamb that sitteth upon the throne.'

This is the day of repentance. But God said, "The age of grace will come to an end."

III. GOD-GIVEN OPPORTUNITIES COME TO AN END

When the disciples came back to the well with food for Him to eat, Jesus said, "I am not hungry."

They asked Him, "Have you eaten?"

He replied, "I have meat to eat that ye know not of." Then He added, "Say not ye, There are yet four months, and then cometh harvest? behold, I say unto you, Lift up your eyes, and look on the fields; for they are white already to harvest." Jesus said, "Don't say you have four months. I have won this woman because it was the last chance for her to be won."

Dear people, I believe to individuals, to preachers, to Christians, to saved men and women, to churches, to spiritual organizations, God gives a moment of opportunity and says, "It is now or never."

What do you think Jesus meant in John 9:4 when He said, "I must work the works of him that sent me, while it is day: the night cometh, when no man can work"? Night cometh! I believe God gives people a moment of opportunity.

I went to Bob Jones College with just a few cents in my pocket. I had borrowed five dollars and bought a railroad ticket from Sheffield, Alabama to Cleveland, Tennessee. But I went with the deep conviction that I was saved and called to preach and sent of God to get some training.

But I had no money. My dear mother made $17.50 a week clerking in a store. Sometimes when I went for the mail I would have three or four dollars from Mother, a fourth of her salary. As I read her letter I would weep. I almost felt it was blood money. Twelve times the treasurer of Bob Jones College, in three and a half years, came to me and said, "Tom, you'll have to go home." Twelve times I walked out on the highway with a broken heart and tears and hitchhiked down across the country to preach and pray and get a little money so I could go back.

One time I had enough money to ride a bus part of the journey. By then I was about ready to give up. Have you ever been ready to give up? If you haven't, I feel sorry for you! It teaches you something.

On that bus trip I sat by a fine young man. I don't know why I even had enough spirituality left to speak to him, but I asked him if he were a Christian.

He said, "Yes, I am. But I am the sorriest one that ever lived."

I said, "No, you're not. I am."

"No, I am." We nearly got into a fight on that Greyhound bus about who was the sorriest Christian!

I said, "Well, why do you say that?"

"God called me to preach. And I went to school and I managed one year. Then I gave up and went out of the ministry. I'm not studying and I'm not preaching and I have given up what I believe was a divine call in my life."

As I sat on that bus by that young man and listened to that story, I said, "If there is a God on His throne, and He answers prayer, I'll never give up."

Thirteen years later, in 1948, I finished four years and walked across a stage and got my diploma.

My friends, God gives us a glorious, golden, glittering moment of opportunity. Sometimes, when it is gone, it is gone forever.

That is true of life.

I think of Esau, that one crucial moment when for a mess of pottage he sold his birthright. The Bible says, "He found no place of repentance, though he sought it carefully with tears." He couldn't reclaim what he gave away in a moment.

The end of our opportunity comes.

IV. THE END OF ALL FLESH CAME

"And God said unto Noah, The end of all flesh is come before me;

for the earth is filled with violence through them; and, behold, I will destroy them with the earth."—Gen. 6:13.

Yes, God destroyed the wicked generation in which Noah lived. It was an age of immorality, violence and materialism. Jesus spoke of this wicked age in Matthew 24:37-39:

"But as the days of Noe were, so shall also the coming of the Son of man be. For as in the days that were before the flood they were eating and drinking, marrying and giving in marriage, until the day that Noe entered into the ark, And knew not until the flood came, and took them all away; so shall also the coming of the Son of man be."

Here Jesus teaches that it will be the same when He comes the second time. Men will have no time for God and will be living as if death and judgment will never overtake them. But man will have a day of reckoning.

In Genesis 6:3, God says, "My spirit shall not always strive with man." God's Holy Spirit will not always strive with you. God pity your poor soul if God gives you up!

The end of your day of grace will come. You need to be saved now while there is hope. Tomorrow could very easily be one day too late.

"An end is come, the end is come: it watcheth for thee; behold, it is come."

V. THE END OF LIFE COMES

I will close with a statement that has been said so many times until people hardly hear you anymore. And that is, the end of life comes. "And as it is appointed unto men once to die, but after this the judgment. . . " (Heb. 9:27).

It is brought to our minds every day. I sat with a group of workers of the adult Bible class a few nights ago. We were discussing two or three different lists of people. One is the active, good group—the group leaders who serve the Lord and visit and call and are on the ball for Jesus. Another was a group of fine people, members of this church, people who used to serve but don't now. There were the reasons. Some—ill. One or two—moved. But do you know why two of them don't serve tonight? It was written on the sheet: "Deceased." Neither was an elderly man, but in recent months God took them both.

Like it was said to old Hananiah, "This year thou shalt die."

People say to me, "You preachers are always telling deathbed stories and telling people they are going to die." One time when someone asked him, "Why are you preachers always trying to scare people?" my preacher friend answered, "I'll tell you what. You promise me that you will never die; and I promise you I will never mention it to you."

The fellow replied, "I can't promise that."

"Then I can't promise you that I will never mention it to you again," the preacher said.

I have had folks ask, "Why do you try to scare people?" I'll give you one good reason: I am scared for you. God pity a preacher who is not afraid in his heart for the souls of people.

The end comes.

Reminisce with me about your boyhood and girlhood philosophy of death. When you were a child, you used to think, "I'll live a long time, so long that my eyes will become so dim that I can hardly see, and my steps so tottering I can hardly walk, and my shoulders bent and my hair as white as snow. The end will come, and on the bed in my home, I call all my family around and I'll say to this one and this one and this one, 'Good-by.' And I'll bequeath something spiritual or material to each. And that's the way it will be when I die."

I have been in the ministry since 1935. I have seen only one saint of God die like that—a dear German lady up there in the thumb of Michigan when I was holding a meeting. One night after preaching like I am preaching now, I went to her home, along with a German pastor. We gathered around the bed and she sang. Her voice was as clear as a bell. She spoke to each of her loved ones and bid her husband of some fifty-odd years good-by. She closed her eyes and went to be with Jesus. That is the only one in thirty years.

I have seen scores and hundreds die, both good and bad, both saved and lost. I have seen the hour come when the eyes are set and the death dew is on the brow and the death rattle is in the throat. I've seen the coma come, and the one dying doesn't know his dearest loved one. I have seen loved ones come and in their ear pour out their love and say, "Daddy, Mama, can you hear me?" Not one bit of response.

I have stood in the hall and looked in the room and back and forth, until some wee hour of the night the nurse comes or the doctor reaches down and takes the old white sheet, pulls it up over the face and comes out into the hall and says, "Would you like to sit down? Your loved one just departed."

That is the way people go.

I have seen them out yonder called to meet God, pulled out of an automobile, and in a bloody, broken mass, hauled to the hospital and so bandaged you could hardly see their facial features. I have watched them go out to meet God with never a chance to repent.

I have seen them burned to a crisp and taken yonder to the hospital to die. All the prayers and tears of people who loved them availed nothing.

The end comes. And it will come for you.

Yes, the end comes. It comes suddenly or slowly. It nearly always comes unexpectedly. It comes whether you are ready or not ready; whether you are saved or lost. Oh, then, now, as we start the new year, I beg every unsaved reader to turn to Christ and be saved.

XIV.

The Land of Beginning Again

**Abraham at seventy-five made a new start, ventured out
into the unknown following God. Here he is held as
our example for the new start.**

BILL RICE

*"Now the Lord had said unto Abram, Get thee out of thy country,
and from thy kindred, and from thy father's house, unto a land that
I will shew thee: And I will make of thee a great nation, and I will bless
thee, and make thy name great; and thou shalt be a blessing: And I
will bless them that bless thee, and curse him that curseth thee: and
in thee shall all families of the earth be blessed."*—Gen. 12:1-3.

Bible scholars call this the Abrahamic covenant. I understand that
this is a great message and promise to Abram (Abraham) and to his
people, the Hebrew race.

But I am interested right now in these Scriptures as they might apply
to you and me.

Abraham was now seventy-five years old. He had already established
himself in the land of Ur. He had thousands upon thousands of acres
of good ranch land and so many cattle that it took some 800 menservants to care for them! He was also rich in silver and gold. Doubtless
he and his beautiful wife Sarah lived in a magnificent home. Yes,
Abraham had security.

Now God wanted him to leave everything—his ranch, his home, his
lands, and at age seventy-five, journey to a far country he had never
even seen, and begin life anew!

It was a tremendous decision for him to make. Should he leave behind
his people, his property, his friends? Doubtless he was perplexed and
burdened about the great decision he faced. Yet he may have thought,

In spite of all my wealth, I have no real rest of heart. Although others may envy me my position and prestige, my life is actually barren — as barren as Sarah's womb.

Abraham was tired of halfway measures, tired of half trusting, half doubting, tired of incomplete obedience. He was tired of burying loved ones who died without hope. Abraham would turn to God and from now on God's way would be his way. He would live where God wanted him to live and be what God wanted him to be. Perhaps he felt like Alice Chase Chinn who wrote:

> **For each of us who have traveled the road**
> **Of sorrow, misfortune and sin,**
> **There's a wonderful place of courage and hope**
> **Called the Land of Beginning Again!**

I. TRUSTING

The biblical description of the days that followed are summed up in a few brief words— *"So Abram departed, as the Lord had spoken unto him."*

The Abraham Ranch was a beehive of activity. Herds were being rounded up for the long march toward Canaan. His 800 menservants and their families were busily engaged in packing the possessions they could carry with them on the long journey. Lovely Sarah worked excitedly from morning till night. Household goods were strapped on the backs of camels and donkeys for the long trip.

At last the great day of departure arrived. Abraham and Sarah took one last look at the home they loved so well before leaving it forever.

"He's Gone Crazy!"

Perhaps some of the neighbors came over to say good-by. I can just see them standing together talking with Abraham.

"I understand it's deer season in Colorado now, Abe. You goin' out there for a little hunting trip?" one of them asked.

"No," Abraham replied. "I have something much more important than hunting on my mind."

"Maybe you figure on spending a couple of months in a fishing trip down in Florida," suggested another.

"No, I have something far more important than fishing to do," Abraham answered.

"I'll bet I know what you have on your mind," shrewdly suggested another. "Since you have spent most of your life gathering riches, I'll bet you're off on a business venture! I wouldn't be surprised if you aren't going down to Texas to buy up some oil land!"

"No," Abraham answered again, "making money will never again be the chief interest of my life. I'm going to make an investment of far greater value than money—I am going to invest my life for God."

"Then where *are* you going?" they asked.

Abraham faced them steadily. "I really do not know where I am going," he said. "God asked me to leave my family, my home and my country and follow Him. I do not know where God will lead me, but I intend to follow Him as long as I live!"

This was the exact truth. He really did not know where he was going. Although I was a very small boy, I can still remember soldiers of the First World War singing:

**I don't know where I'm going
But I'm on my way.**

So it was with Abraham, for Hebrews 11:8 tells us, "By faith Abraham, when he was called to go out into a place which he should after receive for an inheritance, obeyed; and he went out, not knowing whither he went."

Doubtless his friends said, "He's gone crazy over religion!" But actually Abraham had never done so wise a thing in all his life. He was determined to go where God wanted him to go.

How would he care for his family? He would trust God to provide for their needs. How would he defend himself against the enemies he might encounter on the way? He would trust God for protection. Who would repay him for all he had left behind? For what he was to suffer? For giving up a palace to live in a tent? He would trust God to reward him.

So Abraham went—trusting God.

Good neighbor, let's you and I, like Abraham, make a new start today. Let's dedicate ourselves to God. Let's purpose in our hearts that we will trust Him to reward us. Whether men appreciate our ministry or not, we will do what we do for Jesus' sake. We will live sacrificially, honestly, trusting God to lead, protect and reward.

You and LeTourneau

Every summer my famous big brother, John Rice, used to go to

Toccoa, Georgia for a conference. I would go with him. We would conduct a conference on soul winning and revival at the beautiful Lake Louise Hotel and Conference Ground. The lake, hotel and grounds were built and controlled by the famous Christian millionaire, R. G. LeTourneau. Now I never had the good fortune of meeting Mr. LeTourneau. I heard him speak one time when I was a student in Moody Bible Institute and can still remember his powerful message. But although I spoke at Lake Louise time and time again, he never heard me speak and probably never even knew I was alive.

I knew nothing about Mr. LeTourneau and his millions other than what I have read and heard. But I understood that he is extremely wealthy. Rumor had it that he sold his Toccoa Plant to Westinghouse for approximately thirty million dollars, which, alone, would be enough to last him the rest of his life. I do know that he was vitally interested in spreading the Gospel of the Lord Jesus Christ.

Perhaps you did not know him either, but let us do some supposing. Let us imagine that Mr. LeTourneau knew you. Perhaps he slipped into an auditorium to hear you preach. Perhaps he was a visitor in your Sunday school class. Perhaps he heard you sing in the choir. Let us imagine that being strangely attracted by your ministry, he made you the following proposition: you and he would become partners. It would be your job to serve the Lord Jesus at every opportunity. You would put God first in your life. Your church would come before your business; your Sunday school class before your job. It would be more important to you to go to choir rehearsal than to take overtime work. In brief, you were to begin immediately to live the way you felt would be most profitable and pleasing to God.

Mr. LeTourneau, on the other hand, would make money for both you and himself. You would never have any financial worry. If you spent so much time studying the Bible, visiting the sick, attending jail services, teaching Sunday school classes, winning souls from house to house, etc., that your income dropped off, Mr. LeTourneau, with all his wealth, would be there for you to fall back upon. You need not worry about old age, for he would take care of you then. If your children needed to go to college, Mr. LeTourneau would help you to provide for them.

Wouldn't that be wonderful! Wouldn't it be good to make serving God the main concern of your life! Wouldn't it be wonderful to be able to serve Him with an utter abandonment of care and anxiety! How eagerly you would accept such a proposition from Mr. LeTourneau!

Of course, Mr. LeTourneau might die and leave you destitute. Or he might change his mind. Or he might lose every penny he owned in a brief time. But you would gladly take that risk.

You would trust a mere man like Mr. LeTourneau. How tragic that you are not as willing to trust God! God, who has all the wealth of the world, yet you are afraid to trust Him. He never changes, will never die, will never lose His power—and you are afraid to trust Him!

How tragic that so many Christians serve God so little because they feel they cannot afford to do so. Sunday school teachers have no time to prepare their lessons because they feel their work on the farm, in the home, at the office to be of so much more importance. After all, a man gets paid for working in a filling station or a grocery store, but actually he feels he does not get paid for work he does for God!

There are literally thousands of young men who have been called of God to preach but will not do it for fear of starving to death.

Once I drove my car into a garage in Kansas City to have some work done on it. A young man, head of the service department, came smilingly out to greet me, saying, "We may not look like it, Mr. Rice, but actually you and I are just alike! God has called both of us to do the work of an evangelist."

"Fine," I told him, and then asked him where he was preaching.

He replied that he was not preaching anywhere just then. He was holding down two jobs because he was married and had two little children. "I must not let them starve," he explained, but as soon as he could afford it, he was going to do evangelistic work.

"We are not alike at all," I told him. "God called me to preach, and I am preaching and trusting Him to help me care for my lovely wife and four children. God called you to preach, but you are not preaching. You believe the Nash garage can take better care of you than God! Both God and the Nash garage called you, and you decided you would rather trust the garage! Don't say you are like me if you believe the Nash garage will love you better, care for you better and reward you better than God will!"

"I Won't Be Back"

Most of my life I have known that God wanted me to be an evangelist. It was with this in mind that I left the little church in Gainesville, Texas and went, with my wife and baby, to Moody Bible Institute in Chicago.

For more than three years Cathy and I worked and went to school. I went to school in the morning and worked afternoons and nights. I had a job taking sightseers around Chicago. I took visitors with their suitcases and trunks from the railway and bus stations to the Institute and back again.

I had a night job from about six to eleven with the Railway Express. At the same time I became pastor of a church in Dubuque, Iowa, almost two hundred miles away. I would usually get up about three o'clock on Sunday mornings and drive to Dubuque, round up Sunday school youngsters, teach a Sunday school class, preach in the morning service, preach in the afternoon, conduct young people's services, preach that night, then drive back to Chicago, arriving at four or five o'clock the next morning. I worked long hours and hard. (I needed more money than the average student because of the illness and resultant deafness of our first baby Betty Ann.) At the same time, I took the full Pastor's Course, courses in music, children's work, teacher training, radio work, etc. Cathy worked at Marshall Fields, serving tables in the afternoons, and then she babysat at odd hours and went to evening classes. As I look back, I wonder how on earth we went at such a killing pace.

When graduation day finally came, we were both simply exhausted. But, at that, those were wonderful, happy years. I was preparing to do the work of an evangelist! I ate, slept and lived revivals! God had called me, and I could hardly wait for the time to come when my preparation at Moody would be over and I could enter the full-time evangelistic field. In the meantime, I preached, led singing, went on deputation groups, conducted jail and hospital services, passed out thousands of tracts and did personal work on the streets.

After making sure God did not have other educational plans for me at that time, I felt I was now ready to go into full-time revival work.

Then I received one of the greatest surprises in my life. When I asked John Rice to recommend me as an evangelist in THE SWORD OF THE LORD, he said he could not do it! He must be honest, he told me, with his readers. I was young, inexperienced, had not proven myself in the evangelistic field. He did not know if I could conduct a successful revival or not. I was a youngster just out of Bible school. He could not conscientiously recommend to pastors that they have any other student under the same circumstances. And even though I was his brother, he felt it would not be honest to recommend me to pastors when he did not know whether I could deliver the goods!

I was crestfallen but realized that he was entirely right.

However, John said that he would be willing to announce to the people that I felt called to be an evangelist, that I was honest and sincere although inexperienced.

He did put such a statement in THE SWORD, and I thought surely I would receive a flood of revival invitations. But no flood came. It didn't even rain! In fact, it didn't even sprinkle!

Finally one letter of inquiry came from Kenneth Beilby, First Baptist Church of Gas City, Indiana. He had waited too late to get a good evangelist, he frankly told me, and so might have to use someone like me! After an exchange of letters I was definitely invited and accepted the invitation.

I waited for other invitations, but none came. What was I to do? If I resigned the good job I now had with the Railway Express and received no more invitations, how would I make a living for my family? How could I make the last two payments on our new Ford car? How could I pay the rent?

Cathy settled the entire matter by asking me a simple question: "Does God want you to be an express man or an evangelist?" It was as simple as that.

When I went to work that night, I told Mr. Larry, the big boss, I was leaving and told him what I planned to do. He asked what I would do after the two weeks were up, and I told him that I did not know. He urged me to merely take a leave of absence. He said he and other officials had been watching me. They would soon make me a foreman. I could go places if I stayed with the Railway Express. I thanked him warmly but told him I was going to be an evangelist regardless of what happened. If I lost my car, I would just lose it. If my family and I starved, we would simply starve. "I won't be back," I told him. I meant it.

The Gas City campaign lasted three weeks instead of two. During the last week I received another invitation for a revival—this time from the First Baptist Church of Allegan, Michigan. During the second campaign I received an invitation from Orestes, Indiana. During this meeting I received an invitation from another church and another. And so it has gone for these blessed years. Living from "hand to mouth"? Yes, but from God's hand!

He Is Able

Good neighbor, why not begin a new life at the beginning of this year, a new life of trust and faith in God? Serve God—not a board of deacons, not a church, not a group of people. And trust God rather than man to reward you. Do not preach or sing or teach or visit in order that men may pay or praise you. Rather, have an agreement with God that you will do what He will have you do and you will trust Him to reward you in due season. Remember that God is a "rewarder of them that diligently seek him" (Heb. 11:6).

When you are afraid, remember, "The Lord is my helper, and I will not fear what man shall do unto me" (Heb. 13:6).

When you are discouraged, remember God has said, "Let us not be weary in well doing: for in due season we shall reap, if we faint not" (Gal. 6:9).

When you feel helpless, remember, "I can do all things through Christ which strengtheneth me" (Phil. 4:13).

When in need, remember, "My God shall supply all your need according to his riches in glory by Christ Jesus" (Phil. 4:19).

Abraham left the old life of doubting to enter into one of faith and trust in "the Land of Beginning Again."

II. CONFESSING

Abraham loved the Lord. He set out to live a new life of trust and service. But he still had his body of clay, and he was not perfect. There were pitfalls of temptation in his pathway. And there came a day when Abraham fell into sin. He suffered from a famine in the land of Canaan, and "Abraham went down into Egypt to sojourn there."

His beautiful wife Sarah went with him, of course. The king of Egypt desired her; and because Abraham was afraid, he said she was his sister but neglected to say that she was also his wife. The king desired the beautiful woman for a wife and would have taken her had the fact not been revealed that she was the wife of Abraham. Therefore Abraham and his family were sent from the land of Egypt.

Bluntly, Abraham had sinned. He had backslidden. And there were two courses open to him, the same two courses that are open to every backslider. He could be hardhearted, hardheaded and rebellious. He could try to act as though nothing had ever been wrong and go on with his sin unconfessed and, therefore, unforgiven. Or he could humbly confess his sin to God and go back to the place of service God had appointed him.

Abraham chose the latter—he went back to Canaan, back to

"Beth-el, unto the place where his tent had been at the beginning, between Beth-el and Hai; Unto the place of the altar, which he had made there at the first: and there Abram called on the name of the Lord."—Gen. 13:3,4.

The Bible says, "If we confess our sins, he is faithful and just to forgive us our sins, and to cleanse us from all unrighteousness" (I John 1:9).

That is what Abraham did. He was wrong and acknowledged it. He had left Bethel to go into backsliding. He left backsliding to come back to Bethel and confess his sin. Here he found pardon and forgiveness.

The Bible says, "He that covereth his sins shall not prosper: but whoso confesseth and forsaketh them shall have mercy" (Prov. 28:13).

Many churches are cold and formal today because the members are not willing to confess their sins. Many an individual has a cold heart, a barren life, a ruined testimony because of an unwillingness to humbly confess sins. Many a church goes year in and year out with no souls saved, no lives changed, no hearts blessed because of deacons, elders, trustees, teachers and laymen who are unwilling to confess their sins.

Some years ago I went to a church in a small town for an eight-day revival campaign. They told me there had been no conversions for about twenty years in the little church. The building was a lovely one. It was made of brick, had an auditorium seating about 200 and a side auditorium that would seat an additional 175.

The opening night there was just a handful present. The weather was bitter cold. I proposed that the pastor and I begin visiting up one street and down another until every person in the little town had been invited to the revival. He thought the idea was foolish. Besides, he was "very busy," so I went alone in sub-zero weather. God blessed the visitation and in a couple of nights the church was packed.

The messages seemed to be refreshing, yet I could get no one to make a move. Not a soul came forward for rededication or salvation.

On Thursday night a number did raise hands for prayer, but no one came forward. We sang longer than usual during the invitation, but to no avail. Finally when I decided to close, a deacon in whose house I had been staying wept his way to the front. He told the people that he knew why the church was barren, why no souls had been saved in the last twenty years. He said that he, the chairman of the board of deacons, was a thief!

He told how he had defrauded the railroad years before. It seems he had bought a ticket for a little town some twelve miles away. It began to rain and he decided to stay on the train. When the conductor neglected to ask him for his ticket, he made the long trip to Minneapolis on a twelve-mile ticket! Some twenty years had passed, and he said that every time he had tried to pray, the Lord had reminded him that he was a crook. There had been no conversions in the church services; and now, during the special revival campaign, there had been no conversions, although the church was enjoying the largest attendance of its history. He felt like an Achan in the camp and wanted to confess his sin to God and to the people.

When he had finished his story, I again gave the invitation and Christians came forward, one after another, to confess their sins. An invitation was then given to the unsaved, and they literally crowded down the aisles! Seventy-two people came forward that night, over half of them first-time decisions for Christ.

This man told me later that he had often felt God tugging at his heart; but being chairman of the board of deacons, he felt he could not afford to come forward for rededication like an ordinary church member.

Actually, however, it is far more important for those in places of leadership to confess and forsake their sins than it is for the ordinary member of the church.

Good neighbor, if you would know the blessing of God on your life, then be quick to confess your sins to God. Should you confess them publicly? Yes, if the public knows about them. I urge you to return to Bethel, back to the place where you left the Lord. It is entirely possible that you will be a stronger Christian than ever before.

> Their hope, like a cloak that wraps us around,
> Makes stronger our purpose to win,
> And love, truth and faith are easily found
> In this Land of Beginning Again.

III. LOVING

When Abraham went to Canaan, he took his nephew Lot with him. It may be that Lot was the adopted son of Abraham. Probably the boy was already grown when Abraham took him in. Maybe his uncle had given him a start in the cattle-raising business and he had become a man of considerable wealth. He had large herds and flocks. In fact, Lot and Abraham had so many head of livestock that

"...the land was not able to bear them, that they might dwell

*together: for their substance was great, so that they could not dwell
together. And there was a strife between the herdmen of Abram's cattle and the herdmen of Lot's cattle: and the Canaanite and the Perizzite dwelled then in the land."* —Gen. 13:6,7.

It seemed that a range war between the herdmen of the two men
was inevitable. There is little doubt but that the herdmen of Abraham
would have won.

But here we see the great character of this man who had come to
the Land of Beginning Again. Instead of reminding Lot that he was a
trespasser on his uncle's land; instead of accusing the younger man of
ingratitude; instead of driving his nephew off the range, Abraham said
to Lot,

*"Let there be no strife, I pray thee, between me and thee, and be-
tween my herdmen and thy herdmen; for we be brethren. Is not the
whole land before thee? separate thyself, I pray thee, from me: if thou
wilt take the left hand, then I will go to the right; or if thou depart to
the right hand, then I will go to the left."* —Gen. 13:8,9.

How loving and gracious Abraham was!

Two things that motivated his action: first, the "Canaanite and the
Perizzite dwelled then in the land." Unsaved people, heathen people,
were all around them. Abraham and Lot were the only people of God
these lost ones knew. What would their opinion of God be if Abraham
and Lot fought one another!

Good neighbor, there are unsaved people around you, too. Many
a man and woman never attend church, never read the Bible. The
only thing they know of God is what they see in you. Think carefully,
then, before you engage in a fight with your Christian brethren over
personal matters. Perhaps nothing in the world so hinders the work of
the Lord Jesus Christ as does the fussing and fighting of our churches.
All over the land we have churches that have split and then the splits
have split! We have factions and cliques that dishonor God and bring
reproach upon the name of Christ.

And almost every time the fusses are over personal matters. Hardly
ever are the fusses and fights over doctrinal matters. We fuss about who
will sing the solo in the choir, who will be the Sunday school superinten-
dent, who will teach the young married women's class, who will ramrod
the Ladies' Aid, who will play the organ, and every other conceivable
matter. And while we are calling one another names, we wonder why

the unsaved are never interested in our churches, why our testimonies have no more effect on the lost than pouring water on a duck's back.

Remember, Jesus said, "By this shall all men know that ye are my disciples, if ye have love one to another" (John 13:35).

For the sake of the lost, Abraham was willing to suffer ill-treatment at the hands of a brother without making a fight, without any attempt at getting even.

The second reason Abraham gave in to Lot may be found in his words, "we be brethren."

Christian fellowship is sweet and precious. Do not lose the friendship and fellowship of others of like precious faith if you can possibly help it.

Many times we lose friends because we insist on "standing up for our rights" and "saying just what we think." Of course, this often enables us to have our own way—at the price of a friend.

As an evangelist, I have services in churches all over our nation. I tell you now there is nothing as tragic as a split church. There is nothing as pathetic as hard feelings between Christians. Everyone suffers. The ones who carry on the fight suffer the loss of fellowship and friendship that was so pleasant and sweet. Children suffer. The work of the church suffers. Most important of all, the work of the Lord Jesus suffers, for Christians who are busy fussing and fighting hardly ever have time to win souls for whom Christ died.

The Love Chapter

No matter how generously we give of our offerings, no matter how sound we may be in the faith, no matter how beautifully we may speak or sing—if we do not have love for our brethren we are not worth the powder it would take to blow us up!

First Corinthians 13 reminds us,

"Though I speak with the tongues of men and of angels, and have not charity, I am become as sounding brass, or a tinkling cymbal. And though I have the gift of prophecy, and understand all mysteries, and all knowledge; and though I have all faith, so that I could remove mountains, and have not charity, I am nothing. And though I bestow all my goods to feed the poor, and though I give my body to be burned, and have not charity, it profiteth me nothing. Charity suffereth long, and is kind; charity envieth not; charity vaunteth not itself, is not puffed up. Doth not behave itself unseemly, seeketh not her own, is not easily pro-

voked, thinketh no evil; Rejoiceth not in iniquity, but rejoiceth in the truth. . . . "

"You Go Your Way"

When Abraham saw that he and Lot could not get along together, he did not propose a fight. He did not ask for a show of strength. Instead, he graciously suggested that the young man decide where he wanted to live and then he, Abraham, would move to another place. He said, in effect, "Lot, we are brethren. It is not right for us to fuss and fight. If we cannot get along together, then let's get along separately. You go your way and I'll go mine, and we will get along separately."

In spiritual matters I do not say nor believe we ought to compromise with those who are openly unsaved or those who pose as Christians but really are not saved, like the modernist crowd. But certainly those of us who are saved should love and pray for and help other Christians.

> **No grudge in our heart, no malice, no strife,**
> **No words that are ever unkind;**
> **But a smile, and a laugh, and a loving hand-clasp**
> **In the Land of Beginning we find.**

IV. GIVING

In the Land of Beginning Again, Abraham was a tither. Lot was kidnapped by five kings, and Abraham armed his servants and fought to rescue his errant nephew. When he returned from the battle with the five kings, Abraham met a man named Melchizedek and "he gave him tithes of all" (Gen. 14:20). Melchizedek was a type of Christ. He was the "king of Salem" and "priest of the most high God." "Salem" means peace. Jesus is our King of peace, and Jesus is our High Priest.

Tithes, then, should be given to the Lord Jesus Christ.

Tithing is right. It was right in the days of Abraham. It is right for you and for me today. People ought to tithe. And those who love the Lord do tithe. Jesus said, "If ye love me, keep my commandments."

Let me repeat—those who love the Lord keep His commandments, and those who love the Lord give tithes to Him.

Under the Law?

But someone will say, "Tithing was for the Jews under the Law, not for us today." But let me remind you that the Law had not yet been given in the day of Abraham. The Law was given by God through Moses.

And Moses was not born until years and years after Abraham had been buried in the cave of Machpelah. Abraham did not give because of the Law; he gave because it was right. Jacob, too, was a tither.

Later on, tithing was included in the Law. Of course, someone will insist that the Law was abolished when Jesus came. Someone will say that the ordinances were nailed to the cross.

But Jesus did not do away with the Law. He did not come to break it; He came to fulfill it. It is true that ceremonial laws or ordinances were nailed to His cross, since these ceremonies, such as sprinkling the blood of a dove, sacrificing a red heifer, etc., pointed to and pictured Christ. There is no need of the ceremonial laws now that Jesus has come.

But *moral* law was in effect before the Law was ever written, and it is in effect today. The Bible says that Cain was a murderer although the Law of Moses had not even been given at the time Cain killed his brother. And it is just as wrong to murder today. This is moral law, not ceremonial. It is wrong to bear false witness, to commit adultery, to take God's name in vain.

And it is still wrong to steal. And the Bible says that one who does not tithe is a robber. "Will a man rob God?" asks Malachi. "Yet ye have robbed me. But ye say, Wherein have we robbed thee? In tithes and offerings" (Mal. 3:8). A man who does not tithe, then, is a deliberate thief. He is as crooked as a dog's hind leg or a snake with the cramps!

It was right to give tithes in Old Testament times. It was right in the days of Christ; for He said, ". . . ye pay tithe of mint and anise and cummin. . .these ought ye to have done. . ." (Matt. 23:23). And it is right today, for Paul said, 'Give as the Lord has prospered you' (I Cor. 16:2).

If God has given you a dollar, give Him one dime. If He has given you ten dollars, then give Him a dollar. That is a tithe, and it belongs to God. Then give offerings over and above the tithe as God enables you to do so.

Ingratitude

Suppose a destitute brother came to you asking for help. Suppose you had ten dollars in a dresser drawer and you told the friends to go and get nine of those dollars, leaving one for your own needs. But suppose your friend took all ten of those dollars! You would certainly feel he had been guilty of base ingratitude. How contemptible! How *little!* How mean!

How, then, do you believe God feels about you when the cattle on a thousand hills are His and the silver and the gold? He gives you the privilege of opening the drawer of His storehouse in order that you may provide for yourself and your family. He only asks that you use at least one dollar out of ten for Him. What kind of person are you if you do not do it?

I Don't Keep a Record But . . .

Many people feel sure they give as much as, or more than, one-tenth of their income but do not keep record. But if it doesn't mean enough to you to even keep a record of it, I seriously doubt that you give anything like as much as one-tenth of your income to God. More than likely you are a first-rate phony.

What do you believe would happen if you went to your groceryman with the suggestion that you would take all the groceries you needed day after day without keeping any special record of how much you got? You, on the other hand, would pay the groceryman some money occasionally, but there would be no record kept of how much you paid him. How do you believe your groceryman would react to this kind of proposition? Or the manager of the filling station? Do you honestly believe any businessman would agree to this kind of proposition?

Isn't it strange, then, that you feel your business transactions with the Lord are not as important as the ones you have with your groceryman or milkman or laundryman or tailor!

The probable truth is that you do not tithe and you well know it. What is more important, God knows it, for He keeps a record whether you do or not.

Every Christian should set aside at least one tenth of his income for the work of the Lord regularly and systematically.

Not Because of Wieners

Remember there is only one way to finance our churches. Backslidden indeed is the church that sinks to church bazaars, pie suppers, basement carnivals, the sale of ice cream or even—heaven help us—kisses! Do not give your money for a carnival; give it for the Lord.

In a small church in a Texas town I was plagued years ago with a choir director who could get no one to sing in his choir, which had places for sixty people. This man was doing well when he could get ten or twelve to come to the choir. As far as his private life was concerned, perhaps the less said the better. At any rate, here was a choir director without a choir.

Then one Sunday morning he had a brilliant idea, and he announced it to the congregation. "If the choir is full this morning and tonight, we will go on a wiener roast next Thursday night and I will pay for the wieners!"

You should have seen the people flock to the choir! It was a veritable stampede! The choir was not only full; it was overflowing. It was the same way that night. The following Thursday night they all went on a wiener roast, and I understand everyone had a lovely time. (I was not present.)

The following Sunday morning the same thing happened. An appeal was made for choir members, and only a handful responded until the director announced that they would follow the same procedure as that of last Sunday. If the choir was full both night and morning, they would have a wiener roast the following Thursday and he would pay for the wieners.

Before anyone had a chance to respond, I was in the pulpit confronting the chorister: "No, you won't," I yelled. "If anyone is going to sing in this choir, he is going to sing because he loves Jesus Christ, not because he loves wieners! We will have no more of this kind of business."

And that was definitely that!

Good neighbors, let's do what is right for Jesus' sake. Let's give our tithes and offerings because it is right. Let's sing in the choir, teach a Sunday school class, do what we can—all for Jesus' sake, trusting Him to reward us in due season.

V. BLESSINGS

Abraham followed God. He went to the Land of Beginning Again, the promised land, the land of Canaan. He humbly walked with his Lord and became known as a friend of God. He lived close to the Lord and was sensitive to his shortcomings. When he sinned, he confessed it. He loved his brethren and had peace with them as much as lay within him. He gave his tithes and his offerings.

And God blessed him. His name, indeed, became great. All the families of the earth have been blessed through him. God has blessed them who have blessed him and cursed those who have cursed him. By faith Abraham followed God, and it was counted unto him for righteousness.

It worked for Abraham—this journey to the Land of Beginning Again. And it will work for you.

It was true in the life of my own father who has long since been with God. Because it did work for my father, I am writing this message to you today.

My folks died when I was in my early teens. I left the old home place in Decatur, Texas, and went back to the ranch country where I had been born. I lived with my widowed sister Ruth on the Graham ranch between Olney and Archer City, Texas. Ruth taught school on the ranch. There was a two-room schoolhouse. She and her three little boys and I lived in one room, and she taught school in the other. I drove her Ford car the ten miles to Olney every day to finish high school.

When my school days were over, I wanted to go on to college. I had no money. I was of a shy nature. It was during the Great Depression. From every standpoint, my desire to go to college seemed hopeless; yet I was determined to go to college.

I stayed on the ranch after I graduated from high school until it was time to enroll for the fall term. I wanted to go to Decatur Baptist College where John and George and Joe and Ruth had gone.

I sent in for an application and signed up for the fall term. I packed up my meager clothes in an old, battered valise that had been my father's and shipped it to Decatur, Texas.

Then one morning before daylight I went down to the corral, took a lariat rope off the peg and opened the gate. Inside the corral were several horses, one of them a large silver named West that belonged to me. I roped, saddled and bridled her in the morning darkness. Leading her outside the corral, I mounted, waved a silent good-by to the sleeping ranch and turned the pony's head toward the east and Decatur Baptist College, over one hundred miles away.

I left before breakfast without one single penny in my pocket with which to buy food for lunch. I had no supper.

Through the long, hot hours of the day I rode. Sometimes I followed the highways; sometimes I cut across the Texas prairie. Most of the time West maintained a smooth fox trot, and we covered a surprising number of miles.

But they were not happy ones. In the first place, I was tired and hungry. In the second place, I was scared half to death. In the third place, my heart was filled with bitterness. My father had left me a little money when he died, and some of his friends had borrowed it and had not paid it back. I had been a Sunday school boy all of my life, and what had it gotten me? Almost all my friends danced, but I had never even learned—had never been on a dance floor in my life. Many of my friends drank, and I had never touched one drop of liquor. Many of my friends smoked, but I never had. I had kept myself morally clean. Yet here I was, an orphan in the midst of the Depression without one single penny in my pockets. I had told everyone I was going to college, but how could I without a job, without money?

I grew more bitter as the long day drew to a close. Suddenly I became aware of dark storm clouds gathering overhead. Lightning cracked and thunder rolled. Clearly I was in for a good old Texas thunderstorm! My horse and saddle and clothing would get soaking wet. My bitterness increased.

I was back on the highway now. Presently I noticed on the left of the road a large farm home with fine barns and buildings. Turning my horse's head up the lane, I approached the front yard gate and hollered the customary "Hello."

A gray-haired man appeared on the front porch and answered, "Hello yourself. Get down."

I dismounted and walked down the path to meet him. "I am on my way to Decatur where I'm going to college," I explained. "It's going to rain in a few minutes; and if you don't mind, I'd like to sleep in your barn tonight."

The gray-haired man assured me that he did not mind my sleeping in his barn if I would promise to strike no matches. Then, as he looked me square in the face, he asked, "What did you say your name was, son?"

I had not said, but now I told him my name was Bill Rice and repeated that I was on my way to Decatur where I was going to college (proud that I was going to college!).

"Did you say Rice?" he asked. "Are you any kin to the Senator Will Rice who used to live in Decatur?"

When I told him that Senator Will Rice was my father, the old man was delighted. Turning toward the house, he called in a loud voice, "Ma! O Ma!" And when a lovely gray-haired lady appeared at the door, he continued, "Ma, this young fella is the son of Senator Will Rice, and he's going to spend the night with us."

The dear lady ran down the path to meet me saying she was so glad

I had come their way. When she asked if I was hungry, I told her that I had not yet had my supper.

The man and I went to the barn where we unsaddled West and gave her fresh water and oats and hay. Back at the house the dear lady had set the table with good food, and I hungrily ate my breakfast, dinner and supper!

As I ate, they talked. Would this be my first year in college? Did I think I would like it? How were my brothers and sisters?

As I concluded my meal, they excused themselves and put down springs and mattresses on the front porch for a bed. The old man told me I ought to get to bed since I had a hard ride ahead on the morrow. When I suggested going to the barn to sleep, he told me that any son of Will Rice would always have the best bed in his house; but since the storm was over, they felt it would be cool and very pleasant on the front porch.

Before we retired, the two knelt on the front porch to pray. I dropped to my knees, too, and reverently heard him pray for his sons and daughters, for his neighbors and for me. He thanked God for the many good things that had come his way, and he thanked God that I had come to spend that night with them. He prayed that he and Ma might be a blessing to me.

I was a very thankful young man as I pulled off my boots and slipped between the clean, fresh sheets.

It seemed I had hardly fallen asleep when he was shaking my shoulder and telling me to get up. "It will be daylight before long, and you have a long ride today. Ma has breakfast about ready."

I rolled out of bed, dressed and pulled on my boots. I washed my hands and face in the cold water of the old pump behind the house and, as I walked into the kitchen, I could smell fried chicken! Yes, fried chicken, biscuits and gravy for breakfast! Since I ate longer than they did, he had bridled and saddled West and brought her up to the front gate by the time I had finished eating. The good lady made a number of sandwiches so I would not go hungry that day.

They were standing by my chair when I finished eating. He had on a pair of blue overalls and from the bib pocket pulled out a checkbook. "It takes money to go to college, son, and I imagine you are going to need a little help. Just how much do you think you will need this first term?"

I told him I wouldn't need any. He insisted on helping. He said I could call it either a gift or a loan but that he would like to help me. He asked again how much I needed. Again I told him I didn't want to take any money from him. I did not let him give me or lend me one single penny.

As we walked down the path toward the front gate, the early morning sun had just begun to shine on the silver head of this dear couple. I untied the reins, but before I mounted I turned and tried to thank them for their kindness to me. "But why have you been so good to me?" I asked.

The old man explained.

> I was going to tell you about that, Bill. Years ago when Ma and I first came to this place, we invested all the money we had in a down payment. Our children were little. Hard times and drought came. Crops dried up. Our herd of cattle wasted away. Everything seemed to go wrong.
>
> When the time came to meet the note on the place, I had no money with which to pay it. I was granted an extension. But things went from bad to worse, and I still was unable to pay on my note. Finally I was told I would have to pay or lose the place.
>
> I was desperate. I tried to borrow money, but couldn't. I tried to find work, but there was no work to be found. I wondered what in the world would become of my wife and babies. We were in desperate circumstances.
>
> When it seemed there was no hope for us, one day a stranger came riding down this same highway on a horse. He turned up the lane and stopped at my front yard gate, just as you did yesterday. He told me he had heard that I was in trouble, that I was about to lose my ranch, that my family was in need. "I have come to see if I can help you."
>
> I did not know him and he did not know me, but he helped Ma and me to save this place. And he did more than that for us. He told us that we would lose far more than the ranch if we were not careful—we would lose our souls. He told me and Ma about the Lord Jesus Christ, and we gladly became Christians. Our children, too, turned to the Lord that day.
>
> Yes, that cowboy heard we were in trouble, and he came to help us because he was a Christian, and he wanted us to be Christians, too.
>
> Because of him I was able to pay for this ranch. My four children have had good educations. I gave each one a farm on his wedding day. All are saved, and all my grandchildren who are old enough have been saved. God has been so good to me and to Ma. But we would have lost this ranch and lost our souls had it not been for the stranger who came our way that day.

And, Bill [he placed his hand on my shoulder], that stranger was your father!

My dad! God bless him! Years before I was born my father heard of a man in trouble—a man who needed money and who needed Christ. And just for Jesus' sake my father saddled a horse and rode to see this man, this complete stranger. He helped the man and then won him and his family to Christ.

My father never dreamed that some forty years later his baby boy would ride a horse down that same highway. He never dreamed that I would be so backslidden, so scared and so bitter. And he did not dream that the man to whom he had been a blessing—the man he had sacrificially won to Christ—would, in turn, take me in, feed me, give me a bed for the night, offer me money for college tuition and send me on my way reconsecrated to the Lord Jesus Christ!

My father did what was right for Jesus' sake. He trusted the Lord to guide him, to provide for him and to reward him. And God richly rewarded my father's faith; for I mounted my silver horse that morning, waved a grateful farewell to the elderly couple and turned my horse's head toward the east, toward college and the ministry—to the Land of Beginning Again.

MONROE PARKER
1909-

ABOUT THE MAN:

When you meet Monroe "Monk" Parker you meet both an educator and an evangelist, Ph.D. and personal soul winner—a great mind and hot heart!

Parker was a pre-med student at Birmingham Southern College in Birmingham, Alabama, because so many of his family were in medicine. By the same token—in Parker's background was a long history of preachers.

But saving grace does not run in family bloodlines.

Parker attended church and Sunday school regularly but was not converted until he was nineteen. The same week, in his church, he heard Dr. Bob Jones, Sr. tell about a one-year-old school he had organized to teach and train preacher boys. Parker knew this was where God wanted him.

He went to Bob Jones College, where he was called to preach. After graduating, Parker entered evangelism. After five years in the field he returned to BJU to assume directorship of religious activities, a position that eventually led him to become assistant to Dr. Bob Jones, Sr. Even then he conducted ten revivals a year.

In 1949 he re-entered full-time evangelism, a ministry that was interspersed with a pastorate in Decatur, Alabama and presidency of Pillsbury Conservative Baptist Bible College for eight years. Under his leadership, the student body grew 20% annually.

Besides conducting hundreds of campaigns and preaching in scores of high schools, colleges, Bible institutes and seminaries and over many radio stations, Parker has taught in Bible colleges and in seminaries, organized an association of independent Baptist churches in Alabama, served as president of the Minnesota Baptist Convention, developed and built the Christian Dells Bible Camp and Conference Grounds near Decatur, Alabama, and serves now as General Director of Baptist World Mission. He also serves on a host of boards.

You kind of gasp for breath when you read the ministries God has given him, but you also breathe a grateful "Amen!" for the man and his ministry.

Dr. Parker is a preacher of unusual ability, has keen insight into the Word of God, and is loyal to every fundamental.

Aye, we need some more Ph.D.'s like "Monk" Parker!

XV.

Choose Your God!

MONROE PARKER

"And I have given you a land for which ye did not labour, and cities which ye built not, and ye dwell in them; of the vineyards and oliveyards which ye planted not do ye eat. Now therefore fear the Lord, and serve him in sincerity and in truth: and put away the gods which your fathers served on the other side of the flood [literally "river"—the river Euphrates], *and in Egypt; and serve ye the Lord. And if it seem evil unto you to serve the Lord, choose you this day whom ye will serve; whether the gods which your fathers served that were on the other side of the flood* [Euphrates], *or the gods of the Amorites, in whose land ye dwell: but as for me and my house, we will serve the Lord."* —Josh. 24:13-15.

Joshua offered the people the alternative of choosing between Jehovah, the true God of Heaven, or some other god. Everybody worships something. Every person, even the atheist, has some kind of god.

Some years ago I was on my way to Miami to hold a revival meeting in the First Baptist Church. I went down from Jacksonville by bus. A rather portly, sophisticated lady sat down in the seat next to me and began a lengthy explanation to a passenger across the aisle as to why she had condescended to ride with ordinary folks on a Greyhound bus.

After a period of greatly-appreciated silence, she turned and asked me if I were a tourist. I replied that I was an evangelist on my way to Miami to conduct a revival meeting. She seemed rather surprised; she had heard of evangelists but had never actually met one in person; she found it difficult to believe that they actually did exist.

At that time I was connected with Bob Jones University. When I told the lady this, she asked if that were not "a reactionary school." I explained that it was an orthodox Christian university with a positive and aggressive program, although it stands "without apology for the old-time religion and the absolute authority of the Bible."

She said she "did not know that educated people believed in God anymore." I explained that some of the greatest scholars in the world are orthodox and believe the Bible profoundly.

She said, "Incidentally, I received my master's degree from _____ University." She was speaking out loud so she could be heard by everybody on the bus, and she continued, "I received my Ph.D. from _____ University, and every person who got his doctorate when I got mine was an atheist."

I had done some work at that University and was not surprised to hear this comment. I detest loud talk in a public place; but I, too, spoke out loud because I did not want the lady to skin my ignorance before all the people on the bus.

I said, "Lady, everybody has some kind of god."

She said, "I'll grant that there is a kind of universal religious instinct, and you'll find peoples in all parts of the world worshiping their several gods, but some of us have progressed up the scale of intelligence until we have outgrown the antiquated idea of a God."

"Lady, you have a god," I said.

"No, I don't."

"Yes, you do; and I can tell you what your god is."

She said, "All right, what is it?"

"A Ph.D. from _____ University."

A good old sister sitting just behind us said, "Amen!"

Everybody worships something. Your ideal is your idol. One does not have to have an image to be guilty of idolatry. The image is merely a circumstance. The Bible speaks of those who set up idols in their hearts. One does not have to go to a remote part of the earth to find idolatry. You can find it in your own neighborhood.

In ancient times every city and every pursuit of life had a particular god or goddess.

Athens was the city of Minerva, the goddess of wisdom.

Ephesus was the city of Diana, the goddess of the chase.

Rome was the city of Mars, the god of war.

Mariners worshiped Neptune; the war-like worshiped Mars; and female vanity bowed down at the shrine of Venus.

The Goddess of Wisdom

There are those in our modern society who proudly and ignorantly worship these ancient gods. Thousands are bowing at the shrine of Minerva and are sacrificing at the altar of their own intellects. They light the flickering torch of reason in their search for spiritual truth, but it will not yield a clear flame.

The God of Drink

One of the most popular gods in the world today is Bacchus, the awful god of drink. His temples are in every city, town and hamlet. His shrines are erected along the highways of the land and in the homes of millions. See yonder cathedral with its massive columns made of human skulls with dry, ghastly eyeholes. In its sanctuary there are bloody altars with human souls burning upon them in blue alcoholic flames. Thousands are crowding to the shrine to sacrifice on the altars.

Here comes a young man with something held dear. "What have you there, young man?"

"It's my wealth."

"What are you going to do with it?"

"I am going to sacrifice it to my god." Down it goes upon the bloody altar.

Another comes with his health and reputation and character. A young lady sacrifices her virtue. Another gives her children; another, home; another, position.

A young man comes with something shrieking, and I ask, "What have you there, young man?"

He answers, "My soul."

I plead with him to forsake this awful god and turn to the Christ who died to bring peace and victory to that miserable thing he calls his soul.

The God of Lust

Other ancient gods and goddesses flourish today. There is Venus, the personification of lasciviousness, with her millions of devotees in dance halls and nightclubs and theaters and other places of lewd entertainment and in secret places of sin. To her is sacrificed body and soul and spirit and "her house is the way to hell, going down to the chambers of death."

The God of Gold

Plutus, the god of gold, is worshiped by multiplied millions. Oh, the injustice and extortion and gambling and adultery and theft and war and murder committed for money! Indeed, "the love of money is the root of all [kinds of] evil."

Israel's Alternatives

Joshua gave to the people of Israel four choices. They could choose Jehovah, the God of Heaven; or rejecting Him, they could choose from among three other groups of gods. And in either of the three choices, they would worship the gods which their fathers served on the other side of the river.

These were the teraphim, the little household gods like the ones Rachel stole from her father Laban and hid in the camel's furniture which she sat upon when Laban searched Jacob's camp for them. Would you not hate to have a god someone could hide from you by sitting upon it? These teraphim were supposed to have power to protect the household from harm and danger as do the images of certain saints used by the Egyptians (the sun, the Nile, cattle). People could worship the gods of the Egyptians or the gods of the Amorites (the Baalim), with which worship were connected many abominable practices.

Israel's Choice

What could these other gods do for those who worshiped them? What did the teraphim do for the people of Mesopotamia? Had not Abraham been called from that heathendom? and had not Jehovah blessed him abundantly in the Land of Promise?

What did the gods of Egypt do for the Egyptians? They allowed Jehovah to send all kinds of plagues. They allowed Pharaoh's army to be drowned in the Red Sea. Jehovah had demonstrated His superiority to these gods.

What could the gods of the Amorites do for their followers? They allowed them to be driven out of their land by the Israelites. The gods of the Amorites allowed Israel to take the vineyards and the oliveyards which the Amorites planted and the cities which they built. They allowed the Amorites to fall before Israel, and Jehovah gave the victory to His people.

The history of Israel demonstrated that Jehovah was the true God. The people chose Jehovah!

The Justice of God

Bob Ingersoll and others have said that it is not consistent with the idea that God is love for Him to empower Israel to destroy the Amorites, slaughtering even the women, children and babies.

It is a sad fact that in this life the innocent sometimes suffer with the guilty, for the guilty and more than the guilty. However, we must remember that there are two places beyond the grave where things that are uneven in this life are going to be made even. God executes enough justice in this life to demonstrate that He is a God of absolute justice and beyond the grave and in the ages to come He will execute justice and judgment.

In the destruction of the Amorites, God executed justice. God had appeared to Abram and revealed that Israel would dwell in Egypt for a long season; and He had promised that He would then bring them to possess it after four hundred years, "for," said He, "the iniquity of the Amorites is not yet full."

But their iniquity did fill up. Archeologists have dug into the ruins of those old Amorite cities and discovered that the people were so corrupt and so diseased that had God spared them they would have contaminated the entire human race. Their iniquity was full.

America's Iniquity Is Filling Up

And, my friends, the iniquity of America is now just about full. We are living in an evil day. I am no pessimist; but if there ever was a time when revival is needed, it is today. There is such moral decadence, such deterioration of character that even those who have opposed evangelism are now saying that revival is our only hope.

The divorce mills continue to grind out broken hearts and homeless children with ever-increasing momentum—to say nothing of the awful sin of abortion.

Liquor flows like water all over the nation, and we are a half-drunk people.

Modesty is regarded with contempt. Photographs which would have been outlawed in the mails a generation ago, now are used to advertise the movies. Nude dancers are as common as street lights. Sin has been glorified.

The following captions and comments were taken from the theater advertisements on a single newspaper sheet in a comparatively small city recently:

"Born to be bad,"

"When she's bad, she's plenty good,"

"Now! Heartless, glamorous huntress of men,"

"The big Hotcha Girlie show,"

"His camera held the key to 1,000 sinister secrets,"

"Her secret was the mistake that young love brought,"

"Her secret was born of a loveless kiss."

And so it goes.

And, my friends, we have come to sad and evil days when sex perversity among government employees in the national capital is so widespread it becomes a political issue.

God save America! The iniquity of this country is filled up. Surely judgment will fall if we do not turn to God. "Except the Lord of hosts had left unto us a very small remnant, we should have been as Sodom, and we should have been like unto Gomorrah" (Isa. 1:9).

Wisdom of Israel's Choice

God drove out the Amorites and established Israel in the Promised Land. Was not Jehovah mightier than the gods of the Amorites? Were not His benefits more gracious? The Israelites would have been foolish to choose the gods of the Egyptians or the gods of Mesopotamia.

Just as in Joshua's day there were many gods, there are gods today too numerous to mention through which the Devil gives his siren call.

But none of them can do for you what Jesus can do. What have Mohammed and Buddha and Tao and Confucius done for the world? Look at India with her sorrows. Look at China and the teeming, suffering millions of the other Eastern nations. Look at dark, benighted Africa.

Benefits of Christianity

What has Jesus Christ done for the world? Look at America! "America, America, God shed His grace on thee, and crown thy good with brotherhood from sea to shining sea." Of course, it is true that America is a backslidden nation, a drinking nation, a gambling nation and a sinful nation over which impending judgment hangs; but it is still the most humanitarian nation in all the world.

We are the freest people on the earth. America is nearer Christian than any other nation in the world. Yes, our Christianity has almost become a mere tradition, and we have drifted far from the righteousness of our Founding Fathers. But all the elements that make America great emanate from the influence of Jesus Christ in the land.

Christ Incomparable

I do not like the term "comparative religions." It is all right as an academic term, but the incomparable Christ must be contrasted with the false gods of all other religions. Wherever the true missionary plants the standard of the cross he declares that 'Christ has no concord with Belial nor light with darkness.'

Wherein is the religion of Jesus Christ distinguished from other religions? It is the only religious system that can offer pardon to the sinner. Where in all the world is there another religion that can do this? They can feed the hungry, clothe the naked, comfort the fatherless and the widow and promote good deeds; but they cannot pardon the sinner.

> See yonder from the sky above
> Stern justice hurls a dart of wrath.
> The sinner here on earth below
> Is standing in the danger path.
> He'll soon be struck and justly so.
> But bursting through those gates of love
> Sweet Mercy brings a shield of grace.
> That shield is Christ, the Son of God.
> Swifter far than dart can ride
> He flies to take the sinner's place,
> Is struck Himself, and sheds His blood.
> Sinner, 'twas for thee He died.
> Stern Justice now is satisfied.

Let all institutions and systems and councils and theories bow down before Jesus and stack their crowns at the foot of His cross, for they cannot pardon the sinner. "Who is a pardoning God like Thee, or who has grace so rich and free?" All have sinned. You have sinned, and you need pardon. Only Christ can give it to you, my sinner friend. If you will accept Him as your Saviour, you may stand in the presence of God as pure in His eyes as Jesus Himself.

> Near, so very near to God,
> Nearer I cannot be,
> For in the person of His Son
> I am just as near as He.

Jesus Can Make You Happy

Jesus Christ is the only One in the universe who can make men happy. Often I hear young people testify as if they are trying to convey the idea that they are happy even though they are Christians. Perhaps they do not realize it, but it is as though they were saying something like this: "I can still have lots of fun even though I am saved. I can play ball or fly a plane or swim or wear pretty clothes or do certain other things as well as those who are not saved. I am saved, but I can still be a regular fellow. I am happy even though I am a Christian."

Of course, there are many wholesome things that people may enjoy whether they are saved or lost, but those are not the things that make people happy. A Christian may enjoy these things, but he can be happy without them. We are not happy "even though" we are Christians. We are happy *because* we are Christians.

In the first place, we are happy because our sins are forgiven. Sin is the source of sorrow. The sense of guilt which can be lost only when sin is pardoned keeps all sinners from true happiness.

Jesus makes us happy in the second place because He gives us power to rise above sin. The Christian is beset with temptations. He may be defeated, but he does not have to be. The defeated, backslidden Christian is unhappy. Hence David prayed, "Restore unto me the joy of thy salvation."

We are made happy by the assurance that God loves us and also by the assurance that all things work together for our good. We are made happy by the presence of the indwelling Spirit who produces virtues which adjust our lives so that the spiritual is elevated above the sensual, which is the only proper and, therefore, the only happy condition.

Adapted to All

The religion of Jesus Christ is adapted to all people. It is adapted to people of all ages.

I had an old man eighty-seven years of age converted, and at the same service a little boy nine years old was saved. The next night I heard them in conversation. They were both happy in Jesus and understood each other when they talked about it.

The old-time religion was good for Paul and Silas. . . . It was good for our mothers . . . and it's good enough for me. It was all right in the horse-and-buggy days; it was all right in the automobile age. It is all right in the atomic age, too, my friends. It was adapted to Adam and Eve camping in the sight of Eden, and it will be adapted to the last born child this side of the White Throne Judgment.

Jesus is the same for people of all races. "Some from every tongue, and tribe and nation will be there." He is the same for all people circumstantially and socially. He can save the king, and He can save the slave. He can save the moralist, and He can save the wretch sunk in the deepest and blackest bogs of human depravity.

Jesus Loves the Moron

He is the same for all people intellectually. He can save the philosopher, and He can save the fool. I never get alarmed when a moron gives a testimony. Often some poor "dim wit" will get up to testify, and some brother will pull my coattail and whisper, "Don't let that fellow say anything. He is not all there."

Let him testify. Just do not let him take over the service. The other morons will think he has good sense, and they will get a blessing. People with good judgment will also get a blessing. They will say, "It's wonderful. Jesus can save a poor fool, and He can save a philosopher."

Suppose God had put salvation up on a high intellectual shelf where a man had to climb a philosophical ladder to reach it. Most of us would have to go to Hell.

Or maybe you say, "I am too smart to be a Christian." You are a fool! I do not care who you are or how much you have had your brain stretched, you are a fool. You haven't got sense enough to know that God did not put salvation up on a shelf where only intellectuals could get it. That is the way you would have done it.

Christianity is not reason; it is revelation. There are depths in Christianity which the profoundest philosopher has not plumbed. There are realms into which the keenest mind created by God cannot reach. But God reveals Himself to ordinary people like you and me through Jesus Christ.

Jesus Gives Power

The religion of Jesus Christ is distinguished from all other religions because it is the only one that supplies the power to live up to its demands. The religions of the world say, "Do and live." Jesus Christ says, "Live and do."

Someone says, "I want to be a Christian but don't know if I can live it. I believe in a man's living up to his profession."

So do I, but what is my profession? That I am a naturally born sinner, a child of Adam. I am so sinful that I cannot hope to save myself. I must cast myself entirely upon Jesus Christ and on His robe of righteousness as a substitute for the filthy rags of my own self-righteousness.

God looks at the righteousness of Jesus Christ covering me and declares me righteous. And because God is honest, when He writes it down that I am righteous, He has to make me righteous so it will be true, so He imparts something to me. He comes into me in the Person of the Holy Spirit and causes my life to produce fruits of righteousness.

Christ Lives in Me

In other words, my profession is that I am not good. Therefore, He must come and live the Christian life for me. I sometimes think it is almost too good to be true that I know that many years ago the great God leaned over the battlements of Heaven and placed a jewel in a vessel of the poorest clay. That clay was my life, and that treasure was Jesus. I have this gem in an earthen vessel. I have salvation. I have Christ. I have never lived the Christian life, but for these years the Lord Jesus Christ has lived it in me and for me and through me and, sometimes, I am afraid, almost in spite of me.

A Living Saviour

You can have Mohammedanism without Mohammed, Buddhism without Buddha and Confucianism without Confucius; but you cannot have Christianity without Christ. There is no crucifix on this church. Christ is on no cross. He is in no tomb. He is a risen, living Christ. 'He ever liveth and is able to save unto the uttermost all who come unto God by him.'

He is here tonight in the Person of His Spirit. His arms are outstretched. He says, "Him that cometh to me I will in no wise cast out." Why do you not choose Jesus? You have the light. You know what you ought to do. The Spirit of God has spoken. The Spirit of God has brought light to you. "Choose you this day whom ye will serve"!

XVI.

A "Fear Not" for Every Day in the Year

LEE ROBERSON

"But now thus saith the Lord that created thee, O Jacob, and he that formed thee, O Israel, Fear not: for I have redeemed thee. I have called thee by thy name; thou art mine." —Isa. 43:1.

The story is told of a young man who went to New York City to study to be an architect. Later, he became a contractor and builder, making a million dollars in a few years.

Going down the street one day, he met an old man, ragged, dirty. Recognizing him as an old-time friend who had helped him when he first came to New York City, he stopped him and said, "Hello, John. I am glad to see you. Where do you live?"

The old man told him.

"Is your wife living?"

"Yes."

"Well, I'm coming down tomorrow night to see both of you."

The next night he sat in a little room and talked with John and his wife. After finding out their condition, he said to the old man, "If you will cut out the booze, stop your gambling, live an honest, upright life and take care of your wife as you ought to, I'll give you a chance to make some money."

John promised that he would do it.

Then said the young man, "Come to my office tomorrow and I'll give you something to do."

The next day when he appeared at the office, the young man pulled out of the drawer some specifications and a blueprint of a cottage that he wanted built on a lot in the suburbs of the city. He said to his old friend, "Now, I want you to take these specifications and erect this cottage for me. I will pay all the bills. I'll put ten thousand dollars in the bank in your name. You can draw on the money for the house, and I'll pay your salary. When the house is completed, report to me."

The old man went to work. But his native meanness got the best of him. He cheated. Wherever he could, he put in a cheaper material, saving and stealing about five hundred dollars.

When the building was finished, he reported that he was ready to turn the house over. The young man said, "I'll be down at your apartment tonight."

That night he sat and talked with the old couple. Finally he said, "For the sake of the old friendship and due to the fact that you gave me my first opportunity to make some money when I came to New York, I'm going to make you a present of this house and lot."

Feeling so humiliated that he had cheated, the old man broke down and wept. When the young man asked him what was wrong, the old man confessed and pleaded to be forgiven and asked that he be given another chance.

The young man said, "John, I'm going to forgive you and give you another chance. I hope you have learned your lesson, and I am sorry you cheated, for you must live in the house you built."

The application of that story is this: We must live in the houses we build. Build a fearful, trembling life and it is your house to live in.

The Bible has been given to help us. It tells us what to do with these lives of ours. The Bible tells us how to be victorious Christians. The Word of God tells us how to conquer our fears. Every part of life is touched by the Lord's "fear nots."

We have a "fear not" for sorrowful days, a "fear not" for pain-filled days, a "fear not" for days of persecution.

There are three thoughts that I want you to see in this message.

I. THE WEAKNESS OF THE FLESH

A leading secular magazine carried an article by a minister who was a radio counselor and had received thousands of letters from listeners who were in trouble. He has discovered that many troubled souls leap at an opportunity to unburden themselves to a stranger.

In the article he analyzed the letters received and expressed his conclusion that there were four great maladies that trouble people: fear, anxiety, loneliness and unkindness.

There is no solution to these things outside Christ.

It is stated that someone counted 365 occurrences of "fear not" in the Bible. This could mean that there is a "fear not" for every day in the year. It is for us to learn that in Christ we have the solution to fear.

Paul faced his weakness and conquered it—through Jesus Christ. He said:

"We are troubled on every side, yet not distressed; we are perplexed, but not in despair; Persecuted, but not forsaken; cast down, but not destroyed: Always bearing about in the body the dying of the Lord Jesus, that the life also of Jesus might be made manifest in our body."—II Cor. 4:8-10.

As you read in II Corinthians 11 and 12, you are conscious of the apostle's recognition of his weakness. He found himself forced to rest upon the power of God. There was a certain thorn in the flesh about which he prayed three times. God did not remove it but said to him, "My grace is sufficient for thee: for my strength is made perfect in weakness."

I must recognize my weakness—in the flesh. It is when I see this weakness and recognize it that I can be strong in the Lord. Paul meant that when he said, "Therefore I take pleasure in infirmities, in reproaches, in necessities, in persecutions, in distresses for Christ's sake: for when I am weak, then am I strong."

In the recognition of my weakness, I am not to be pessimistic.

A Scotchman had the habit of saying, "It might be worse." When his wife ran away with another man, a friend went to comfort him, thinking that this was one time he couldn't say, "It might be worse." But when his friend spoke to him about the tragedy, the Scotchman, true to form, said, "It might be worse."

His friend said, "How could anything be worse than having your wife run off with another man?"

The Scotchman replied, "She might come back."

I must recognize the tendency to fear. Fear is a common ailment of this day. All who are in the flesh must face the difficulty, the problem and the weakness of fear.

Elijah had great power with God. It is not pleasant to contemplate, but Elijah had fears. After the great victory on Mount Carmel, he ran for his life. Jezebel threatened him, and he went a day's journey and sat under a juniper tree and cried out, "It is enough; now, O Lord, take away my life; for I am not better than my fathers." Elijah was afraid!

The New Testament affords the story of fear also. When Jesus was being tried, Simon Peter sat in the outer courtyard. When a certain maid said, "This man was also with him," Simon Peter denied this three times, saying, "Woman, I know him not." What was wrong? Peter was afraid.

Again, I must recognize that worry is sin. Worry is the lack of faith. Worry is a dependence upon the flesh. Worry points downward. Worry puts us on the toboggan slide.

Come, my friend, and recognize the weakness of your life. Self-sufficiency will not hold you. Abundance of material possessions will not protect you. Weakness can only be answered by dependence upon the Almighty God.

II. THE WISDOM OF MY SAVIOUR

He knows my need. How blessed is this thought, that my Saviour knows my need, my weakness, my fears, my proneness to fail. But He knows something else: through His power I can conquer.

But wait a minute! Though He knows my weakness, He waits for me to call upon Him. This is God's way. If a man fail in life, he has no one to blame but himself. James tells us, "Ye have not, because ye ask not" (4:2).

When I see my need, I must come to the all-wise Saviour and seek the blessing and help of One who never fails!

Second, He is ever near. The all-sufficient, all-wise One is ever near me.

On one occasion the disciples were crossing the Sea of Galilee when a storm arose. They were fearful. Then Jesus came walking on the water. He came to them that He might help.

On another occasion, they were crossing the lake. Jesus was with them in the ship asleep. When a storm came, they cried out to Him for help. He arose and rebuked the wind and the raging water. There came a calm. Jesus turned to them and said, "Where is your faith?"

He was near to Daniel when he was put in the lions' den. Daniel stood for his convictions and because of the king's foolish promise to Daniel's adversaries, he was cast into the den of lions. In the early morning the king came out and called unto Daniel, who answered, "O king, live for ever. My God hath sent his angel, and hath shut the lions' mouths, that they have not hurt me."

He is ever near. He was near to Paul and Silas in the jail in Philippi.

At midnight, they prayed and sang praises unto God, and the Lord answered and released them from the prison.

He is ever near. He was near to the Apostle John on the isle of Patmos. You could almost hear him shout, "And this is the victory that overcometh the world, even our faith."

What made John write like this? Because he was conscious of the presence of God. An old man, broken, and about to die, could still shout the victory song. John knew about the Devil and the Devil's power, but he knew better still the power of the Almighty God.

Third, He cannot fail.

"He shall not fail nor be discouraged, till he have set judgment in the earth: and the isles shall wait for his law."—Isa. 42:4.

This is real assurance. Friends may fail, circumstances may change, but He cannot fail and He cannot change.

"For I am the Lord, I change not; therefore ye sons of Jacob are not consumed."—Mal. 3:6.

"Jesus Christ the same yesterday, and to day, and for ever."—Heb. 13:8.

My Saviour is wise. He knows my need. He is ever near. He cannot fail. This the Lord said to me,

"Peace I leave with you, my peace I give unto you: not as the world giveth, give I unto you. Let not your heart be troubled, neither let it be afraid."—John 14:27.

III. THE WAY TO VICTORY

We have discussed: first, the weakness of my life; second, the wisdom of my Saviour; now, third, the way to victory. Let us understand some things about fear.

Fear is an enemy to health. Fear produces death to energy, death to tissue and death to growth. When you bring a child up in a home of fear, that child is touched by this tragic enemy. The health will be impaired. The life will be weakened. Fear affects the chemical composition of the body.

Fear is an enemy to happiness. No person can enjoy life fully if the soul is filled with fear. There cannot be a joyous, happy life when you are depressed by fears and worries. Anticipation of the troubles of tomorrow will take away the joy that God intends you to have today.

Fear is an enemy to successful living. The person who thinks failure cannot succeed; the person who is afraid to step out on faith will be robbed of success today.

Someone said, "Fear blurs the vision, stampedes the nerves, paralyzes the reason, and does not change anything for the better."

Now let us turn to the Word of God for a few moments and read some verses to strengthen our hearts.

"Fear thou not; for I am with thee: be not dismayed; for I am thy God: I will strengthen thee; yea, I will help thee; yea, I will uphold thee with the right hand of my righteousness."—Isa. 41:10.

"Be careful for nothing; but in every thing by prayer and supplication with thanksgiving let your requests be made known unto God. And the peace of God, which passeth all understanding, shall keep your hearts and minds through Christ Jesus."—Phil. 5:6,7.

"Humble yourselves therefore under the mighty hand of God, that he may exalt you in due time: Casting all your care upon him; for he careth for you."—I Pet. 5:6,7.

"There is no fear in love; but perfect love casteth out fear: because fear hath torment. He that feareth is not made perfect in love."—I John 4:18.

Satan has a double objective: to damn souls and to deceive the saints of God. He desires to cast as many into Hell as he can. But if souls escape him and come to the Saviour, then he desires to blacken their lives, weaken their testimonies, defeat their lives and cause them to stumble in their Christian walk.

But we can be victorious now!

We can overcome fear now! God has given us a way, and the way is to cast every care upon Him and to know that He cares for us. Fear—the wrong kind of fear—can defeat us; but God will give us the victory.

I have read the beautiful story of Jenny Lind many times. Jenny Lind was the world-renowned Swedish singer of the last century. She came to New York City to give concerts. In the course of these concerts, she paid a visit to a boat in the New York harbor. This boat was the chapel of a man named Pastor Olaf Hedstrom.

It was in 1851 that Jenny Lind came to New York, and at the height of her fame and influence in the musical world, she paid a visit to the ship and heard Pastor Hedstrom preach.

At the conclusion of the service, she went into the pastor's study where the man of God talked to her faithfully about her need of salvation. Soon they were kneeling and Jenny Lind wept and called on the name of the Lord and was gloriously saved. The pastor did not mince words. He talked about Heaven and Hell. He talked about sin and judgment. He pointed her to the Lamb of God who takes away the sin of the world.

After this occasion, Jenny Lind wrote the pastor many times and expressed her appreciation for the fact that he led her to the Lord. After awhile she wrote him that she would never again appear in the theater. She decided to leave the operatic stage.

Because of this, many expressed strong words against her religion and against Pastor Hedstrom, but she kept her promise. She never again appeared in opera. She only sang at concerts for some definite philanthropic purpose.

Some years after all of this happened, a visitor found Jenny Lind reading her Bible. The visitor said, "Why did you leave the stage?"

Looking toward a beautiful sunset, the singer said simply, "Because it blinded my eyes to that." And then looking down at her Bible, she added, "And because it blinded my eyes to this."

At the time of her conversion, Jenny Lind had said, "There is no peace in created things. They cannot give happiness, but only increase my anxiety. There is no peace, O God, until my soul finds peace in Thee."

Many people have discovered that the only peace that means anything is the peace that comes from Jesus Christ the blessed Saviour. Some have not discovered this yet, but you can discover it right now. By repentance and faith, you can come to the Lord Jesus and have everlasting life. Christ is able to satisfy your heart and give you a peace and a joy unspeakable.

Will you receive Him as your Saviour?

"Verily, verily, I say unto you, He that believeth on me hath everlasting life."—John 6:47.

JOHN R. RICE
1895-1980

ABOUT THE MAN:

Preacher...evangelist...revivalist...editor...counsellor to thousands...friend to millions—that was Dr. John R. Rice, whose accomplishments were nothing short of miraculous. Known as "America's Dean of Evangelists," Dr. Rice made a mighty impact upon the nation's religious life for some sixty years, in great citywide campaigns and in Sword of the Lord Conferences.

At age nine, after hearing a sermon on "The Prodigal Son," John went forward to claim Christ as Saviour. In 1916, with only $9.35 in his pocket, he rode off on his cowpony toward Decatur Baptist College. He was now on the road to becoming a world-renowned evangelist, although he was then totally unaware of God's will for his life.

There was many a twist and turn before Rice rode through the open door into full-time preaching—the army, marriage, graduate work, more seminary, assistant pastor, pastor—then FINALLY, where God planned to use him most—in full-time evangelism.

Dr. Rice and his ministry were always colorful (born in Cooke county, in Texas, December 11, 1895, and often called "Will Rogers of the Pulpit" because of their likeness and mannerisms)—and controversial. CONTROVERSIAL—and correctly so—because of his intense stand against modernism and infidelity and his fight for the Fundamentals.

Dr. Rice lived and died a man of convictions—intense convictions. But, like many other strong fighters for the Faith, Rice was also marked with a sincere spirit of compassion. Those who knew him best knew a man who loved them. In preaching, in prayer, and in personal life, Rice wept over sinners and with saints. But there is more...

Less than seventy-one hours before the dawning of 1981, one of the most prolific pens in all Christendom was stilled. Dr. John R. Rice left behind a legacy in writing of more than 200 titles, with a combined circulation of over 61 million copies. And through October of 1981, a total of 24,058 precious souls reported trusting Christ through his ministries, not counting those saved in his crusades nor in foreign countries where his literature has been translated.

And who but God knows the influence of THE SWORD OF THE LORD magazine which he started and edited for forty-six years!

And while "Twentieth Century's Mightiest Pen"—and man—has been stilled, thank God, the fruit remains! Though dead, he continues to speak.

XVI.

Come Back to Bethel

Like Jacob of Old, We Need to Return to Early Christian Joy, to Sweet Promises, to Meet God Afresh, Be Newly Commissioned and Renew Holy Vows

JOHN R. RICE

(Written New Year's Day, 1958)

"And God said unto Jacob, Arise, go up to Beth-el, and dwell there: and make there an altar unto God, that appeared unto thee when thou fleddest from the face of Esau thy brother. Then Jacob said unto his household, and to all that were with him, Put away the strange gods that are among you, and be clean, and change your garments: And let us arise, and go up to Beth-el; and I will make there an altar unto God, who answered me in the day of my distress, and was with me in the way which I went. And they gave unto Jacob all the strange gods which were in their hand, and all their earrings which were in their ears; and Jacob hid them under the oak which was by Shechem. And they journeyed: and the terror of God was upon the cities that were round about them, and they did not pursue after the sons of Jacob. So Jacob came to Luz, which is in the land of Canaan, that is, Beth-el, he and all the people that were with him. And he built there an altar, and called the place El-Beth-el: because there God appeared unto him, when he fled from the face of his brother."—Gen. 35:1-7.

John Wesley had a never-to-be-forgotten experience at Aldersgate. There he felt his heart strangely warmed, and by faith he knew that he, even he, was forgiven and justified.

Saul of Tarsus met the Lord Jesus Christ on the road to Damascus with a light brighter than the sun. There his proud heart surrendered to the Saviour whom he had before hated. He was saved, then called to carry the Gospel far hence to the Gentiles.

Neither John Wesley nor Saul of Tarsus could forget his crisis experience.

Jacob had his Bethel, an experience as tremendous as that of John Wesley or Saul of Tarsus.

Jacob, after many weary years, is called back to Bethel, back to a renewal of his vows and to a new fellowship with God, a new call to be the head of a nation and the ancestor of the Seed of Abraham—the Lord Jesus.

Every man who knows Christ as Saviour has had his place of blessing, his place of Christian joy and assurance, his place of holy vows. And all of us might well, like Jacob, hear the call of God to come back to Bethel to receive afresh the promises of God and to renew the holy vows we made before and the fellowship once so sweetly enjoyed.

I. THAT EARLIER MEETING WITH GOD AT BETHEL

Jacob had a twin brother, Esau.

In answer to the beseeching prayer of Isaac, his barren wife, Rebekah, conceived. When the twins struggled within her, she prayed and God revealed this to her:

"Two nations are in thy womb, and two manner of people shall be separated from thy bowels; and the one people shall be stronger than the other people; and the elder shall serve the younger."—Gen. 25:23.

So before they were born, God had planned to make Jacob the head of the promised nation and the ancestor of the Seed which He had promised Abraham, the Saviour through whom all nations should be blessed.

1. How Jacob Got the Birthright and the Blessing

God, who made such plans, had put some holy hunger in the heart of the boy Jacob. He believed what he had heard his father Isaac tell that ownership of the land of Palestine, the headship of the nation, the ancestry of the blessed Seed, was to come through Abraham and Isaac and one of these boys.

Without knowing how God had planned to work it out, Jacob traded the hungry, tired Esau (born first) "bread and pottage of lentiles" for the birthright which was expected to go to the firstborn.

Later when Isaac was an old blind man, he instructed Esau, the firstborn, to bring in venison and prepare it "such as I love, and bring it to me, that I may eat; that my soul may bless thee before I die" (Gen. 27:4).

Rebekah overheard. She knew what God had told her—"the elder shall serve the younger." So she schemed with Jacob to pretend to be Esau, to dress in Esau's garments and serve quickly prepared meat of kids instead of the venison.

So old and blind Isaac was deceived and gave to Jacob the blessing which he thought he was giving to Esau.

God had intended Jacob to have the blessing, and it was a prophetic blessing, but it need not have been sought by deceit and fraud.

Esau penitently sought now to get back the birthright which he had bargained away and the blessing which he had missed. But on this matter he repented in vain. God had chosen Jacob to be the head of the Jewish nation and to enter into the covenant made with Abraham and Isaac.

We can imagine how angry Esau was with his crooked brother; for we read, "And Esau hated Jacob because of the blessing wherewith his father blessed him: and Esau said in his heart, The days of mourning for my father are at hand; then will I slay my brother Jacob" (Gen. 27:41).

Dreading the wrath of Esau for her favored Jacob, Rebekah arranged to have Isaac send the young man back to Padan-aram to get a bride from the daughters of Laban, Rebekah's brother, lest he should marry some heathen woman among the Canaanites. So Jacob, running from the wrath of his brother and shamed before his father, left home and headed northwest.

It must have been a sad journey—away from the mother he loved and from his old father whom he had deceived and from familiar surroundings. He had no money, no company. When dark came upon him, he was near a place called Luz. There was no inn, no friendly home, no pleasant bed available, so he gathered rocks together to prop his weary head and slept on the ground!

2. The Ladder From Heaven, the Angels of God, and God's Covenant With a Homesick Man

As sad and lonely Jacob slept the sleep of weariness, in a dream Heaven opened. There was a ladder set up on earth reaching to Heaven. The angels of God ascended and descended. God stood above the ladder and said:

"I am the Lord God of Abraham thy father, and the God of Isaac:

*the land whereon thou liest, to thee will I give it, and to thy seed; And
thy seed shall be as the dust of the earth, and thou shalt spread abroad
to the west, and to the east, and to the north, and to the south: and
in thee and in thy seed shall all the families of the earth be blessed.
And, behold, I am with thee, and will keep thee in all places whither
thou goest, and will bring thee again into this land; for I will not leave
thee, until I have done that which I have spoken to thee of."*—Gen.
28:13-15.

Jacob woke up, his soul shaken, partly with the fear that sinful mor-
tals must have when they come into God's presence and partly with
the glory of God's presence and promise. He said, "How dreadful is
this place! this is none other but the house of God, and this is the gate
of heaven" (vs. 17). God was in the place where the lonely man lay
his weary head and slept, and he knew it not!

*"And Jacob rose up early in the morning, and took the stone that
he had put for his pillows, and set it up for a pillar, and poured oil upon
the top of it. And he called the name of that place Beth-el: but the name
of that city was called Luz at the first."*—Vss. 18,19.

The Hebrew word *beth* means "house." *El* is the Hebrew word for
God. So Jacob called this place "the house of God."

Then we read:

*"And Jacob vowed a vow, saying, If God will be with me, and will
keep me in this way that I go, and will give me bread to eat, and raiment to put on, So that I come again to my father's house in peace;
then shall the Lord be my God: And this stone, which I have set for
a pillar, shall be God's house: and of all that thou shalt give me I will
surely give the tenth unto thee."*—Vss. 20-22.

Oh, how could Jacob ever forget that holy night—the awe-inspiring
scene of angels who are usually invisible to mortal eyes; the glory of
God shining above the stairway to Heaven; the voice of God speaking
to his heart!

And what glorious promises, that he should have a multitude of seed
and ". . . in thy seed shall all the families of the earth be blessed." That
promise could only be fulfilled by the coming of the Saviour, the Seed
of Abraham, of Isaac and of Jacob.

And the promise was not only to his descendants, but God had promised to be with him and to keep him and bring him again in peace to this land of Canaan.

On the basis that God would do what He had said, would care for his needs and bring him again to his father's house in peace, Jacob had made three lifetime promises:

First, "Then shall the Lord be my God" (vs. 21). Is this the time when Jacob first knew forgiveness of sin and opened his heart to the saving grace of God? Is this the time when his heart was renewed and changed, when he became a child of God? Perhaps it was. We know that he had believed in the God of his father, had wanted the spiritual heritage of the firstborn, but now there is an outright decision: "Then shall the Lord be my God."

Second, the stone that had been his pillow—he set it up and poured oil on the top. Henceforth this stone, this place, was to be to him the house of God! So he called it "Beth-el," the name which has remained these thirty-seven hundred years.

Last of all, Jacob made the holy vow, "Of all that thou shalt give me, I will surely give the tenth unto thee."

This was the first of two or three climactic spiritual mountaintops in Jacob's life. How could he ever forget the presence of God, the holy promises, the serious vows which involved all his loyalty, all his will, all his love, all his possessions!

3. We, Too, Have Had Our Bethels

Dear Christian reader, did you not have a Bethel also? It may have been when you were saved.

How can I ever forget the events connected with my own turning to Christ! First, there was the time when I stepped out in the faith of a nine-year-old boy to trust the Lord Jesus and claim Him openly. A few years ago I drove through Gainesville, Texas early on a summer Sunday morning. On a sudden impulse I drove to the First Baptist Church. The doors were open. Soon the throngs would be coming to Sunday school.

I went in and sat in the same seat where I had sat as a boy. Then I imagined good old Brother Ingram preaching again on the prodigal son and telling the story of his experience as a runaway boy and his return to the loving, forgiving arms of his father. I remembered again the invitation and how I slid off the pew and walked down that aisle to take Christ as Saviour.

Then I remember the time when, after three years of troubled, un-
sure heart, I found the blessed promise of God, "He that believeth on
the Son hath everlasting life." Then, thank God, I had it! Full assurance
flooded my soul, and from that time to this I have known that my sins
are forgiven, that I, unworthy sinner that I am and was, am received
by God's grace and pardoned and saved!

I remember when I was baptized in the old railroad "tank" or pond
near the little cow town of Dundee, Texas. I remember that, as we came
out of the water on that cold November day and stood in a line beside
the water, all sang together,

> **O happy day that fixed my choice**
> **On Thee, my Saviour and my God!**
> **Well may this glowing heart rejoice**
> **And tell its raptures all abroad.**
>
> **Happy day, happy day,**
> **When Jesus washed my sins away!**

All our big family couldn't ride in the seats of the two-seated hack,
so I prepared to stand in the back, as I usually did. But my father, anxious that I not be chilled in my wet garments, wrapped me in a quilt
and had me sit in a seat. My heart was so warm I did not feel the brisk
November wind. Oh, that was a Bethel to which my heart often goes
back!

I remember so well the day when I knelt under a thorny bush in the
"brakes" near our home in West Texas. With a burning in my heart,
I felt I must go to college and get ready for the work God might have
me to do. So I made my decision.

With some $9.35 in my pocket, I rode away on a January day toward
Decatur College. With borrowed money, I started toward the long hours
of toil and eventual training in Baylor University, the University of
Chicago, and Southwestern Baptist Theological Seminary. Oh, that day
when I told God I would preach or sing or be a missionary or do anything
He wanted me to do, if He would take me as I was and help me through
school!

It was a Bethel of blessing. That chaparral bush where I knelt and
prayed was to me the house of God.

Again, my heart goes back to that holy time in 1921 when I knelt
in the Pacific Garden Mission with my arms around a drunken bum and
won him to Christ. He was so wonderfully transformed that my heart
was enthralled. I had made my life plans to be a college teacher and

had taught one year in Wayland College. Now suddenly I felt there was far more for me than being a college teacher.

I offered myself to God, and in response to the blessed invitation of Romans 12:1, 2, I presented my body a living sacrifice. By faith I took the call, the place of service which I now know God had laid upon me from the day I was born and in answer to the holy prayers of my father and mother. Oh, kneeling on that floor beside the bum who found Christ was to me the never-to-be-forgotten house of God!

Strangely enough, one of those times I met God, one of those times which became to me a veritable Bethel, a true house of God, was when, under strong temptation and serious threats of denominational men, I decided I must be true to my convictions. I must oppose modernism and evolutionary teaching in Baylor University where I had graduated and where my teacher, Dr. Dow, had been a bone of contention because of his teaching of evolution.

Facing the threats that I would be blackballed and branded and that I would never be invited to hold revivals, that I would have no chance as an evangelist, I told God that if I were serving a God who could not look after His preachers unless they kowtowed to the leaders, unless they sought to please men and played politics with the brethren, I would leave His service. But I told Him that I was willing to risk everything to prove that the God who called me could care for me.

Oh, what a day of decision! I lost overnight friends of a lifetime. I was a marked, a branded man.

But in some strange way, when I ceased to care so much for the opinions of men, the Word of God became to me new and sweet. In some strange way, now the drunkard, the harlot, the profane swearer, the convict, the infidel came to hear me. Before I had had children and young people saved. Now I began having many, many of the hardest sinners saved.

O thou Bethel, thou house of God, where I made holy vows that I would put God before all men, and God promised me that He would care for His own! And He has!

What was that time when God revealed Himself to you, when He called you, when He encouraged you, when there was repentance or holy vows or a new start?

You, too, doubtless have had your Bethels, your places of blessing, those times of special divine call and intervention and those times of

holy vows and new surrender. I trust that you will remember your Bethels
as I remember mine.

How often I have thanked God for that time in 1926 when I felt I
must give up all salary and never make any requirement about my own
income. I gave up $10,000 in insurance. I made God the proposition,
"Lord, You look after my business, and I will look after Yours."

I left the pastorate to become an evangelist. He alone knows how
sadly I have failed in my part, but He has never failed in His!

Oh, that Bethel is as real to me as the time when Jacob promised
God his tithe and that that stone should be to him the house of God.

Then I go back to 1941. I was in the field of full-time evangelism.
The dear Lord had pressed on my heart so heavily the burden for revival.
And now in the large Bethany Reformed Church on the south side of
Chicago, I conducted a Conference on Revival and Soul Winning.
Among the speakers helping me were Dr. H. A. Ironside, Dr. Oswald
J. Smith and, as I remember, Dr. Hyman Appelman.

In my room in the Roseland YMCA I stayed on my face until two
o'clock in the morning while God and I made a bargain. I promised
Him that at any cost I would see that mass evangelism was brought
back to America and that America again would see great citywide revival
campaigns. At two o'clock in the morning God assured me that He
would let me see that long-desired day.

I did not know then that He would use me in great citywide revival
campaigns in Buffalo, Cleveland, Seattle, Chicago, Miami, Winston-
Salem, San Pedro and elsewhere. But I knew even then that He would
bring again mass evangelism to the front in America.

We have not seen what we ought to see and what I trust we will see,
but this generation knows now that the living God has not done away
with those He has called evangelists nor done away with His method
of preaching the Gospel and calling sinners to repentance!

Oh, that little cheap YMCA room was to me a Bethel, a house of God!

Some who read this stood by a mother's deathbed and promised to
meet her in Heaven. One who reads this went forward when his heart
was burning under the impact of a message from some prophet of God
and laid his life on the altar. You promised to go wherever God would
lead you. It was a time of surrender, of dedication, of consecration.

Some who read this remember the time when you promised God
to tithe, that neither business, nor friends, nor anything else would come

before God; and the token would be the tithes and offerings you would give in His name.

Do you remember the time you laid some sin on the altar and felt His healing, cleansing touch and heard the Lord say, "Son (or daughter), thy sins are forgiven thee"?

Do you remember the time that you felt led to launch out in some new work when, humanly speaking, there were obstacles too great to overcome, but you believed God and by faith went in to take the promised land?

Do you remember the time when you vowed you would have upon you continually the breath of God, the power of the Holy Ghost? And perhaps you set apart a time for the morning watch. You kept a rendezvous with God in the secret place of prayer.

Oh, all who read this who are saved have some Bethel which you ought to go back to.

I do not doubt that to many a heart who reads this God has said, "Arise, go up to Beth-el, and dwell there: and make there an altar unto God, that appeared unto thee . . . ." You ought to answer to all your family and those about you, "And let us arise, and go up to Beth-el; and I will make there an altar unto God, who answered me in the day of my distress, and was with me in the way which I went" (Gen. 35:3).

II. THE WANDERING, BACKSLIDING, TROUBLED JACOB NEEDED BETHEL AGAIN

According to Ussher's chronology, it was twenty-eight years after Jacob's experience at Bethel when the Lord appeared to him in Genesis 35:1 and said, "Arise, go up to Beth-el, and dwell there: and make there an altar unto God, that appeared unto thee when thou fleddest from the face of Esau thy brother." But it was likely even longer than that.

After that Bethel experience Jacob had joined Laban's household and fallen in love with Rachel. Then he had worked seven years for a wife, was cheated by being given the wrong girl, Leah. Then Leah had borne six sons despite a period of barrenness. Then had come Dinah, the only girl, who had grown to young womanhood and had been led into sin and promised in marriage. Probably more than thirty years had gone by since Jacob made his vows at Bethel and had promised God that that would be to him the house of God. And as far as we know, he had never been back to that holy place.

O Jacob, Jacob, how could you so long neglect the house of God!

How could you so long forget that place of holy vows and promises?

Jacob needed to go back to Bethel. He needed to erect an altar and dwell there! He had been too long away from the place of blessing.

And think of all the reasons that indicate how badly Jacob needed Bethel and the presence of God.

1. A Broken Heart Over a Ruined Daughter Called Back to Bethel

First, there was his daughter who had gone wrong. I know how dearly a father loves a beautiful daughter. Someone has said that a man's son is his pride, but his daughter is his joy. I do not know, having never had a son, but I know that Jacob's heart was broken when he found that his daughter had been deceived and violated.

Jacob had bought a bit of ground at Shalem and there had made his home. It was only some twenty miles from Bethel. How strange that he tarried here away from that place of blessing! And here his daughter went out to see some of the daughters of the land and Shechem. The young prince saw her, loved her and led her into sin. How sore the heart of Jacob when they told him!

2. His Murdering Sons Had Shown the Price of His Neglect

But the wild young sons of Jacob had gone too long without the influence of Bethel. We suppose their busy father had not found time to teach them about God. When they heard of their sister's ruin, they made a wicked scheme of revenge. Pretending to be friends and promising intermarriage with the young prince Shechem, his father and their city, they had all the men of Shechem's city circumcised. Then while the men were sore and incapacitated, they came and killed every man and looted and spoiled the city!

If you want to know how Jacob felt about the murdering rage of Simeon and Levi, read the word in his dying charge and blessing.

"Simeon and Levi are brethren; instruments of cruelty are in their habitations. O my soul, come not thou into their secret; unto their assembly, mine honour, be not thou united: for in their anger they slew a man, and in their self will they digged down a wall. Cursed be their anger, for it was fierce; and their wrath, for it was cruel: I will divide them in Jacob, and scatter them in Israel." —Gen. 49:5-7.

The grief of Jacob over his daughter was now made more dreadful by the grief over his wicked sons.

Moreover, there was a real danger that the people of the land would now combine against Jacob and these deceitful and wicked sons and kill them all. Jacob was troubled about the matter.

3. His Idolatrous Wives Show How Far Jacob Had Drifted

There is another indication of how badly Jacob needed to go back to Bethel and rear an altar and dwell there. His two wives, Rachel and Leah, daughters of Laban, worshiped idols. At least, when Jacob left his work with Laban and took his family away from Padan-aram, Rachel stole her father's idols, hid them in the stuff and took them with her. Now, when God called Jacob to return to Bethel, he knew about these strange gods and told his family, "Put away the strange gods that are among you." And we are told, "And they gave unto Jacob all the strange gods which were in their hands . . ." (Gen. 35:2,4).

Oh, Jacob was a man of energy, of foresight, ingenious and hard-working, a man of leadership. But alas, all these great qualities were put to increasing his flocks and herds, his wealth and prestige. He had no time to teach and guide his family in the religion of the true God whom he had vowed to serve and worship.

Some who read this today will doubtless, upon reflection, find you have left your wives and children to be absorbed in the things of the world. You have idols instead of God. It may be that to one of you the idol is pleasure; to another, clothes or a house or clubs. One may put society first and another, your home. How sadly lacking is the home where Father has not taken time to lead his family with him to the blessings of his Bethel!

Lot down in Sodom loved God and grieved his righteous soul over the wicked things that went on in Sodom. But it seems he had no time to lead his family. He could not take with him even his wife when he left Sodom, and to his sons-in-law he was as one that mocked!

The man who has pleasure-crazy daughters, wild, uncontrolled sons and a worldly wife cannot be a good Christian. He may have met God at some Bethel in the past, but alas, the years have been wasted, as in the case of Jacob.

Jacob had amassed wealth. When he came to that Bethel some years before, he had only a walking stick and perhaps stale bread and a flask of oil. Now he has a great family and is rich in flocks and herds. But he is a disillusioned, disappointed man. His children have gone the way of sin; his wives have gone into idolatry.

4. Oh, the Backsliding Brought by Being Too Busy! We Need Bethel!

Jacob himself has worn out his soul with hard work.

There is something noble about labor. I have the highest regard for the thrifty man, the one who works and schemes and saves and prospers. But all of us who have energy and push, all of us who feel a delight in doing, in work, in accumulation, need to beware. That way is the way to leanness of soul and to the loss of our joy.

The dear Saviour said that some Christians, those represented by the seed which fell among thorns, "are they, which, when they have heard, go forth, and are choked with cares and riches and pleasures of this life, and bring no fruit to perfection" (Luke 8:14). Oh, the care of this world and the deceitfulness of riches and the weariness of long labor and the distraction of constant pressure—these can keep a Christian from happiness, from meeting God, from prayer, from Bible study and from Christian joy.

Jacob had gone too long without being back to Bethel. He had worn himself out for the things of the world, all of which mean so little!

I have one fear, one matter about which I warn myself continually. As Paul buffeted his body to keep it under subjection lest he should, after having preached so long to others and with such blessing, be "cast away," that is, laid on the shelf and lose his usefulness to God, so I feel a constant need to beware lest constant labor, long hours, many plans, the incessant pressure of work, should take away my joy in the Lord, my times of secret devotion and cause me to lose the song in my heart.

O dear Lord Jesus, forgive us, and watch over us more gently, and over all who have heavy burdens and much work to do, even for Thee! A man may be so busy working even for God, doing the highest and best work in the world, that he does not take time to meet God, does not take time to enjoy the Lord and have the refreshing and blessing which are the privilege and duty of every Christian.

With all the burden of raising hundreds of thousands of dollars each year to keep the Lord's work going, with the constant pressure of a deadline for copy for THE SWORD OF THE LORD, the pressure of many, many preaching engagements and much study which is a weariness of the flesh but which is inevitable for a good preacher—oh, what if with all this toil and my writing and traveling and planning, I should be too busy to pray enough? What if I should lose the passion and tears in my preaching and the burden for souls? What if I should no longer have a bubbling forth of song in my heart? What if this blessed Book, which has been to me the mine of the richest treasure all these years, should become as barren as a played-out mine, as fruitless as an arid field without rain? O God, protect all of us from losing our Bethel and the blessings of Bethel!

Yes, Jacob needed to go back to Bethel and to take time for worship and to lead his family for God. He needed time for holier things than the sheep, goats, camels, donkeys and cattle which had so driven him day and night for thirty years!

5. But There Was With Jacob the Constant Urging of God's Spirit That Made Him Seek Bethel Again

It is a precious truth that every Christian now has the blessed Holy Spirit dwelling within to represent Christ in his body. In Old Testament days, Christians did not have the Spirit dwelling in the body as we have now, as I understand from many Scriptures. But surely God's Spirit was with Jacob and kept tenderly calling him back to fellowship with God.

We know that even in his boyhood Jacob had longed for and sought the birthright and had traded with his brother to get it. Even though his methods were wrong and he need not have thought deceit would be necessary to get the blessing he so greatly coveted, Jacob was right in desiring the blessing. He wanted to be the head of a great nation for God. He wanted to be the ancestor of that blessed Seed of Abraham through whom all the nations of the world should be blessed.

Even in far-off Padan-aram when he worked with unstable Laban, the God he had met at Bethel was with him. First, Laban said, "I have learned by experience that the Lord hath blessed me for thy sake" (Gen. 30:27).

God was with Jacob as a herdsman. The angel of God had appeared and reminded him of how whatever part of the flocks Jacob had chosen, had multiplied under God's blessing. God had said, "I am the God of Beth-el, where thou anointedst the pillar, and where thou vowedst a

vow unto me: now arise, get thee out from this land, and return unto
the land of thy kindred" (Gen. 31:13). That was years before our text.
But even then God was calling him back to the land of Canaan and
back to worship.

Then in Genesis 32:1 we learn how "Jacob went on his way, and
the angels of God met him." We learn how Jacob tarried all night and
wrestled with the angel until the angel blessed him and gave him a new
name, Israel, which means "Prince." Thus God warmed the heart of
Esau, and enmity was removed, and they met as brothers beloved. Even
at Shalem, where he had lived some years and where Dinah had gone
wrong and where Jacob's sons had killed and looted a whole city, Jacob
had erected an altar to God.

You see, God had chosen Jacob and would not let him go.

We are told that "the gifts and calling of God are without repentance"
(Rom. 11:29). God had chosen Jacob and would keep him safely. And
stirring in Jacob's heart was a hunger for God, the Spirit always prod-
ding him. Jacob had the call to come back to Bethel, and when God
spoke to him and gave him solemn invitation and commandment to
"arise, go up to Beth-el," his own heart condition called him to go back.

So it is with many who read this. Your own heart is hungry for the
blessing of God to be renewed. Oh, then, do not wait! Make your way
back to Bethel.

III. THE WONDERFUL GOD WHO GIVES
ANOTHER CHANCE!

It seems a strange and wondrous thing that God would still want
Jacob, would still plan to use him, would remember his covenant! Now
after some thirty years away from the place of blessing, Jacob is called
back to Bethel to rear an altar and to abide there.

Oh, the grace of God! How wonderful is His dealing with lost sinners
when He seeks them so long and saves them! How wonderful is God's
dealing with His own children that He bears with us so long and never
lets us go!

So God is calling Jacob again after weary, wandering, money-mad
years, after disappointment and disillusionment have wrecked his peace
of mind. God still wants Jacob, still calls him back.

We find this attitude of God throughout the Bible. No wonder David
said by divine inspiration:

"The Lord is merciful and gracious, slow to anger, and plenteous

in mercy. He will not always chide: neither will he keep his anger for ever. He hath not dealt with us after our sins; nor rewarded us according to our iniquities. For as the heaven is high above the earth, so great is his mercy toward them that fear him. As far as the east is from the west, so far hath he removed our transgressions from us. Like as a father pitieth his children, so the Lord pitieth them that fear him. For he knoweth our frame; he remembereth that we are dust."—Ps. 103:8-14.

1. God Mercifully Spared Lot in Spite of His Compromise

God remembered Lot down in Sodom, and the angels of God complained that they could not do anything at all about destroying the city until Lot came out! Poor, worldly Lot! Poor, compromising Lot, who called the wicked his brethren! Poor Lot, who neglected his family until his religion was a mockery to his sons-in-law! Poor Lot, who took two daughters out of Sodom, but could not get Sodom out of his daughters! Lot down in Sodom was dear to God, and He would not give him up.

God gives His children another chance. He may punish us, but He loves us. He may chastise His own most severely, but He never gives one up.

2. God Did Not Cast Away David When He Sinned Grievously

Isn't it amazing that God, who had chosen David to be king and, like Jacob, to be in the ancestral line of Jesus, would not give up David when he sinned!

David was a man after God's own heart, a man of faith. By faith he risked all and killed the giant Goliath through God's power on his little sling. David, the sweet singer of Israel, was inspired to write the Psalms of David. The Lord was not ashamed to be called "the son of David." And the angel promised Mary that God would give to Jesus "the throne of his father David" (Luke 1:32).

We know that David led Bathsheba into sin. Then, lest his adultery be found out, he had her husband, Uriah the Hittite, slain with the sword.

God did punish David with heartbreaking severity. His baby died. His daughter was raped by her half-brother, a son of David. Then Absalom, brother of Tamar, avenged her wrong by killing wicked Amnon. And David grieved over the murder of a licentious son by another son. Then Absalom himself stole the throne and David ran for his life until Absalom was killed in battle.

Yet God called David back to his Bethel. God sent Nathan the prophet to rebuke David for his sin and to offer him mercy. And David's heartbroken prayer in Psalm 51 tells us how he came back to Bethel pleading for cleansing, acknowledging his sin and making holy vows that he would teach transgressors God's way and that sinners would be converted.

Oh, how God's dealing with David should comfort us wayward Christians! Not all of us, of course, have experienced the same kind of sin David experienced, but all of us have sinned. We may not have had the same tragedies in our family which David had, but all have had tragedies and failures, God knows. And God calls us back to confession, new vows and sweet fellowship, as He called David.

When God called Jacob back to Bethel, He was calling him not only to fellowship but to preparation for the headship of a nation. God is merciful to give us a new chance for joy and fellowship. He is equally merciful to give us a new chance to serve Him.

3. Our Merciful God Gave Rebellious Jonah a Second Chance

The word of the Lord came to Jonah, the son of Amittai, saying, "Arise, go to Nineveh, that great city, and cry against it; for their wickedness is come up before me" (Jonah 1:2). But in effect Jonah said, "Nothing doing, Lord; that bunch of fish worshipers? Why, I'm afraid some of them would get converted."

So Jonah bought a ticket on an ocean-going vessel and ran away from the call of God.

You know the story of the mighty wind and the great fish that God prepared, and the gourd and worm. It is enough to say that God dealt with Jonah by a storm at sea when he was thrown overboard and swallowed by the great fish. And after three days in the belly of the whale (typifying Christ's three days in the grave as told by our Lord in Matthew 12:40), Jonah was vomited out on dry land.

Jonah may have smelled like fish, but he certainly felt more like preaching! And here is the wonderful, wonderful truth again: God gave Jonah a second chance! "And the word of the Lord came unto Jonah the second time, saying, Arise, go unto Nineveh, that great city, and preach unto it the preaching that I bid thee" (Jonah 3:2). It is Jonah's call back to Bethel! "Jonah, you are called as a prophet of God. There have been holy vows and divine revelations! Now God calls you again to preach the Gospel as He had called you before."

"So Jonah arose, and went unto Nineveh, according to the word of the Lord" (Jonah 3:3). And God gave one of the most marvelous revivals of all history, when hundreds of thousands repented in sackcloth and ashes, and turned to God for mercy and forgiveness.

God gave Jonah a second chance.

4. Peter, Cursing and Denying Christ, Was Restored to Fellowship and Wonderful Service

Peter is another example of a man who needed another chance. Peter, who had vowed to die for Jesus, went in and sat by the fire with the soldiers who would crucify the Saviour before nine o'clock the next morning. And as it always happens with those who rest in bad company, Peter's courage ebbed away. They "put no strings" on him, but he was hindered nonetheless. And when he was challenged, he cursed and swore, "I know not the man." Then, as Jesus had predicted, the cock crowed. Peter, suddenly facing the ruin of his ministry, the breaking of his vows and public disgrace in the eyes of the disciples, went out in the dark that cool April morning and wept bitterly.

Well, Peter would naturally think, *I'm all washed up. Who would hear me preach the Gospel now, a man who has no courage and lies and denies Jesus and curses and swears?* So Peter gave up the ministry. I can imagine him thinking, *I have a big family and my mother-in-law lives with us. I'll go back to the fishing business for a living.*

So back up to the little Sea of Galilee went Peter. Because he was a leader, the other disciples went with him. (When we fail God, we may lead many others to failure, even though not meaning to.) The disciples again had their boat and nets. They toiled all night but caught nothing. In the morning One stood by the seaside and said, "Children, have ye any meat?" (His voice was like an angel's, but they knew Him not.)

They had caught nothing all night. But this Stranger told them to let down the net on the other side of the boat. When they obeyed, suddenly the net was filled with 153 great fish!

John the Beloved, the more spiritually-minded of the group, perhaps, recognized Jesus. Had He not given them a great load of fishes, two boats full, once before? And when Peter realized who He was, he turned the nets loose. They could draw in the fish or they could let them go. What were fish beside a chance to see Jesus and get his sin and failure straightened out!

So Peter put on his coat and jumped in to swim to the shore. Boats are too slow when you've been so long away from your Bethel, so long out of fellowship, so long out of the will of God!

You remember how they ate the breakfast Jesus had cooked around the fire and then how the searching question was put to Peter and how he answered: "Lord, thou knowest that I love thee." Jesus recommissioned Peter, and soon we see him on the Day of Pentecost standing before thousands and preaching the Gospel with power and seeing 3,000 souls added to the church that day!

Oh, we serve the God who gives a second chance or a third chance. We serve the God who seeks us so long and pleads with us to come back to the Bethel of blessing, back to the renewing of our call, the re-signing of our commission!

5. The Prodigal Son Story Shows How Willingly God Forgives

It may be that one reads this who is not even saved. Or perhaps you have gone so far in sin that you do not feel any assurance of salvation. Then remember that blessed story of the prodigal son as told by our Saviour in Luke 15.

A certain man had two sons. One was given the portion of goods that belonged to him and took his journey into a far country and wasted it in riotous living. As gamblers and drinkers and harlot-chasers do, he came to want and, having no friends now, he got a job feeding pigs.

There in want and hunger, his proud heart broke and he came to his senses. That prodigal boy resolved:

"I will arise and go to my father, and will say unto him, Father, I have sinned against heaven, and before thee, And am no more worthy to be called thy son: make me as one of thy hired servants."—Luke 15:18,19.

And he did go back to his father, who saw him a great way off. (How long his father had watched the road and longed for the boy's return!) He ran to meet his son and fell on his neck and kissed him. The boy started confessing his sin, but the father hushed him up and called for a robe to take the place of his rags, servants to bring shoes for his bare and sore feet, and a ring of sonship to go on his finger.

They killed the fatted calf long prepared for this contingency. The neighbors were called in, and what a feast of rejoicing! The boy who was dead is alive again! The boy who was lost is now found! No wonder they began to be merry!

O sinner, you are not far from God. Come home! O backslider in heart, the Father never ceases watching the road, waiting for your return! Before ever you can confess how unworthy you are and how little you merit His blessings, the Father will take you in His arms, kiss and forgive you.

God wants to take off the soiled robes and put on you the white garment of His righteousness. He wants to give you the manifest token, the ring of sonship. He wants your feet shod with the preparation of the Gospel of peace.

O backslider, God cannot give you up! As He called Jacob back to Bethel, so He calls you back to forgiveness, blessing, joy and fellowship. God does not forsake His own.

Will you, too, come back to Bethel, which is but another way of saying to draw near to God, for He will surely draw near to you as He has promised? Come for forgiveness, for He offers it free. He wants you, not as a hired servant but as a son. Oh, come boldly to that throne of grace! Come back to Bethel today!

IV. HOW JACOB AND HIS FAMILY WENT BACK TO BETHEL

God called Jacob back to Bethel—only a distance of twenty or twenty-five miles. He ought to have gone long ago.

"Then Jacob said unto his household, and to all that were with him, Put away the strange gods that are among you, and be clean, and change your garments: And let us arise, and go up to Beth-el; and I will make there an altar unto God, who answered me in the day of my distress, and was with me in the way which I went. And they gave unto Jacob all the strange gods which were in their hand, and all their earrings which were in their ears; and Jacob hid them under the oak which was by Shechem."—Gen. 35:2-4.

1. They Put Away Their Idols

First, Jacob commanded his household and workers, "Put away the strange gods that are among you. . . ."

So the idols that had been cherished these years, the idols Rachel had stolen from her father, and perhaps other idols were brought to Jacob and solemnly surrendered; they were disowned and put away!

Does God really have first place in your life? Remember that He said, "For I the Lord thy God am a jealous God" (Exod. 20:5). And when God, in fury, destroyed Israel, killing many by the hand of Nebuchadnezzar's army and carrying the rest away captive, He revealed to Ezekiel that it was "this image of jealousy" which wicked people had put in the entry of the Temple which had broken His heart and aroused His fury against His sinning people (Ezek. 8:5)!

Oh, put away your idols! Unless you do, you cannot properly go back to Bethel, back to the place of blessing, back to the renewal of power, back to the holy vows.

Preacher, have you pleased the denomination more than God? Put away your idol!

Businessman, have you put your business, your job, ahead of the house of God, ahead of the Bible, and before the time you should have taken to teach your children the Word of God and win them? In Jesus' name, put away the idols!

Some woman loves her children more than she loves God. She thinks more of their happiness, their popularity, their prosperity, than she thinks about the Word of God, winning souls and the secret place of prayer. Oh, if you would come back to Bethel, put away your idols!

That job, that loved one to whom you may be engaged, that denomination upon whose promotion and endorsement you depend—whatever that thing which has infringed upon the crown rights of Jesus Christ, upon the singleness of heart with which He demands that you serve Him—put that idol away! If you would go back to Bethel, then idols must be destroyed.

It may be that the idol which has come between you and God is your own will. You want your way, as did the prodigal son. Then if you would come back to the Bethel of blessing, your will must be given up to God's sweet will.

Years ago when Grace, my oldest daughter, was three or four years old, she rebelled at some command. Sadly I spanked her very hard and made her do what she was told to do. Then I had to leave town. When I left, I did not tell her good-by. She still sulked for a little bit over her spanking, but then she was penitent. She began to say to her mother, though I was already gone, "Good-by, Daddy! Good-by,

Daddy!" When she took her afternoon nap, half-asleep and with tears running down her little face, she would say, "Good-by, Daddy!" She was tired of her own way. She was sorry for her rebellion. She wanted to make right what she had done wrong.

So your stubborn will must be given up if you would have the fullness of God's blessing. Do not hesitate to pull that idol of self-will out by the roots and let God have His way, if you want to live at the place of blessing.

2. They Washed Themselves and Put on Clean Garments

Jacob commanded, "Put away the strange gods that are among you, and be clean, and change your garments" (Gen. 35:2). It is a good practice to bathe and put on fresh garments when we go to the house of God. One should dignify his going to church and make it an high occasion. As one puts on his best clothes to go courting or to meet important visitors, so it is proper to dress the best we can in order to honor Jesus Christ.

But Jacob had in mind here a cleaning up before going to Bethel. Surely a lot of bathing was going on among the large family of children and servants. That symbolizes that we need to be clean—clean of dirty habits, clean of filthy thoughts, clean of bad associations—if we would truly go back to Bethel, back to the place of blessing.

I had a letter from a dear woman who heard me regularly on the radio saying she had become convicted about dipping snuff. She wrote how some visitors had come to her house and had rung the doorbell. She had snuff in her mouth and didn't have time to run to the kitchen to spit it out, so she swallowed the snuff, wiped her mouth and went to the door!

But the nicotine in that mouthful of snuff had made her sick. She had felt greatly ashamed that she had a habit she dared not let her neighbors know about. She was ashamed that she had a secret that she must hide from those who would be offended by it. She had heard me preach about how a Christian ought to keep his body as a holy temple of the Lord and had resolved to quit the snuff.

It had a vice-like hold upon her—a habit which it seemed almost impossible to break.

When she gave up the snuff, she became sick. Lying on her bed, desperately sick, she prayed, "O God, I will never touch the filthy stuff again! If I die, I will die clean!" But God raised her up, and she was free from the habit. She had come again to Bethel, the place of blessing. Her letter was one of triumph.

3. They Laid Aside Ordinary Ornaments and Pleasures for Bethel

Now here is a strange thing: God did not tell Jacob all the details of preparation they should make to come to Bethel. It was Jacob, knowing about the idol gods, who commanded that they be put away. It was Jacob who said to his family, "Be clean, and change your garments." God someway inspired these people of Jacob's household to do more than they were commanded. They not only brought the strange gods but "all their earrings which were in their ears; and Jacob hid them under the oak which was by Shechem" (Gen. 35:4).

God did not here say it was wrong to wear earrings. And He did not tell them to leave off their earrings, even, as they were to come up to Bethel to worship.

Earrings are not necessarily wrong. When Abraham sent his servant to get a bride for Isaac, he sent along rich golden earrings and other jewels for the dear girl who would be a bride.

Christian women are commanded that their adorning should not be "that outward adorning of plaiting the hair, and of wearing of gold, or of putting on of apparel." The real adornment of a good woman is "the hidden man of the heart," that "meek and quiet spirit, which is in the sight of God of great price" (I Pet. 3:3,4).

We do not think it wrong to plait the hair. Certainly it is not wrong to wear garments. But a woman's beauty doesn't depend upon her garments or on her golden jewels or on the way she dresses her hair.

I think something of this was put in the hearts of Jacob's household by the Holy Spirit. Before they went to Bethel, they laid aside the earrings. Sometimes when we wait on God for revival and pray for the power of God or pray for some answer in a time of distress, we put aside food. Eating is not wrong, but sometimes God's people ought to fast. Sleeping is not wrong at the appointed time to sleep, but sometimes His people ought to watch all the night through and call on Him. Ordinary businesses of life are not necessarily wrong, but there comes a time when they must give way to a special time of seeking God. Pleasures and games are not necessarily wrong, but sometimes they should be laid aside for better things. So these laid aside their earrings, although they were not commanded to do so.

I beg you, do not let even the good things, even those things which are perhaps harmless, keep you from the fullness of blessing. Paul properly said, "All things are lawful unto me, but all things are not expedient..." (I Cor. 6:12). And surely if we take time to seek God's face, many things which might ordinarily be permissible and proper ought to be laid aside. If it means giving up sleep or food or missing time for business or giving up a sweet companionship in order to have the better companionship of God, I beg you that in this spiritual sense you lay aside whatever those earrings represent in your life and go up to Bethel empty, to receive the fullness God has for you.

4. The Whole Family Went to Bethel Together!

It is blessed that Jacob had been at Bethel alone when he had no family. It is doubly blessed that now he takes the whole family. Joseph was a small boy; now Joseph goes to Bethel. Who knows but that the older sons might have been more blessed of God had they early been taken to Bethel, the house of God, the place of blessing, and the altar there.

Don't try to keep the blessing for yourself. See that wife and children, that husband and loved ones enter into it, too. All the family went together to Bethel, including the servants. All alike gave up their idols, washed their bodies, changed their garments—and their ways. It was a revival time for the household of Jacob when all together went up to Bethel and there met God.

It may not be in some great revival service; it may not be under the preaching of the Word of God by some Spirit-filled man; it may be that alone, at home or in your office or on your farm or in a rented room in a lonely city, you will go back to Bethel and to the God of Bethel. I beg you, do it today, no matter where you are.

These words are written in a lonely motel room on New Year's Day. Today my family goes for happy fellowship with one of our daughters and her family in Moline, Illinois. Had I been there, I would have gone, too. But duty called. In a few minutes I will go to the pulpit to preach my first sermon of the new year. Hungry hearts are waiting. So in this motel room, with a heart that is lonely and feeling a little the constant pressure of the work that is upon me day and night, I have sought God.

In this motel room today I have gone back to Bethel. I have gone back in my mind and heart to the old experiences; I have laid aside idols; I have taken off earrings (spiritually, of course); I have renewed vows. This motel room has been filled with the angels of God and I have felt, even if I have not seen, the ladder reaching to Heaven.

Jacob, after he had been to Bethel, called it not only Bethel, the house of God, but El-Bethel, the God of the house of God. No longer did Jacob think just of the stone upon which he had poured oil, but he thought now of God who met him in person, the God who renewed all the promises He had given to Isaac and Jacob, the God who heard him in the time of distress and delivered him. Jacob met God again.

Will you today have a Bethel of blessing and renewing? Will you lay aside idols? Will you repent of sins and be clean? Will you break the ties that hinder? Will you renew your vows and accept the renewed commission from God for the work He called you to do?

Oh, may God let the altar fires burn at many a renewed Bethel as you read these words.

XVIII.

How to Have a Happy, Prosperous New Year

CURTIS HUTSON

"Blessed is the man that walketh not in the counsel of the ungodly, nor standeth in the way of sinners, nor sitteth in the seat of the scornful. But his delight is in the law of the Lord; and in his law doth he meditate day and night. And he shall be like a tree planted by the rivers of water, that bringeth forth his fruit in his season; his leaf also shall not wither; and whatsoever he doeth shall prosper. The ungodly are not so: but are like the chaff which the wind driveth away. Therefore the ungodly shall not stand in the judgment, nor sinners in the congregation of the righteous. For the Lord knoweth the way of the righteous: but the way of the ungodly shall perish."—Ps. 1:1-6.

God is the giver of many new things. We come to Him by faith; and He gives us a new birth, a new nature, a new heart, new life, new hope, a new task; and someday when our bodies are raised, a new body where we will dwell with Him forever in a new Heaven. No wonder He says, "Behold, I make all things new."

Now, as we close the gates of the old year and enter the portals of the new, God has given to you and me a brand new page. There is not a dirty page on the new calendar, and we can make it all it ought to be if we make up our minds and work at it.

This is the season when friends and acquaintances are wishing for each other a happy and prosperous new year.

Several years ago a popular song went something like this:

> **Wishing will make it so;**
> **If you wish long enough,**
> **Wish strong enough,**
> **You will come to know**
> **That wishing will make it so.**

But contrary to the lyrics of the song, neither happiness nor prosperity comes to one simply by wishing. For every effect there is a cause, and there are certain things that affect happiness and prosperity in one's life.

I. THE WAY TO HAPPINESS

Everyone longs to be happy. I can't recall having ever met an individual who enjoyed being unhappy.

A man walked up to a taxi driver in Atlanta and asked, "Where is Happyville?"

The startled driver exclaimed, "Man, I wish I knew!"

He later learned the man was looking for the city of Hapeville.

Nearly everything we do and every decision we make has our happiness in mind.

I just purchased a new suit the other day, and I chose a certain color and style because it was what I thought I would be happy with.

We eat at a certain restaurant because we are happier eating there.

We sit at a certain place in church because we are happier sitting there.

Happiness is important to us, and God wants us to be happy.

The word *happy* is found 26 times in the Bible, and there are several important suggestions concerning how to be happy.

1. Trusting the Lord Brings Happiness

Proverbs 16:20 states, ". . . and whoso trusteth in the Lord, happy is he."

The happiest day of any person's life is when he trusts Jesus Christ as Saviour. Of course, this does not solve all his problems, but it does solve the sin problem and puts him in touch with One who can solve every problem he will ever face.

But the Christian life not only begins with faith; it continues in faith. "Therefore being justified by faith, we have peace with God through our Lord Jesus Christ," says Romans 5:1. But once we are justified, Romans 1:17 says, "The just shall live by faith."

Happy is the Christian who looks to God for everything.

No matter what the problem, we trust Him, knowing that "all things work together for good to them that love God."

No matter what the need, we trust Him, knowing that "my God shall supply all your need according to his riches in glory by Christ Jesus."

No matter how severe the trial, we trust Him, resting in the promise, "There hath no temptation taken you but such as is common to man:

but God is faithful, who will not suffer you to be tempted above that ye are able; but will with the temptation also make a way to escape, that ye may be able to bear it."

No matter what the sorrow, we refuse to let our hearts be troubled because we believe in Him, we trust Him.

No matter what situation in life the believer may face, there is an appropriate Bible promise to stand on. You can trust Him. His Word never fails.

> **Simply trusting ev'ry day,**
> **Trusting through a stormy way;**
> **Even when my faith is small,**
> **Trusting Jesus, that is all.**
>
> **Trusting as the moments fly,**
> **Trusting as the days go by;**
> **Trusting Him whate'er befall,**
> **Trusting Jesus, that is all.**

2. Obedience Brings Happiness

Jesus said in John 13:17, "If ye know these things, happy are ye if ye do them."

It is not the acquisition but the application of truth that makes one happy.

There is a song in our hymnbook which says,

> **Trust and obey, for there's no other way**
> **To be happy in Jesus,**
> **But to trust and obey.**

Someone once asked William Booth the secret of his great joy. His reply was, "I never say no to the Lord."

If you are an unhappy Christian, then there is a good chance that you are disobedient in some area of your life. Since trusting Christ as Saviour, have you made a public profession of your faith? Did you obey Him and receive believer's baptism? Are you obeying Him in giving the tithe back to the Lord? What about soul winning and church attendance, Bible reading and prayer? Are you obedient in these areas? You may as well try to beat back the tide with a pitchfork as to try to be a happy Christian without being obedient.

II. HAPPINESS COMES FROM NOT FOLLOWING THE ADVICE OF THE UNGODLY

The first verse of Psalm 1 says, "Blessed is the man that walketh not in the counsel of the ungodly." It could be paraphrased, "Blessed, happy, fortunate, prosperous is the man who does not get counsel from the ungodly, does not follow their advice."

It is always wise for the believer to make sure he seeks the counsel of godly people. Now one may be very brilliant and normally give good advice; however, if he is an ungodly person, the believer is not to seek his advice.

1. Godly Living Produces Happiness

Let's read all of Psalm 1:1: "Blessed is the man that walketh not in the counsel of the ungodly, nor standeth in the way of sinners, nor sitteth in the seat of the scornful."

The expression, "nor standeth in the way of sinners," could mean one of two things. Perhaps it means we are not to block sinners from coming to Christ. I know of those who refuse to trust Jesus Christ as Saviour because of some Christian's inconsistent life. I have heard people say, "If he's a Christian, then I don't want to be one!" We should live such a godly and pure life that no sinner will point to us as an excuse for not being a Christian.

But perhaps that expression, "nor standeth in the way of sinners," means we are not to stand where sinners stand and walk as sinners walk. We are not to go in the way of the sinner, doing the things he does, saying the things he says, living the way he lives.

To make sure we are obeying the verse, I suggest we practice both. First, make sure our lives are not bad testimonies that will keep sinners from coming to Christ; second, make sure we are not living as the sinner lives.

". . .nor sitteth in the seat of the scornful." If one is to be blessed and happy, he must not sit down and relax where the scornful and mockers gather. Stay away from the scornful, the mockers.

2. Meditating in the Word of God Brings Happiness

Psalm 1:2 reads, "But his delight is in the law of the Lord; and in his law doth he meditate day and night."

The blessed or happy man delights in the law of the Lord and meditates in it day and night.

A preacher friend of mine wasn't exactly sure what that verse meant, so he decided he would spend some time every morning reading and meditating in the Word of God. And to be sure, he was doing all the verse taught: he read and meditated in the Word of God some every night.

If you want to have a happy new year, then plan now to spend some time in the Bible every day.

G. Campbell Morgan informed his members that the Bible could be read through in sixty hours. One came to him after the service and said, "Mr. Morgan, I disagree with your statement that the Bible can be read through in sixty hours."

"Well," said Morgan, "the burden of proof lies with you."

Some time later the banker came back to Mr. Morgan and said, "You were wrong about reading through the Bible in sixty hours; it can be read through in forty hours."

Mr. Morgan smiled and replied, "I wasn't talking about bankers' rates; I was talking about pulpit rate!"

The average reader can read through the Bible in a year by reading fifteen minutes a day. If you have never read the Bible through, verse by verse, from beginning to end, I challenge you to make it one of your New Year's resolutions and then never let another year go by without renewing that vow.

The Bible has much more to say about happiness. Psalm 127:3,5 says, "Lo, children are an heritage of the Lord. . . . Happy is the man that hath his quiver full of them." Somewhere I read the statement that the father is the head of the home; the mother, the heart; the children, the happiness.

Proverbs 14:21 promises, ". . . he that hath mercy on the poor, happy is he."

Some time ago in a *Reader's Digest* article the author said, "Man needs three things to make him happy: someone to love, something to do and something to hope for."

Christians have all three. SOMEONE TO LOVE—I John 4:19: "We love him, because he first loved us."

SOMETHING TO DO. There are the poor and needy who need help, lost souls to win, burdens to lift. The child of God who is faithful to his local church has more to do than he has time for.

SOMETHING TO HOPE FOR—the blessed hope: Titus 2:13, "Looking for that blessed hope, and the glorious appearing of the great God and our Saviour Jesus Christ."

Ours is more than a desire; it is a well-grounded, well-founded expectation for the future. Jesus is coming. The dead in Christ are to be raised; and the living saints are to be changed in a moment, in the twink-ling of an eye, then we will be caught up together to meet the Lord in the air, and so shall we ever be with the Lord. What a hope!

Happiness can be ours in the new year if we will take the advice given in the Bible. But happiness is not something one stumbles into in a blind alley; it is usually found in the pathway of duty.

A man wrote his Congressman and asked, "Where is this happiness that our Constitution guarantees?" The Congressman wrote back, "The Constitution does not guarantee happiness; it guarantees only the pur-suit of happiness; you must pursue it for yourself."

III. THE WAY TO PROSPERITY

Psalm 1:3 promises, ". . . and whatsoever he doeth shall prosper." The same things that promise happiness in verse 1 also promise pros-perity in verse 3.

I have often said to businessmen, "If you will obey the first three verses of Psalm 1, you will prosper."

Here God lays down four simple things. First, a man is not to take advice from the ungodly. Second, he is not to stand in the way of sin-ners. Third, he is not to sit in the seat of the scornful. And fourth, he is to delight in the law of the Lord and in God's law meditate day and night.

Then verse 3 promises, "And he shall be like a tree planted by the rivers of water, that bringeth forth his fruit in his season; his leaf also shall not wither; and whatsoever he doeth shall prosper."

But the Bible has much more to say about prosperity.

It is said of Joseph in Genesis 39:23, "The Lord was with him, and that which he did, the Lord made it to prosper."

The Bible says of King Uzziah in II Chronicles 26:5, "As long as he sought the Lord, God made him to prosper."

Daniel 6:28 states, "So this Daniel prospered in the reign of Darius, and in the reign of Cyrus the Persian."

I have already shared four things that produce prosperity from Psalm 1; now let me give some additional suggestions regarding prosperity.

1. Giving Produces Prosperity

I have often said that we can have anything we want and as much of it as we want. My reason for saying so is based on the promise in Luke 6:38, "Give, and it shall be given unto you; good measure, pressed down, and shaken together, and running over, shall men give into your bosom."

When we read this verse, we usually think of money. But "money" is not mentioned. As a matter of fact, the verse doesn't tell us what to give; it simply says, "Give, and it shall be given unto you...." Whatever we give will be given unto us. If we give money, then money will be given.

John Bunyan once said,

> **There was a man in our town;**
> **Some folks did think him mad.**
> **The more he gave away,**
> **The more he had!**

And I have often heard it said that we cannot outgive God. God says if we give, He will give back to us; but when He gives back, it will be "good measure, pressed down, and shaken together." In other words, when the measure is full, He will put some on top for good measure; then He will pack it or press it down. Once it is pressed down, He will shake it together.

If you have ever picked a bushel of green beans and shaken them down, you know what "shaken together" means. I thought I had a full bushel; but after my daddy shook down the beans, it was only half full!

God says He will give back to us "good measure, pressed down, and shaken together." But He continues, "...and running over." Once it is pressed down, shaken together, then God promises to run it over; then He adds, "...shall men give into your bosom."

In Bible days, men wore long, flowing robes; and when one purchased grain, the seller placed a container in his bosom and wrapped the robe over the container so as not to lose one grain. In Luke 6:38 our Lord promises that if we give we will receive back in the same measure, only good measure, pressed down, shaken together and running over. And He promises that we will not lose it. What a deal!

We read in II Corinthians 9:6, "He which soweth sparingly shall reap also sparingly; and he which soweth bountifully shall reap also bountifully."

Our prosperity in the new year will depend largely upon how we give and how we sow. If you want love, then give, and it shall be given you— only good measure, pressed down and shaken together and running over. If you want understanding, then give understanding, and it shall be given you. If you want smiles, then smile, and smiles shall be given you. Whatever you want, give it away, and it will come back in greater measure than you gave it.

2. Obedience to God's Word Brings Prosperity

The promise in Joshua 1:8 is, "This book of the law shall not depart out of thy mouth; but thou shalt meditate therein day and night, that thou mayest observe to do according to all that is written therein: for then thou shalt make thy way prosperous, and then thou shalt have good success."

What a wonderful verse for the one who wants to be prosperous and successful! This is almost the same as the promise of Psalm 1, only here the verse adds, ". . .that thou mayest observe to do according to all that is written therein." Simple obedience to what God commands brings prosperity.

Read the Bible. Attend a good Bible-believing church. Listen for the sake of learning, and learn for the sake of doing. When you see clearly from the Scripture that God expects a certain thing of you, then be obedient, and God promises, ". . . then thou shalt make thy way prosperous, and then thou shalt have good success." I might add—only then will God make your way prosperous and only then will you have good success.

In his footnote in the Rice Reference Bible, Dr. John R. Rice says,

> The sure success promised to Joshua is similar to the promise found in Psalm 1:1-3. He was to keep all the commandments of the covenant given to Moses; he was to talk of it continually; he was to meditate therein day and night.

Then Dr. Rice adds, "We may claim the same promise."

I challenge our readers to obey Joshua 1 and Psalm 1 and claim the promise that the new year will be prosperous.

3. Honesty With God About Our Sins
Brings Prosperity

Proverbs 28:13 warns, "He that covereth his sins shall not prosper: but whoso confesseth and forsaketh them shall have mercy."

Here it is stated that the man who covers his sins shall not prosper. We must be honest and open with God about our sins. The Bible promises in I John 1:9, "If we confess our sins, he is faithful and just to forgive us our sins, and to cleanse us from all unrighteousness."

Martin Luther, the great reformer, once said, "We must keep short accounts with God," by which he meant that we are not to allow sin to pile up in our lives. The only way to obtain forgiveness and cleansing is to be open and honest with God and confess our sins to Him. The blessed promise is that if we confess our sins, He is faithful and just to forgive and cleanse us. But we also are warned, "He that covereth his sins shall not prosper."

I wish I could live this new year without one mistake, without committing one sin; but that is impossible. There are no perfect people. But if we do sin, we can have forgiveness and cleansing.

I make it a practice to confess and ask forgiveness the moment I am aware of any sin in my life. I trust you do, too.

The Bible has much more to say about prosperity, but I can only share an additional thought.

4. Material Prosperity Must Not Exceed
Spiritual Prosperity

The third epistle of John, verse 2, states, "Beloved, I wish above all things that thou mayest prosper and be in health, even as thy soul prospereth."

We are to prosper even as our souls prosper. Material prosperity should never get ahead of spiritual or soul prosperity. When God begins to bless a man materially, sometimes he has a tendency to neglect Bible reading, prayer and church attendance. And while his bank account swells, his soul shrivels.

I have prayed with businessmen when they were not quite so successful and heard them make glowing promises to the Lord; but when they began to prosper materially, they gradually drifted away from the Lord.

Luke 12:16-34 records the parable of the rich fool. When his ground brought forth plenty, he thought within himself, "What shall I do, because I have no room where to bestow my fruits?" And he said, "This will I do: I will pull down my barns, and build greater; and there will I bestow all my fruits and my goods."

Nothing wrong with this man's prosperity, nothing wrong with tearing down the old barns and building greater ones in which to bestow all his goods. The problem comes in verse 19, "And I will say to my soul, Soul, thou hast much goods laid up for many years; take thine ease, eat, drink, and be merry." He cultivated his crops to the neglect of his soul.

Make sure when prosperity comes that you do not make the mistake of saying, "Soul, take thine ease." Be sure that your soul prospers, that you prosper spiritually, that your spiritual growth keeps up with your material growth. God wants us to prosper even as our souls prosper and no more.

Now this is not to say that all rich men are spiritual and that all spiritual men are rich; it is simply saying that God does not want our material prosperity to exceed our spiritual or soul prosperity.

I have given a few scriptural principles and guidelines that produce happiness and prosperity, but a happy and prosperous new year can only be realized if we are willing to follow these principles and abide by these guidelines.

XIX.

Time

FRED J. MELDAU

Another year has gone and the mystery of time again challenges us. Job said, "My days are swifter than a weaver's shuttle" (Job 7:6); and as one looks backward it seems almost as if the years pass swifter than a weaver's shuttle.

The Origin of Time

First, God created light (Gen. 1:3), and then He created measured time by dividing light into periods of day and night. In the first few verses of the Bible, we have the origin of measured time: "God called the light Day, and the darkness he called Night. And the evening and the morning were the first day" (Gen. 1:5).

The Measuring of Time

We measure time by clocks and watches. Since the dawn of history mankind has made an effort to measure time. Some of the earliest devices for measuring time are the sun dial (Isa. 38:8); the water clock, which was made similar to the sand hourglass—water dripped through a small hole from one bowl to another; and the sand through a hole in the hourglass. The ancient Babylonians told time by the stars, by the signs of the Zodiac. In China they used a burning knotted rope, each knot representing another segment of the day. Another was the marked candle, each mark representing a segment of the day or night.

Today we have modern watches and clocks that are extremely efficient and accurate. A Naval Observatory clock has a daily variation of less than 1/100 of a second!

But all clocks and timepieces, whether ancient or modern, tell out the same inexorable, relentless story; time moves on, and someday, for all of us, time will merge into eternity.

Time is a strange thing. Let us consider some of the important lessons that "time" should teach us.

1. Time never moves backward. It cannot be recalled. We never grow younger. The sands of time keep trickling. The deeds we do and the words we say can never be recalled. How careful we ought to be in what we do or say!

2. Time had a beginning and time will have an end. Genesis 1:5 tells us of the evening and the morning of the "first day." And time will have an end. After the judgment of the Great White Throne, when God will create the new heavens and the new earth, God Himself will move His throne down to the new earth; and God and the Lamb will be the light of the world in a literal sense: Revelation 21:23—"and there will be no night there." Strange as it may seem, time is especially connected with the history of man. God made time for man's convenience.

3. Time will merge into eternity for all of us. This is one of the most serious and solemn thoughts ever to occupy the mind of man: time will merge into eternity. Time stops for each of us when death overtakes us. Every tick of the clock someone passes into eternity, where time shall be no more.

Every day ends; every night ends; every week ends; every year ends; every life ends. But when we pass out of time we enter a state of being that has no end and is not measured by time. There will be no clocks in eternity; eternity is as endless as a ring, as lasting as the Person of God.

The Bible reveals that all mankind is destined to one of two places in eternity: Heaven or Hell. Man has a body that decays and gets decrepit with age; but he also has a soul that has endless being.

Some people say there is no Hell; the Lord Jesus Christ, all-knowing Son of God, said there is, and He warned men to flee from it. Christ knows; earthly man either guesses or thinks or supposes. We better take His Word for it, heed His warning and call on Him for His salvation. There is a Hell as surely as there is a Heaven. We should do all within our power to get others saved from an awful Hell.

Hear Christ's solemn words in Matthew 25:46: "These shall go away into everlasting punishment; but the righteous into life eternal."

4. Time is measured, time is short, for all of us. When Japan surrendered, Admiral Halsey sent a radio message to Japan, warning, "Your time is short." He was right. The time of Japan's fighting days was very short; shorter than they thought.

God warns every unsaved person: "your time is short"; better repent and get right with God by accepting Christ as your personal Saviour.
Stop and think! Would you exchange a few short years of sinful pleasure
on earth for an eternity in Hell?

Time is short for Christian service. The Lord is coming soon! Death
is headed our way. What we do we must do quickly. The Apostle Paul
reminds us that "the time is short" (I Cor. 7:29). Let us "redeem the
time," for the days are evil. Let us do our best to win souls for Christ
before it is too late.

A man came rushing up to a Staten Island ferry some time ago,
breathless, after running at a terrific pace. He got there just as the
gateman shut the door in his face. A bystander remarked, "You didn't
run fast enough." The disappointed man answered, "I ran fast enough,
but I didn't start in time."

To accomplish the most for God in a lifetime one must start in youth!
Let us urge all Christian young people to take up their cross and follow
the Lord.

**5. Time and material things are closely associated, and will
both pass away.** "We look not at the things which are seen: for the
things which are seen are temporal" —connected with time— "but the
things which are not seen are eternal." Where are you looking? At stocks,
bonds, dollars, buildings, lands, produce, furs, new automobiles? We
need and can use some material things in the service of Christ; above
and beyond the things we actually need, let us look to Christ and the
things of His kingdom and righteousness.

Most children in this country are provided for materially, but millions
are neglected spiritually. What is wrong with the parents who take no
interest in the spiritual and moral welfare of their children?

**6. We should remember the exhortation, "Redeeming the
time, because the days are evil"** (Eph. 5:16). The word translated
"redeem" means to "go into the market and buy up." Every man in
Adam is sold under sin. When redeemed by Christ, we are to fully use
and buy up the time for Him. Outside of the needed rest and recreation required to keep our bodies and minds fit, we should use every
waking hour for Christ and His service.

7. God is above time. God made time for man, not for Himself.
"One day is with the Lord as a thousand years, and a thousand years
as one day" (II Pet. 3:8). God had no beginning; He will have no end.

He lives in the unruffled calm of infinity and eternity—save for the episode of man's sin and redemption on earth.

The Lord Jesus Christ also lives in eternity. Therefore, He gives eternal life, and everything connected with Him is not temporal but eternal. How wise are they who turn from the things of time and link up with the eternal One.

Just now, before our eyes is placed
    A page most white and fair,
And when this year from us is passed
    What shall be written there?
Upon it, we with eager hands
    Might write a schedule there
With joy and love for every month,
    And days most bright and fair.
'Tis true, we'd write upon this page
    The words of faith and prayer
And deeds of love to those in pain—
    But lo! a voice we hear.
A Hand that's pierced now holds a pen
    Ah, wilt thou trust it there
Upon this page to write His plan,
    For you this coming year?
" 'Tis better that thou knowest not
    The path that lies before,
For then I'll lead thee by the hand,
    And thou shalt trust Me more."

                                —Selected

Happy New Year

I do not know, I cannot see
What God's hand prepares for me,
Nor can my glance pierce through the haze
Which covers all my future ways;
But yet I know that o'er it all
Rules He who notes the sparrow's fall.

I know the Hand that hath me fed
And through the year my feet hath led;
I know the everlasting arm
That hath upheld and kept from harm.
I trust Him as my God and guide
And know that He will still provide.

So at the opening of the year,
I banish care and doubt and fear,
And clasping His kind hand, essay
To walk with God from day to day,
Trusting in Him who hath me fed,
Walking with Him who hath me led.

Farewell, Old Year, with goodness crowned.
A hand divine hath set thy bound.
Welcome the New Year, which shall bring
Fresh blessings from my God and King.
The Old we leave without a tear,
The New we hail without a fear.

Author Unknown

A Prayer for the New Year

Lord, I would ask for a holy year,
   Spent in Thy perfect will:
Help me to walk in Thy very steps;
   Help me to please Thee still.

Lord, I would ask for a busy year,
   Filled up with service true;
Doing with all Thy Spirit's might;
   All that I find to do.

Lord, I would ask for a dying world;
   Stretch forth Thy mighty hand,
Scatter Thy Word—Thy power display
   This year in every land.

Lord, I would ask for a year of hope,
   Looking for Thee to come,
And hastening on that year of years
   That brings us Christ and Home.

                    A. B. Simpson

One Day at a Time

One day at a time, with its failures and fears,
With its hurts and mistakes, with its weakness and tears,
With its portion of pain and its burden of care;
One day at a time we must meet and must bear.

One day at a time to be patient and strong;
To be calm under trial and sweet under wrong;
Then its toiling shall pass and its sorrow shall cease;
It shall darken and die, and the night shall bring peace.

One day at a time—but the day is so long,
And the heart is not brave and the soul is not strong.
O Thou pitiful Christ, be Thou near all the way;
Give courage and patience and strength for the day.

Swift cometh His answer, so clear and so sweet;
"Yea, I will be with thee, thy troubles to meet;
I will not forget thee, nor fail thee, nor grieve;
I will not forsake thee; I never will leave."

Not yesterday's load we are called on to bear,
Nor the morrow's uncertain and shadowy care;
Why should we look forward or back with dismay?
Our needs, as our mercies, are but for the day.

One day at a time, and the day is His day;
He hath numbered its hours, though they haste or delay.
His grace is sufficient; we walk not alone;
As the day, so the strength that He giveth His own.

Annie Johnson Flint

A Psalm for New Year's Eve

A Friend stands at the door;
   In either tight-closed hand
Hiding rich gifts, three hundred and threescore;
   Waiting to strew them daily o'er the land,
Even as seed the sower,
   Each drops he, treads it in and passes by:
   It cannot be made fruitful till it die.

O good New Year, we clasp
   This warm shut hand of thine,
Losing forever, with half sigh, half grasp,
   That which from ours falls like dead fingers' twine:
Ay, whether fierce its grasp
   Has been, or gentle, having been, we know
   That it was blessed: let the old year go.

O New Year, teach us faith!
   The road of life is hard:
When our feet bleed and scourging winds us scathe,
   Point thou to Him whose visage was more marred
Than any man's: who saith,
   "Make straight paths for your feet," and to the opprest,
   "Come ye to Me, and I will give you rest."

Yet hang some lamp-like hope
   Above this unknown way,
Kind year, to give our spirits freer scope
   And our hands strength to work while it is day.
But if that way must slope
   Tombward, oh, bring before our fading eyes
   The lamp of life, the hope that never dies.

Comfort our souls with love—
   Love of all human kind;
Love special, close, in which like sheltered dove
   Each weary heart its own safe nest may find;
And love that turns above
   Adoringly; contented to resign
   All loves, if need be, for the love divine.

Friend, come thou like a friend,
   And whether bright thy face,
Or dim with clouds we cannot comprehend,
   We'll hold out patient hands, each in his place,
And trust Thee to the end,
   Knowing Thou leadest onwards to those spheres
   Where there are neither days nor months nor years.

Annie Johnson Flint

For a complete list of books available from the Sword of the Lord, write to Sword of the Lord Publishers, P. O. Box 1099, Murfreesboro, Tennessee 37133.

For Reference

Do Not Take From the Library